Chinese Religions in
Contemporary Societies

Chinese Religions in Contemporary Societies

EDITED BY JAMES MILLER

Santa Barbara, CA • Denver, CO • Oxford, UK

Library of Congress Cataloging-in-Publication Data

Chinese religions in contemporary societies / edited by James Miller.
     p.   cm.
   Includes bibliographical references and index.
   ISBN 1-85109-626-4 (hbk. : alk. paper)—
   ISBN 1-85109-631-0 (ebook)
   1. China—Religion—20th century. I. Miller, James.
BL1802.C54775 2006
200.951'09051—dc22

                                        2006001695
10 09 08 07 06   10 9 8 7 6 5 4 3 2 1

Acquisitions Editor: Steven Danver
Production Editor: Martha Ripley Gray
Editorial Assistant: Alisha Martinez
Media Editor: Ellen Rasmussen
Production Coordinator: Ellen Brenna Dougherty
Manufacturing Coordinator: George Smyser

Text Design: Cynthia Young, Sagecraft, LLC

This book is also available on the World Wide Web as an eBook. Visit http://www.abc-clio.com for details.

ABC-CLIO, Inc.
130 Cremona Drive, P.O. Box 1911
Santa Barbara, California 93116–1911

This book is printed on acid-free paper.

Manufactured in the United States of America

Acknowledgments

When first planning this book I did not intend that so many of its authors should have some connection to Canada—whether by birth, residence, or education—but it has certainly turned out that way. Perhaps Canada's contemporary idea of itself as a multicultural mosaic is in part to be thanked for providing a stimulating environment in which to contemplate narratives of modernization and globalization. I would also like to acknowledge the advice and friendship of Emily Hill at Queen's University, who helped me better understand the late imperial and republican periods in Chinese history and who provided extensive comments on Chapter 2. Grateful acknowledgments are also due south of the border to Frank Korom at Boston University for first suggesting this book to me, to Eric Tang, who read and commented on drafts of the introductory chapters, and especially to Steven Danver and the production team at ABC-CLIO, whose guidance helped bring this complex project to fruition.

James Miller
Queen's University, Canada
February 2006

ROMANIZATION

THIS BOOK GENERALLY USES the Hanyu pinyin system to transliterate Chinese terms into Roman script. Some Chinese terms, however, are more commonly known in English according to other systems of romanization. In those cases, both the pinyin and the traditional versions are usually given.

Contents

TIMELINE OF CHINESE DYNASTIES

B.C.E.

1500–1150	Shang
1150–770	Western Zhou
770–221	Eastern Zhou
403–221	Warring States Period
221–206	Qin
206–6	Former Han

C.E.

23–220	Later Han
220–265	Three Kingdoms
265–317	Western Jin
317–420	Eastern Jin
420–589	Six Dynasties
589–618	Sui
618–907	Tang
907–960	Five Dynasties
960–1126	Northern Song
1126–1279	Southern Song
1279–1368	Yuan (Mongol)
1368–1644	Ming
1644–1911	Qing (Manchu)
1912–	Republic (on Taiwan only since 1949)
1949–	People's Republic

Timeline of Modern Chinese History

1839–1842	First Opium War
1842	Treaty of Nanjing
1850–1864	Taiping Rebellion
1855–1873	Muslim rebellions
1858	Treaty of Tianjin
1894–1895	Sino-Japanese War
1895	Treaty of Shimonoseki
1897–1901	Boxer Movement
1898	Hundred Days' Reform
1905	Sun Yat-sen establishes the Revolutionary Alliance
1911	Qing dynasty collapses
1912	Last emperor Pu Yi abdicates; Republic of China established; Yuan Shikai becomes first president
1919	May Fourth Movement
1921	Chen Duxiu and Li Dazhao found the Chinese Communist Party (CCP)
1924	Nationalists and communists establish a united front
1927	Chiang Kai-shek massacres members of the CCP and others in the labor movement
1937	Japan invades China
1945	World War II ends; island of Taiwan is restored to China by the Allies following Japanese occupation since 1895
1949	Nationalists flee to Taiwan, where the Republic of China continues
1949	Chairman Mao establishes People's Republic of China on the mainland
1958–1960	Great Leap Forward
1966–1976	Cultural Revolution
1976	Death of Mao
1978	Deng Xiaoping is recognized as paramount leader
1989	Tian'anmen Square massacre
1997	Hong Kong is returned to China
2001	China joins the World Trade Organization
2008	Beijing Olympics

Map of China. (Digital Wisdom)

General Introduction

The AIM OF THIS BOOK is to introduce the stunning diversity and complexity of Chinese religions in contemporary societies across the world. In addition to presenting a wealth of data, much of it the result of original research, the book also raises important theoretical questions about the way in which Europeans and Chinese have constructed interpretations of Chinese religions. Above all, the book tells the story of the place of religion in China's quest for modernization. It asks how it was possible for Chinese intellectuals to dismiss Buddhism, Daoism, and Confucianism as being associated inextricably with China's traditional past. It charts the demise of a simplistic paradigm of "tradition" versus "modernity" and the consequent formation of new frameworks for interpreting the place of religion in a variety of social, political, and cultural contexts. Those contexts range from rural mainland China, struggling to identify the proper place for its local traditions in the modern world, to the vast Chinatowns of San Francisco and Toronto, where ethnic Chinese immigrants from Taiwan, Indonesia, and Vietnam construct transnational religious identities at once new and traditional, global and local.

The Scope of Chinese Religions

Amid this emergent complexity it is worthwhile examining whether the term "Chinese religions" has any validity at all. Surely the term panders to an outdated, racialist view of religion, one that ties religious belief and practice to specific ethnicities and cultures. Does it not also further an increasingly strident nationalist rhetoric, a rhetoric that welds the future identity of China as a nation-state to the Han Chinese people? In the Chinese news media, one increasingly notes the use of the racial phrase "Han people" (*Hanzu*) as a direct equivalent for the political term "China" (*Zhongguo*). Such an equation of racial and political identity furthers the quest of the People's Republic of China to be legitimately regarded as the motherland of all Chinese people everywhere—regardless of their status as Americans, Vietnamese, or Taiwanese. It also furthers the marginalization of the fifty-five official minority nationalities that make up slightly more than 7 percent of China's population.

Further complicating this situation is the fact that the Han people themselves display a remarkable linguistic and cultural diversity, even within a single province. Other anomalies include the group of people known as Hakka, who are conventionally regarded as a separate ethnicity but who for official purposes are counted among the Han. On the other hand, members of the Hui minority are often indistinguishable from their Han cousins—except for the fact that they practice Islam.

China's history adds further problems. From 1279 to 1911, a period of 632 years, China was under the authority of Han people for only 276 years, during the Ming dynasty (1368–1644). The previous dynasty—the Yuan (1279–1368)—was Mongolian, and the subsequent dynasty—the Qing (1644–1911)—was Manchu. Add to that the aggression of colonial powers in the nineteenth century, and it is not surprising that Han Chinese should seek to compensate by bolstering their national ethnic identity in the present era.

On the religious scene, as Chapter 1 indicates, China's religious heritage is also a complex mix of local customs; apocalyptic rebellions; the historical traditions of Daoism, Confucianism, and Buddhism; as well as the imperial cult that lasted until the fall of the empire in 1911. Perversely, one of the most popular and widespread of so-called Chinese religions is Buddhism, a foreign import; what is more, the religion that is receiving a high degree of press attention right now in China is Protestant Christianity.

In assessing the complexity of Chinese religions, however, this book does not aim to be totally comprehensive. First and foremost, it does not focus on the religious lives of China's minority nationalities, and therefore there is no mention of Tibetan Buddhism, Islam, or the religious practices of China's minority peoples. That is not meant to imply they are unimportant aspects of religion in the People's Republic of China. This book, however, does not employ "Religion in China" as its topic or theme. For excellent studies of Chinese religions in that framework, see the book edited by Overmyer (2003). The scope of this book, by contrast, is the religious lives of the majority Han Chinese people across the world, and the adoption of "Chinese religions" by non-Chinese people.

Although it adopts the title and category of "Chinese religions," this book does so only as a heuristic device. It aims to explore what that term covers but it does not intend to legitimate the term as a category of religious studies. Rather, by exploring the complexity of Chinese religions across a variety of social and political contexts, it intends to expose the dual meaning of the term, denoting on the one hand the religious lives of the Han Chinese, and, on the other, the traditions historically and culturally associated with them. In so doing it demonstrates that "Chinese religions" cannot be reduced to a single ethnic or racial factor. Clearly, the traditional customs and civilization of China are a significant influence on the day-to-day religious life of the Han people. But equally important are the historical traditions and social contexts that have a life of their own above and beyond questions of race or ethnicity. This book demonstrates, for instance, how Chinese Buddhists study under Theravada Buddhists in Sri Lanka; how Chinese people are adopting Christianity and making it their own; how Daoism is becoming a world religion and influencing the culture and traditions of non-Chinese people; how Confucianism is being reinvented as a global spiritual tradition. Even the revival of local customs in rural China is being influenced by the frameworks for interpreting religion that were derived from Western philosophies such as Marxism, or by economic movements such as socialism and capitalism. All of these developments demonstrate how Chinese religions in contemporary societies have fundamental elements that are not Chinese in any ethnic or racial sense.

The Approach to Chinese Religions

This book begins with two chapters that offer the reader an orientation to the history and content of Chinese religions. They provide background information useful to those readers who have no previous knowledge or experience of Chinese religions or the history of modern China. These chapters paint a picture of the ways in which Chinese religions have been studied by scholars in the West, and the way in which Chinese people in the twentieth century have come to understand and interpret their own religious history. Thus these chapters raise important theoretical questions about modernization, secularization, and the place of religion in contemporary society.

The remainder of this book consists of chapters written by specialists that focus on one particular aspect of religions in contemporary societies. These chapters begin in mainland China and, following migration patterns, proceed across the Pacific Ocean to California, Ontario, and Massachusetts. They are written in a style that aims to be as clear and accessible as possible, free of obfuscating academic jargon, yet without ignoring important details or significant theoretical and methodological questions. Obviously that is a fine balancing act—one, however, that is of prime importance for academics like me who are committed to modern, democratic ideals of scholarship and reject the priestly hocus-pocus of self-important "experts" in their elitist ivory towers.

It is important to state that the specialists' chapters do not necessarily aim at giving comprehensive descriptions of the topics they cover. It would be foolish to imagine, for instance, that anyone could give a synoptic overview of all aspects of local religions throughout mainland China. Any such synopsis would have to be necessarily vague. Rather, most chapters in this book use case studies, interviews, and fieldwork to convey vivid details about particular aspects of their topic. In fact, one of the more unusual accomplishments of this book is that these details are frequently based on firsthand, original, unpublished research by the authors—something that is quite rare outside of technical scholarly monographs. These details, however, are woven into a more general presentation of the topic, so that the reader can acquire both a general understanding of the important issues as well as some specific details and characterizations.

The Content of Chinese Religions

Our survey of Chinese religions in contemporary societies begins with Tam Wai Lun's essay on local religions in mainland China. Professor Tam reports on fieldwork conducted in southern China and describes the ways in which rural Chinese, in the context of recent openness toward religion on the part of government officials, are rediscovering their religious heritage. His essay also points to the role played by Daoist priests in presiding over local rituals, and how the revival of such customs may also be helping to legitimate Daoism as one of China's official religions.

Ven. Jing Yin, an ordained Buddhist in charge of Hong Kong University's Buddhist Studies program, offers a fascinating insider's perspective on the single most important problem facing Buddhist monasteries in China today: how to balance economic and religious activities. His essay places the revival of Buddhism firmly in the context of China's contemporary economic situation, and it highlights the important and frequently problematic relationships between religion and economics. As his essay demonstrates, this has been a perennial problem in Buddhist history, but one that has acquired new characteristics in the present phase of China's economic development.

The third essay turns to Daoism, China's organized, indigenous religion. It focuses not on the questions of economics and tourism that are just as important for Daoist monasteries as for Buddhist monasteries, but on a more explicitly religious question—namely, the content of the liturgical prayer in Daoist monasteries belonging to the Complete Perfection (Quanzhen) order. Kim Sung-hae's analysis points to the way in which these prayers incorporate elements of Buddhist and Confucian philosophy and yet preserve the unique Daoist emphasis on immortality and cultivation of the Dao.

Alison Marshall, a scholar of Taiwanese religion, offers an exciting look at contemporary shamanism and mediumship. Her essay shows not only how these ancient traditions are surviving in the modern world but also how they are being influenced by specific issues relevant to Taiwanese society. Those issues include Taiwan's occupation by Japan between 1895 and 1945, its close political relationship with the United States, and questions of identity among its aboriginal, native Taiwanese, and postwar Chinese communities.

David A. Palmer's essay, in Chapter 7, offers a comprehensive history and analysis of a recent religious phenomenon centered on various forms of *qi* exercise that gained mass popularity in China and across the world in the 1980s. The story of these movements is complicated by the political repression faced by one such movement, Falun gong, at the hands of the Chinese government. His essay offers a fascinating case study, not only of a contemporary new religious movement but also of the complex relationship between religious and political authority in mainland China.

Chapter 8 examines the history of China's newest world religion: Protestant Christianity. After surveying the troubled history of Christianity in China and its relationship to European imperialism in the modern period, Francis Ching-wah Yip goes on to raise some important questions that Chinese Christians are currently discussing: How Chinese is Chinese Christianity? What is the difference between the official Chinese churches and the so-called house church movement? What are the affinities between contemporary Chinese Christianity and popular Chinese rituals of healing and exorcism? Is praying to Jesus really any different from praying to Buddha? Although it is not yet possible to draw conclusions regarding these questions, the chapter reveals a stimulating discussion that will engage Chinese Christians in the twenty-first century.

Tak-ling Terry Woo examines Chinese religions in contemporary societies from the perspective of women's life stories. She tells the stories of women as revealed in autobiographies and interviews across a wide range of social contexts. Of special note are three such figures: Julia Ching was a prominent Confucian Christian intellectual who lived in China, Australia, and Canada; Ayya Khema, born in Germany, studied Tibetan Buddhism but received ordination from a Chinese Buddhist order because Tibetan monasteries do not ordain women; and Dharma Master Zhengyan, one of the most influential Buddhists of the last century, founded the Tzu Chi Compassion Relief Society, now a worldwide organization.

In the last three chapters, we move across the Pacific to examine Chinese religions in North America. Jonathan H. X. Lee tells the history of Chinese American religious life, focusing on California. He offers case studies from Chinese temples in Mendocino and San Francisco and then examines the formation of transnational religious identity through organizations that in various ways connect Chinese Americans to their East Asian roots. He demonstrates how they serve to unify the immigrant communities and also reach out to non–Chinese Americans.

Elijah Siegler's history of the reception of Chinese religions by Euro-Americans tells the other side of this story. He recounts how non–Chinese Americans have consumed and appropriated Chinese traditions, forming new understandings of Chinese traditions such as *fengshui* or *taiji* (t'ai-chi). His chapter contains important case studies of prominent purveyors of Chinese religious practices to Euro-Americans, including Maoshing Ni and Mantak Chia. It concludes with a discussion of "American Daoism" as a new form of Chinese religion.

The final chapter of this book tells a rather different story, one that focuses on Confucianism, a tradition that some might say does not warrant a place in a discussion of Chinese religions inasmuch as it exists in the twenty-first century chiefly as the intellectual creation of a group of elite scholars in China and America. Nonetheless, this chapter examines the way in which one group of scholars is positioning Confucianism, if not as a religion then as a tradition capable of addressing the pressing spiritual questions of our day. Chief among these is the question of the relationship between human beings and their environment. The chapter shows how New Confucians interpret an ancient Chinese tradition as spiritual wisdom for an ecological age.

Conclusion

All of the evidence points to the fact that it is not yet possible to draw any lasting conclusions about Chinese religions in contemporary societies. China began its policy of openness and modernization in the late 1970s, and the effects of that change on the religious scene are too recent to assess. Certainly the enormous social changes that are taking place in China—notably the mass migration from rural to urban areas—will have a profound effect on religion. So too will the growing globalization of religions, whether in the form of formal establishment of transnational religious organizations or the informal adaptation of religions in new cultures and societies. Today technology, economics, and geopolitics are in a phase of rapid change, making this an exciting time to study Chinese religions. On the other hand, religions such as Christianity and Buddhism have thrived over the centuries on their adaptability and the universality of their appeal. Perhaps Chinese religions in the present century will in some ways repeat the history of earlier years, when strangers from India came to China with strange stories of foreign gods, or when Korean and Japanese intellectuals fell under the spell of Neo-Confucian metaphysics. The chapters in this book offer a stimulating introduction to questions that have the potential to reshape not only China's religions but also the religious cultures of the world.

James Miller

References
Overmyer, Daniel L., ed. 2003. *Religion in China Today. China Quarterly* special issues. Cambridge: Cambridge University Press.

The Historical Legacy of China's Religious Traditions

JAMES MILLER

Introduction

In the span of little more than 150 years, China has felt the full impact of an encounter with modernity that took Europe more than four centuries to digest. Between 1839 and 2001, China underwent colonial invasions, the collapse of an imperial political structure, a republican revolution, a civil war, a communist revolution, a cultural revolution, secularization, desecularization, nationalism, an enormous population increase, massive migration from rural to urban areas, emigration of Chinese peoples across the world, environmental devastation, accession to membership in the World Trade Organization, and the emergence of one of its cities, Shanghai, as perhaps the most innovative, vibrant, and exciting urban center on the planet. In the face of this extraordinary and novel transformation, it is entirely understandable why many Chinese people have completely accepted the revolutionary rhetoric of a "new China," a China so completely defined by its embrace of the modern that it has no place for the past.

After I gave a lecture on Daoism at Fudan University, Shanghai, in 2003, a student told me that she simply could not understand how someone could be interested in a way of thinking and acting that so clearly had nothing to do with the real world. It seemed that for her the only thing that was real was what was actual and modern. In the logic of modernity, the past is simply unreal: it has no presence, no power, no existence. As one of the most important engineers of industrial modernity, Henry Ford, famously declared, "History is bunk." And if history is bunk, religion is even more so: not only are history and tradition the very substance of religion, but the fact that religion takes as its focus the invisible world of gods, ghosts, and spirits serves only to compound its seeming unreality and irrelevance. How could a sane, intelligent, and modern person be wasting time on the unreality of the past and the fantasy world of the spirits?

Yet one of the most curious aspects of this powerful rhetoric of secular modernity is that modernity itself is contingent upon the peculiarities of history and culture that have come to shape it. As the Canadian philosopher Charles Taylor has so clearly demonstrated (1989), the modern sense of self—of being an autonomous, rational individual free from the coercive orthodoxies of tradition, hierarchy, and faith—is a notion that arose in a particular European historical context and was itself subject to change and transformation. In the future, modernity will be history. There is an important sense, therefore, in which the Chinese encounter with modernity can be described as a historical encounter with a particular constellation of historical European ideas, European science, and European politics. This is an ongoing and highly contested story about which it is not yet possible to draw any conclusions.

The task of the next chapter is to outline the contours of this encounter and to prepare the way for understanding the transformation and diversity of contemporary Chinese religions that this book sets forth. The task of the present chapter, however, is to outline the history of China's religions in their traditional, premodern forms. To do so runs the risk of accepting the seductive logic of "tradition" versus "modernity" that so informs our modern way of thinking and that so easily slides into the racial and cultural constructions of "China" versus "West" and "Asian" versus "Caucasian." What is portrayed below, therefore, is not so much the historical reality of Chinese traditional religion (as though it were possible to determine what that might be) but rather the ways in which traditional sinology, and the history of religions as Western academic discourses, have sought to construct a view of Chinese tradition that fits neatly into the binary logic of tradition and modernity. As the subsequent chapters in this book demonstrate, the contemporary Chinese religious scene is vast and complex. While the logic of tradition versus modernity carries a high degree of interpretive power, it does not explain the full complexity of Chinese religions in our contemporary networked, globalized, and commodified world.

Below I outline three frameworks for understanding the nature of traditional Chinese religion. The approach of the history of religions is to attempt to understand continuities and discontinuities, tradition and transformation, in the historical evolution of religions. That approach privileges an understanding of religion as a tradition—that is, a body of ideas, beliefs, and practices that are handed down from one generation to the next. The danger of such a way of viewing religion is that it attributes to a tradition an essence or an identity that in reality is hard to justify. It seems as though the tradition has a life of its own, a vital essence or unique personality that becomes manifest in the concrete actuality of history. We begin to speak of the "Buddhist view of suffering" or the "Confucian notion of filial piety" as though those ideas were disembodied constructs that somehow perpetuate themselves unchanged throughout the history of human consciousness.

The approach of the sociology of religions, by contrast, is to construct a view of traditional Chinese religions in terms of their culture and society. This view pays attention not so much to the theological ideas and their material expression but to the social roles played by religious figures, whether priests, nuns, or lay people, and to the ways in which religions both reflect the social realities of Chinese culture and structure that reality, reinforcing certain systems of authority and power while challenging others.

The third approach considered below seeks to construct a description of religion in reference to the geographic locations in which it is found. In such a view we may speak of urban religion, rural religion, coastal religion, or mountain religion, and it becomes possible to formulate an interpretation of traditional Chinese religious life in reference to its habitats and sacred spaces.

By overlapping these three approaches I hope to construct a picture of traditional Chinese religions that will be useful to the reader of this book, but without giving the impression that the picture is somehow independent of the perspectives used to create it. Rather, all three approaches are valid and necessary ways of generating a complex understanding of Chinese religions.

History

The most conventional way of explaining traditional Chinese religions is to speak of the "three traditions." As Tam Wai Lun explains in Chapter 3, such an approach is fraught with interpretive difficulties that I will leave him to explain, but it does help to orient us toward a basic feature of Chinese religious life—namely, that since the beginning of the common era, China has been a religiously plural culture. Whereas Europeans tended to embrace a single religion, Christianity, with a tripartite deity, the Chinese people have embraced a trinity of traditions with an even more complex pantheon of gods, ghosts, and ancestors that vie for the spiritual allegiance of the living. Those three traditions—Buddhism, Confucianism, and Daoism (also spelled Taoism)—have been the principal repository of the beliefs and practices that have shaped the evolution of Chinese religious and cultural history.

The second basic feature of traditional Chinese religious life it is important to explain is that it is hard to make a sharp distinction between religion and culture. Confucianism certainly contains spiritual elements, but Confucius was not a religious figure. Daoism is a complex religion that exists in a priestly form and a monastic form practiced by only a handful of people today, yet its concepts and values and many of its practices are deeply embedded within traditional Chinese culture. Buddhism, originally considered a "foreign" religion by the Chinese, subsequently took on distinctively Chinese characteristics and is now one of the most widespread and visible forms of Chinese religious practice. Its idea of karma and its complex cosmology of hells, demons, paradises, and saviors have become standard features of popular Chinese thought, even among people who would not consider themselves Buddhists.

These three "religions"—Buddhism, Confucianism, and Daoism—are understood in Chinese terms as "traditions" (*jiao*), a term that has a broader range of meaning than the English word "religion." A tradition, both in Chinese and English, is something that is handed down from one generation to another. It denotes not just something from the past but something that is made present again and again in a historical process of transmission. The religious aspect of a tradition comes from the way in which people situate themselves in relation to the tradition as a whole. A tradition is not a "religion"; it is what people do with it that makes it religion.

Confucius (traditional dates: 551–479 B.C.E.) famously declared himself to be a transmitter and not a creator. He lived in the period of the Warring States, during which time the Zhou empire had disintegrated and China experienced turmoil and disunity. Confucius's aim was to recover the tradition of former times so as to attain a national unity and a peaceful and stable society. His thought is thus more akin to a moral philosophy, a way of life, but one that certainly has been regarded in what we might anachronistically call "spiritual" terms (see Chapter 12). Although Confucius was respectful of the spirits, he did not make the spirit world the focus of his life. Rather, he was concerned with the practical matters of virtue and governance. What Confucius realized was that the principles of virtue and ethics could not be stated in an abstract, philosophical form in any way that would be ultimately satisfactory. He did not engage in the kind of logical argumentation that developed in the Greek philosophy of Plato and Aristotle. Rather, he understood that it was the shared conventions and customs of a culture or civilization that created a virtuous and harmonious society. So long as people knew how to treat each other with civility, deference, and respect, they would be able to debate the finer points of philosophy and politics till the small hours without resorting to violence, brutality, or the excesses of power.

What Confucius created, therefore, was not a system of ideas but a method for human relations that zoned in on the most contentious areas of social conflict: relations between husbands and wives, between siblings, between kings and ministers, between fathers and sons, and between friends. Domestic relations, sibling rivalry—that is to say, power imbalances generally—are the most difficult psychological and personal problems for human beings to grapple with. If individuals were able to negotiate and manage those relationships, that would tend toward the creation of a stable and harmonious society. But as soon as husbands treat their wives cruelly, older brothers assert their power unfairly over younger brothers, or employers treat their employees with disregard for their feelings, trouble is bound to erupt. Civility turns into vicissitude and violence. Harmony is ruptured, and society descends into chaos.

Confucius's ideas were never implemented in his lifetime, but they were taken up again and again throughout the course of Chinese history by philosophers and intellectuals. Under the influence of the Neo-Confucian philosopher Zhu Xi (1130–1200), they became the substance of political orthodoxy and the form of official Chinese culture that dominated the civil service, charged with the actual business of running the country. The politicians and intellectuals who were versed in the tradition of reading the ancient classics and reinterpreting them for their own time were known as the *Ru*, a term that is perhaps as contested as "Confucianism" but which may be translated as "scholars" or "classicists." They did not think of themselves as belonging to a particular "religion"—they were simply scholars and intellectuals who sought to articulate a spiritual and ethical tradition capable of effectively addressing the abstruse logic of Buddhist metaphysics.

Confucius (Kong Fuzi), Chinese philosopher (551–479 B.C.E.). (Bettman/Corbis)

These scholars developed concepts such as principle (*li*), the Way (*dao*), vital energy (*qi*), sincerity (*cheng*), and benevolence (*ren*) through reading the ancient classics associated with Confucius and reinterpreting them for their own time. When Jesuit missionaries came to China in the sixteenth and seventeenth centuries, they baptized this tradition "Confucianism," for they believed that what they had encountered was an "ism"—that is, a type of religion, founded by someone they called Confucius, the Latinized form of Kong Fuzi (Master Kung). Their creative misrepresentation has shaped an entire field of academic study in the West, which is focused on the person of Confucius and the tradition he inspired. Some scholars (for example, Jensen 1997) even argue that the entire tradition of Confucianism was effectively a Western invention. Certainly, no one in China would say that "Kong Fuzi-ism is my religion," or that "I practice Kong Fuzi-ism."

Thanks mostly to the Jesuits, what people in the West today call Confucianism has in fact come to denote a way of life synonymous with traditional Chinese culture as a whole. It stands for respect for one's parents, a concern with ethical obligations and ritual customs, the priority of the group over the individual, and reverence for one's ancestors. In short, Confucianism came to mean nothing more than tradition—that is, the old way of doing things. In the logic of modernity wholeheartedly embraced by the Chinese reformers and revolutionaries of the twentieth century, "Confucianism" was precisely what was wrong with Chinese society. It had to be extirpated, annihilated, and replaced with science. But with the renewal of interest in traditional Chinese systems of thought that began to emerge in the late twentieth and early twenty-first centuries, Confucianism is once again being reinvented as a form of moral being and religious concern founded on a reverence for life and personal spiritual development (see Chapter 12).

At the same time that Confucius's intellectual heirs, Mencius (372–289 B.C.E.) and Xunzi (310–237 B.C.E.), were fleshing out the philosophic details of what would later be understood as "Confucianism," there arose an alternative worldview centered on the experience of life as an irrepressible flood of vital energy (*qi*) and a mystical wonder at the operations of the Dao (Tao), its unfathomable cosmic wellspring. Some of the key ideas of this movement were compiled in aphoristic form in the text known as the *Way and Its Power* (*Daode jing; Tao Te Ching*), which remains one of the most influential works of wisdom literature in the world. This mystical experience coalesced some four hundred years later in the religious movement known as the Way of Orthodox Unity, which revered as its god a legendary figure known as Laozi, the "Elder Master," the reputed author of the *Way and Its Power*. In this tradition, the operations of the Dao came to be mediated symbolically in the form of a network of cosmic powers and deities, of whom the Supreme Lord Lao (*Taishang laojun*) was chief, and by a parallel priestly hierarchy headed by a "celestial master." Zhang Daoling, the first of these celestial masters, founded the Way of Orthodox Unity in 142 C.E., in what is today Sichuan province in the west of China. Sichuan was an area far from the central authorities and rich in natural resources, and for some seventy years Zhang and his successors established a religious community based on the covenant that he established with Lord Lao. The covenant made provision for priestly communications between the deities and Zhang's followers and, in particular, a ritual of confession that was designed to restore harmony and healing to the body and to the community. Although Zhang's theocratic community did not last long, his followers established lineages of transmission that continue to the present day. Daoist priests learn from their teachers how to make communications with the gods and how to set right the relations between the world of the living and the world of the deceased. They are ordained into a ritual tradition and invested with scriptures and talismans that to this day give them privileged access to the spirit world.

As the original Daoist community dispersed through China, new forms of Daoism began to emerge. In particular Daoists began to develop a form of meditation exercises that sought to refine and purify the vital *qi* energy that courses through the body. The aim of this tradition was to engage in an alchemical process in which the organs of the body and its fluid energies are transmuted into an elixir of immortality. A body thus transfigured would be able to survive the trauma of death, viewed as the slow but certain dissipation of the body's earthly (yin) and heavenly (yang) life forces, and continue intact as a spiritual being composed of pure cosmic energy. The various traditions of meditation and visualization that emerged in the Six Dynasties period were eventually formalized in a type of monastic training known as the Way of Complete Perfection, which was founded by Wang Chongyang and his seven disciples, six men and one woman, in the Yuan dynasty. This monastic tradition is the other main form of Daoism that continues to the present day.

Buddhists came to China as early as the first century C.E., earlier even than the creation of the Daoist Way of Orthodox Unity. They brought a vast store of Buddhist sutras, a tradition of male monasticism, and an intense spiritual discipline that aimed toward the total liberation of the self from the chains of karma and rebirth. Alongside that elite religious tradition arose a popular form of religious expression founded upon the recitation of spells and formulas that appealed to popular deities known as bodhisattvas—powerful cosmic beings who had attained liberation but who, out of compassion, had vowed not to enter nirvana—the total extinction of the self—until all living beings had been similarly freed.

Unlike the somewhat fictive creation of Confucianism, Buddhism was more evidently founded on the vision of a single man, Siddhartha Gautama, an Indian prince who left his wife and son to pursue intense ascetic practices in the company of other wanderers. Finding that the extreme mortification of the flesh did not produce the enlightenment he was seeking, Siddhartha developed his own techniques of meditation and discipline that eventually resulted in his enlightenment. Thus wakened to the true nature of existence, he became known as the Awakened One, or Buddha. He assembled his fellow seekers and began to teach them the Buddhist dharma, the teachings that lead to awakening. The Buddha, the dharma, and the sangha (or Buddhist community) are together known as the three jewels of Buddhism.

Buddhists established monasteries, competed with Daoists and Confucians for imperial favor, translated Buddhist scriptures into Chinese, and developed new forms of meditation and popular practice. Chief among those was the tradition we know in the West from the Japanese term *Zen*, a translation of the Chinese term *Chan*, because it was Japanese Buddhists who first introduced this form of religious discipline to the West. Chan Buddhism became established as a separate institutional form in the twelfth century but constructed an account of itself that went right back to the teachings of the Buddha. Paradoxically, the content of this transmission was held to be entirely devoid of substance—that the Buddhist teaching of emptiness (*sunyata*) precluded any step-by-step progress along the path toward enlightenment. Rather enlightenment was to be grasped in an instantaneous understanding of the absolute emptiness of all forms of existence. It is also paradoxical that this novel and institutionally subversive "antidoctrine" was institutionalized in a rigid form of discipline and training that continues to this day.

The conventional historical account of Buddhism is similarly constructed around such sects and lineages of transmission and has focused on specific sutras or doctrines. All of these narratives, however, are retrospective constructions, either by Buddhists who wish to place their teachings in a line of transmission and authority going back to the Buddha himself or by scholars who have privileged a view of Buddhism that centers on its elite scholastic forms (Teiser 1996, 20). Such accounts have less frequently paid attention to popular Buddhist religious expression, which has focused on the use of mantras and other ritual formulas to obtain succor from the cosmic pantheon of buddhas and bodhisattvas and rebirth in a "pure land."

Society

In contrast to the historical traditions described above, a sociological account of Chinese religions is helpful because it pays attention to the different forms of Chinese religiosity in terms of the structure of traditional Chinese society. To be sure, any description of so-called traditional Chinese society is itself a generalization that is bound to be false in certain respects and in certain historical periods. However, the value of this way of construing Chinese religion is that it reveals certain features and details that might otherwise be overlooked.

The first point that needs to be made is that Chinese society in imperial times was a hierarchical and patriarchal society. The country was ruled by a hereditary male emperor who was advised by a staff of male civil servants and whose will was executed throughout the country by a network of male magistrates and governors. The emperor claimed his title by divine mandate and saw himself as the father of his people and the supreme mediator between them and the gods of heaven and earth. There was thus a particular religious system associated with the emperor, and he himself was revered as a quasi-divine being so awesome that his name was taboo. His religious functions included making animal sacrifices every year to the gods of heaven and earth so as to ensure a plentiful harvest and peace in the empire. He also employed a vast staff to conduct court rituals with due reverence and protocol so as to ensure the outward radiance of harmony from the capital to the far corners of his dominion.

While it was the emperor's duty to entreat the sovereign deities of heaven and earth, it was the duty of his governors and magistrates to maintain order in the provinces and the cities. Each city had its own tutelary deity or city god whose duty it was to ensure the city's prosperity and ward off baleful spirits. The city magistrate, appointed directly by the court from a pool of men who had been successful in the civil service examinations, performed sacrifices at the local city temple as well as overseeing the execution of the imperial will. The magistrate thus exercised his power through the discharge of a variety of ritual functions that spanned the spectrum of what we would today call religion, politics, and law.

In this centralized monarchy, large estates were owned by gentry families that had been given title to it by imperial favor, but land was also freely bought and sold. The earth was worked by farmers who either were tenants of the large landowners or were themselves owners of small estates. From time to time sons would be taken away to perform military service, road-building, or other labors. Peasants lived in villages led by a headman who was the liaison between the workers and the landowners.

The chief religious concern of the male gentry lay in maintaining their genealogical status and lineage. Homes contained a shrine that recorded the names of male ancestors in an unbroken lineage as far back as possible. The ancestors watched over their progeny and worked in an unseen way to ensure the continued prosperity of the male line and the birth of sons who would continue the tradition of ancestral veneration into the future. Society was thus patrilineal and virilocal: only the male line of descent was important; daughters were to be married out and sent to live with their new husbands; sons were to marry in suitable wives whom they would bring to live in the family home. The fertility of women, animals, and crops was ensured by supplication to ancestors who, like the city gods in the towns, guarded against natural disasters such as floods, plagues, and famines.

Occasionally certain ancestors were so well known and their spiritual powers so well regarded that they were in effect deified—that is, made the object of sacrifice and worship by people to whom they were not genetically related. Such figures became local gods; they were enshrined in their own public temples and were spiritually responsible for an entire region or class of people, not just a single clan.

In this social structure Buddhism and Daoism found important niches. The monastic forms of Buddhism and Daoism at first generally worked outside this system, because they required monks and nuns to leave their families—that is, to place themselves outside of the structures of patrilineal descent and ancestral veneration. Later, however, temples found a way to insert themselves into the system by providing shrines in which the names of the dead could be recorded and by providing funeral services. (Marriages generally did not take place in a formal religious setting but in the family home.) Both Buddhists and Daoists, however, developed a repertoire of rituals that were designed to assist ordinary people with the everyday problems of peasant life. They wove themselves into the religious fabric of popular society to the extent that by the Qing dynasty it was often difficult to tell whether rituals were "originally" Buddhist or Daoist, or what tradition various religious practices actually "belonged to." Such rituals included funerals, exorcisms, and methods for feeding the hungry ghosts—those deceased persons who had no descendants to provide them with spiritual sustenance or who, because of their karma, were languishing in various Buddhist hells. Indeed, there developed a class of professional ritual specialists who continue to the present day and who are able to perform all manner of religious services, whether Daoist, Buddhist, or anything else, depending upon the needs and wealth of their clients.

Such practices were predicated on a popular cosmology that included gods, ancestors, and demons in the ranks of the unseen world. Gods were powerful cosmic forces such as the gods of the earth or the heaven, Daoist immortals, or Buddhist bodhisattvas. All were imbued with a mighty spiritual power that could be invoked for the protection and benefit of the whole people. Ancestors were the deceased, who continued to exist as unseen spirits for perhaps as long as seven generations before their spiritual integrity finally decayed into the cosmic ether. Demons were either hungry ghosts or nature spirits that could inflict psychological or physiological harm on the unsuspecting living. They were the cause of random illnesses, mysterious deaths, or anything for which there was no visible material cause. They could be exorcised, banished, or subdued by appeal to more powerful deities through ritual formulas or the magical efficacy of Daoist talismans or Buddhist relics. Today, for example, people commonly hang such talismans from their car mirrors to prevent automobile accidents—the random and unwanted interventions of mischievous demons.

As an alternative, and sometimes as an accompaniment, to Daoist exorcisms, it was also common for people to consult the services of a spirit medium—a religious specialist who was able to communicate with the unseen world and to divine answers to problems afflicting the earthly sufferer. Such inquiries on behalf of the living would produce answers to specific problems, especially dealing with sickness and misfortune. These ritual practices drew on a long-standing tradition of shamanism that at times was opposed by the formal traditions of Buddhism, Confucianism, and Daoism and at other times accepted. Opposition to these practices and the denigration of them as "superstitious cults" by the religious and political elite continues to the present day.

In addition to benefiting from the professional services provided by religious specialists, lay people also engaged in a wide variety of sexual, health, and longevity practices that were related to the more alchemical practices and martial arts undertaken by Daoist monks and nuns. Records of such gymnastic practices go back more than two thousand years and continue today in various *qigong* (ch'i-kung) and *taiji* (t'ai-chi) practices that are popular around the globe. Such popular cultural practices have been loosely labeled "Daoist," though they need have no specific religious or spiritual focus.

Although it may be tempting to think that Chinese religion served chiefly to support the status quo in terms of the authority of men and the continuance of the imperial system, religion was also a mechanism for social subversion. As in medieval Europe, women who were unwilling to submit to the requirements of marriage were able to assert their will by entering a monastery. The monastic system provided a means for the education and training of people outside the standard male Confucian model of classical studies, examinations, and a career in the civil service. Moreover, sectarian cults arose focused on the advent of a future Buddha or Daoist savior. Such cults attracted mass followings with their claims to establish heaven on earth rather than provide the way for humans to attain paradise after death. When such notions of future salvation were understood to be imminently available, religion became a powerful tool for subverting the existing dynastic power structure. Such movements helped hasten the end of the Han, Yuan, and Qing dynasties and were generally viewed with suspicion by the authorities whenever they occurred throughout Chinese history. Not only were they ambiguous with regard to the existing political order but they also tended to undermine existing social structures by proclaiming radical notions such as the equality of the sexes or the dissolution of traditional blood ties in favor of newly invented sectarian fraternities. Religion was thus not simply the means of maintaining the existing social structure; it also was a mechanism for forming new social arrangements. Traditional Chinese society was frequently able to tolerate such dissidence within its own structures, but when religious movements were seen as threatening to the foundations of society, they were inevitably put down with blood and the sword.

Geography

A third and perhaps less common way of viewing traditional Chinese religions is in terms of their geography. Here it is useful to think in terms of some customary oppositions: Chinese religion versus foreign religion; central religion versus peripheral religion; urban religion versus rural religion; and mountain religion versus coastal religion. Inherent in all these dualisms is the general function of religion to create oppositions that can be expressed spatially. In the specific context of Chinese traditions this construction of sacred space also made reference to the concept of China as the "middle kingdom" (*Zhongguo*), the Chinese word for "China." This term, which originated in the Warring States period, originally was understood in the plural, referring to the various "central states" that shared the culture of writing in characters that distinguished them from the outer regions. After unification under the first Qin emperor, these "central states" became the "middle kingdom"—that is, the single China that is familiar to us today. At the center of this middle kingdom was the capital, and at the center of the capital was the imperial palace; at the center of the imperial palace was the court from which the emperor governed the distant corners of the empire. This cosmology was replicated everywhere. The magistrate had his offices in a courtyard at the center of the city. The city was surrounded by walls. Outside the walls was the countryside, which provided the food to keep the city functioning; beyond the countryside was the wilderness, inhabited by bandits, beasts, and barbarians. Similarly, the heavens were viewed as a circular canopy rotating around a central ridge-pole beneath the pole star. The most significant deities were the ones of the Big Dipper (Ursa Major), which lit the way to the apex of heaven and around which the lesser constellations revolved. Chinese religion, then, was concerned with the construction of space, with structuring in a certain way the relations of human beings with their surroundings so as to promote a cosmic vision of order and harmony.

Central to this worldview was a network of sacred mountains that symbolized the center and the four corners of the empire. In addition, both Buddhists and Daoists claimed their own sacred mountains and established monasteries and retreat houses there. At certain times and in certain locations, these sacred geographies overlapped each other. The Ming emperors, for instance, patronized the Daoist sacred site at Mt. Wudang, home of a deity known as the Perfect Warrior (*Zhenwu*). Through imperial favor the Daoist site was raised in importance, and a vast complex of temples was erected; it remains one of the most prominent of sacred mountains to the present day. Another example is Mt. Tai in Shandong province, the Eastern mountain of the imperial cult and today sacred to both Buddhists and Daoists. On this mountain, the Qin emperor who reunited the country following the dissolution of the Warring States period instituted new sacrifices to the supreme cosmic rulers. Only the emperor was permitted to offer these *feng* and *shan* sacrifices. Through this exclusive ritual the emperor asserted his own personal connection to the cosmic powers that govern heaven and earth. He established himself not only as the chief mediator between the gods and the people but also as an indispensable element in the theological geography that constituted the Chinese understanding of their place in the universe.

The Wu emperor of the subsequent Han dynasty reinstated these sacrifices and built a temple at the base of the mountain where the entire cosmic pantheon could assemble to witness the rituals over which the emperor personally presided (see Bokenkamp 1996). The imperial cult thus served to reinforce the authority of the emperor over his people, an authority vested in the ancient notion of the Mandate of Heaven, by virtue of which imperial power was divinely constituted. Equally significant, however, was that the rituals served to construct a sacred space by means of which the nation could orient itself in relation to the heavens above and the peripheral spaces to the north, south, east, and west.

This sacred cosmography was replicated in miniature at all levels of the state government, including especially the construction of cities along north-south and east-west axes, with the city temple and magistrate's quarters at the center. Interestingly, however, the human body was also conceived of as a sacred landscape ruled over by the heart (standing for the emperor) and with the major organs (heart, liver, lungs, spleen, and kidneys) standing for the five sacred mountains and the five directions (the center plus the four cardinal points). In this way the imperial topography based on a numerology of five directions, or a three by three square, became the single map upon which the body, the state, and the cosmos could be located (see Miller 2003).

Daoist priests sought to unite these three dimensions of existence (the body, the state, and the cosmos) into a single metaphysical framework predicated on the refracted, multiple energies of the evolving Dao. To perform their rituals they erected temporary altars, sacred spaces in which the "orthodox unity" of the Daoist cosmos could be imposed upon the relative disharmony of mundane existence. Through ritual movements and internal meditations they brought into alignment the complex and disparate elements of the various landscapes into a singular harmonic vision, thus restoring peace, health, and longevity to the communities they served. In some instances, however, the Daoist vision of a sacred landscape went beyond the idea of restoring harmony and stability and aimed toward a more transcendent state. Daoists developed techniques of meditation in which the landscape of the body could be harmonized with the constellated powers of the night sky. In so doing the body's fluid energies were transmuted into a radiant body of precious florescence compared in the literature to a flawless, dazzling jewel. Unlike the state religion, which was designed to evoke a unitarian monolithic order, the Daoist vision tended toward a more subtle and ethereal glory.

The major problem faced by Buddhists was that their religious system could not so easily be integrated into this monolithic Chinese vision. Their religion, known in Chinese as *fojiao,* had a clearly foreign name, and their mythology made reference to strange people living in distant areas. Clearly the success of world religions such as Christianity, Islam, and Buddhism has historically lain in their ability to transcend the geographic and cultural limits of their origins. Buddhists have done so by presenting their tradition as an answer to the fundamental problems of human existence that are shared by all who live and die. Although couched in the culturally strange dialectic of emptiness and the transmigration of souls, Buddhist teaching was relatively easily translated into terms that Chinese people were able to grasp, even though their grasping of them may have amounted to a creative misunderstanding of the Sanskrit and Pali originals. But in order to plant Buddhism firmly within the Chinese cultural landscape it was necessary for Buddhists to overcome the ideological antipathy toward the periphery that was implicit in the sacred imperial vision of the Chinese state. That was achieved through promoting Buddhism as an ally of the court and as a supporter of the emperor. Buddhist rituals to benefit the state were translated from their original Indian context and formed the basis of a "National Protection Buddhism" (Orzech 1996, 372). In such a way Buddhist teachings, Buddhist institutions, and Buddhist mountains gained a place in the sacred geography of the state and came to be accepted without question as part and parcel of the Chinese religious landscape.

A second aspect of the geography of religions that needs to be considered is the way in which China's various environments have nurtured a corresponding variety of religious expressions. Already mentioned are the local deities that oversee specific geographic and existential domains. Chapter 10 of this book details the way in which Mazu, the goddess sacred to coastal communities in southeast China, has accompanied her devotees to North America's Pa-

Pagoda with Dragon Snow Mountain in the distance. (PhotoDisc, Inc.)

cific coast. Chapter 6 tells of the way in which Japanese and Western deities are now revealing themselves through the voices of Taiwanese spirit mediums.

Beyond these coastal religions, and island provinces subject to frequent commerce and migration, China's agricultural heartland also enjoyed its own religious expressions and local cults centered on local temples and ancestral shrines—as well as the pan-Chinese Buddhist or Daoist traditions. Beyond the domesticated countryside, the sacred mountains were always sites of tourism and pilgrimage attracting visitors and monks from the surrounding rural areas and towns. And beyond the hillside monasteries, the rugged wilderness of forests, caves, and mountains served their own religious clientele in the form of Buddhist and Daoist hermits on extended solitary retreats.

The solitude of living in caves and the direct experience of nature provided an environment which nurtured a unique religious experience that was institutionally sanctioned but that effectively took place beyond the bounds of traditional religious norms (see Porter 1993).

The third way in which geography and religion interacted in traditional Chinese society was in the connection between the earth and the realm of the dead. In traditional Chinese popular religion, death was not understood as an instantaneous, on-off process, but rather as a lingering affair in which the body of the deceased, though no longer animate, was still a reality for the living and could not be disposed of simply by cremation or exposure to the elements. Rather, it had to be placed carefully in a new home in the earth and tended to through regular ministrations at the annual Qingming, or grave-sweeping, festival. Of particular importance was the gravesite: it had to harmonize with the contours of the earth and the flow of *qi* energy through the local landscape. The system for determining appropriate gravesites was known as *fengshui*. Although *fengshui* has since been adapted into a knowledge system designed to maximize good fortune in all manner of situations, in its most original form, *fengshui* masters were required to design not houses for the living but burial spaces for the dead (see Bruun 2003; Field 2001). In the popular worldview that constituted the rationale for the traditional Chinese view of death and burial, the earth was not simply "dirt" or inert "material" but a living organism that interacted with all its inhabitants. Just as the body was imagined as a landscape with organs for mountains and *qi* meridians for streams, so also the landscape was envisaged as a body through which energy flowed in subterranean channels whose locations had to be properly divined and taken into consideration.

All this suggests that the Chinese sacred landscape at the local level did not sit well with the grand monolithic scheme envisioned by the imperial state cult. Rather, it was a fluid landscape whose contours shifted with time and whose basic features were subject to a process of evolution, transformation, and even erosion. Local religious specialists paid attention to their micro-environments, and hermits inhabited the stark solace of mountain grottos. While the imperial vision sought to subordinate the various elements of the disparate Chinese landscape into a totalitarian vision, and the Daoist priests ritually incorporated all manner of deities into a rich and complex pantheon headed by the Jade Emperor, these were religious tasks that could never be complete and that required constant and repeated ritual actions.

Divinity or Divination

Through the three brief sketches above I have attempted to portray a vision of traditional Chinese religion that is consistent with traditional scholarship and that will serve as the backdrop to the discussion in the next chapter of the advent of European modernity and the corresponding Chinese response to it. But there is one aspect of traditional Chinese religions that has not yet been covered in detail—namely, the close association between Chinese religious traditions and traditional Chinese knowledge systems such as *fengshui,* traditional Chinese medicine, physiognomy, and divination. Perhaps one of the most basic aspects of Chinese traditions that needs to be emphasized is that theology was not an important mode of religious expression. That is, Chinese scholars did not compose vast scholastic tomes on the topic of divinity—the nature of the gods, the creation of the universe and the afterlife, and so forth. Those topics have been central to Christian and Islamic ways of thinking about religion, but it is a safe generalization to say that they were not essential to the traditional Chinese ways of thinking. (The next chapter will show that, because of this, the conflict of tradition with modernity will take a different expression in China than in Europe.) In lieu of divinity, then, as an important form of religious expression, stood divination, a drive to negotiate and master one's fate.

The most powerful example of this difference can be observed through comparing Christian churches with Chinese temples. In a Christian church one of the main forms of religious expression is the reading of scriptures and the teaching through sermons. That is because Christianity is a religion centered on a book, the Bible, and one that developed in its early years in conversation with the Greek philosophy of Plato and Aristotle. Jesus himself was understood by early Christians not just as a personality, a figure about whom stories were told, but as "the Word"—that is, as a theological concept. From its inception, therefore, the Christian religion has been a conceptual religion, and membership in the religion was codified not just in terms of a ritual (baptism) but also in terms of a creed, a set of statements that expressed the fundamental beliefs of the tradition. For this reason, in European languages, there is a high degree of overlap between the words "religion," "creed," and "belief." A religious person in the West is commonly known as a *believer.*

In traditional Chinese temples, by contrast, there are no "believers" who assemble for "teachings" or who recite a "creed" together. Rather, individuals come to the temples because they are concerned with their fortune. One of

A fortune-teller gives a reading to a young family in the Wong Tai Sin Temple of Kowloon,
Hong Kong. (Earl & Nazima Kowall/Corbis)

the main functions of temples is thus to provide a space in which it is possible
for individuals to grapple with fortune or destiny. There are two main ways
that takes place: one is through prayer for good fortune, whether to Buddhist,
Daoist, or local deities; the other is through divination practices such as the
Yijing, in which individuals cast lots or use some other game of chance to divine their fortunes. This is not to say that the fundamental differences in the
Buddhist or Daoist belief systems are irrelevant. Rather, they are less relevant
than might be suspected by someone schooled in exclusivist Western religions that have historically coalesced around, and distinguished themselves
by, specific theological doctrines.

To pray for good fortune and to know one's fortune are thus ultimate concerns of Chinese religious practice, and Chinese cultural and religious traditions are full of methods for addressing those ultimate concerns. Historically,
Western religions have distinguished themselves from such "superstitions" as
tarot or astrology, regarding them as a debased form of spiritual expression

or as a type of pagan magic. (Despite this, various forms of divination have remained persistent, though marginalized, features of the Western cultural landscape.) Chinese religious traditions, however, have been more closely woven into this culture of divination and fortune-telling. A brief look at the life of a traditional Chinese saint, Chen Tuan (fl. tenth century), will serve as a useful example.

Chen Tuan was a figure of the Song dynasty who was widely renowned by Daoists and Confucians alike and became a well-known figure of popular culture. His skill at prognosticating future events through physiognomy endeared him to the court; his exposition of the principles behind this system became central to the development of Neo-Confucian philosophy; and his practice of certain forms of internal alchemy was legendary among Daoists (Kohn 2001, 16). In the legends and traditions that grew up around him he came to be revered as a saint and a mystic—not because of any asceticism or moral sacrifice, nor because of any theological wisdom, but because of his legendary success at divining the future based on the patterns of *qi* energy in the cosmos and, in particular, in an individual's face and body. One could say that Chen Tuan was a doctor of divination, not of divinity.

Chen Tuan was universally lionized in his time and after his death because he had mastered skills that were highly prized by the cultural elite. Divination was vital to the dynastic courts because it provided cosmological confirmation of the legitimacy of their rule—especially after the overthrow of a previous dynasty and at the start of a new one. Divination practices such as astrology and physiognomy were thus part and parcel of the ideological system that underpinned traditional Chinese society, comparable to the role of the papacy in legitimating the rule of European monarchs. With the onslaught of colonialism and European modernity in the nineteenth century, traditional forms of Chinese religion would be called into question precisely because they were so intimately allied to the traditional systems of knowledge that were deemed to be unscientific and politically backward. "Science" would be seen as replacing "superstition," and religious leaders would seek to distance themselves from practices such as divination and to modernize their traditions so as to conform more easily to the ideological contours of modernity.

References
Bokenkamp, Stephen. 1996. "Record of the Feng and Shan Sacrifices." Pp. 250–260 in *Religions of China in Practice*. Edited by Donald Lopez, Jr. Princeton: Princeton University Press.

Bruun, Ole. 2003. *Fengshui in China: Geomantic Divination between State Orthodoxy and Popular Religion.* Honolulu: University of Hawai'i Press.

Field, Stephen L. 2001. "In Search of Dragons: The Folk Ecology of Fengshui." Pp. 185–200 in *Daoism and Ecology: Ways within a Cosmic Landscape.* Edited by N. J. Girardot, James Miller, and Liu Xiaogan. Cambridge: Harvard University Press.

Jensen, Lionel. 1997. *Manufacturing Confucianism.* Durham, NC: Duke University Press.

Kohn, Livia. 2001. *Chen Tuan: Discussions and Translations.* eDao series. Cambridge, MA: Three Pines.

Miller, James. 2003. "Daoism and Nature." Pp. 393–410 in *Nature across Cultures: Non-Western Views of Nature and Environment.* Edited by Helaine Selin. Dordrecht: Kluwer Academic.

Orzech, Charles. 1996. "The Scripture on Perfect Wisdom for Humane Kings Who Wish to Protect Their States." Pp. 372–380 in *Religions of China in Practice.* Edited by Donald Lopez, Jr. Princeton: Princeton University Press.

Porter, Bill. 1993. *The Road to Heaven: Encounters with Chinese Hermits.* San Francisco: Mercury House.

Taylor, Charles. 1989. *The Sources of the Self.* Cambridge: Harvard University Press.

Teiser, Stephen F. 1996. "The Spirits of Chinese Religion." Pp. 3–37 in *Religions of China in Practice.* Edited by Donald Lopez, Jr. Princeton: Princeton University Press.

2

The Opium of the People:
Religion, Science, and Modernity

JAMES MILLER

CHEN DUXIU (1879–1942) was one of China's most influential advocates of revolution and modernization and a founder of the Chinese Communist Party (CCP). In 1915 he penned a famous "call to youth" in the journal *New Youth* (*Xin qingnnian*), which he edited. In that article he called for a new type of young person to lead China into its future, a young person with four chief characteristics: someone who was independent, not servile; progressive, not conservative; aggressive, not retiring; and cosmopolitan, not isolationist (see Lawrance 2004, 2–3). Chen's description of the young leader of the future precisely marks out the values embraced by China's modernizers, their worldview, and their self-identity. It does so not only by defining what Chen saw as desirable and modern but also, significantly, by repudiating what he saw as traditional. This chapter seeks to explain how the values of "modernity" were constructed over and against the values of "tradition," and what their impact was on Chinese religions in the twentieth century. To do so, the chapter first presents a brief summary of China's history from 1839 to the present. Next it analyzes more carefully the ideology of radical modernity espoused by Chen and his successors and the reasons for their opposition to traditional Chinese values. It ends by questioning the value of the binary paradigm of tradition versus modernity and offers the alternative paradigm of globalization as a theoretical framework for interpreting the complexity of the contemporary Chinese religious situation that the reader will encounter in subsequent chapters.

Historical Background

The Chinese historian Immanuel Hsü has been criticized for presenting the view that the Chinese encounter with modernity was fundamentally an encounter with European values and ideas (see Cohen 1984). Research has indicated a wealth of transformation and vitality within the intellectual and economic life of the Qing dynasty (1644–1911), and also a significant impact of Chinese ideas on Western philosophy in the Enlightenment period (Mungello 1999). The relative vitality of Chinese religions documented by the subsequent chapters of this book also suggests that the distinctly European embrace of secularization has failed to take hold completely in the Chinese cultural world. Indeed the resurgence of China as an economic and political power in the late twentieth and early twenty-first centuries has also entailed an accompanying resurgence of traditional Chinese cultural and religious values. But despite those important caveats, it is impossible to tell the story of Chinese religions in the twentieth century without explaining the concrete impact of European thought on the way Chinese people view their own cultural and religious heritage. This story is bound up with the history of European colonialism and with the European Enlightenment.

Until 1833 the British East India Company held a monopoly on the import of all tea into British territories. The source of much of this tea was China, which had created an arrangement known as the Guangzhou system, by which certain authorized foreign enterprises were permitted to do business in carefully demarcated areas known as factories outside the city of Guangzhou (Canton). Although the trade was hugely profitable for the East India Company, the British thirst for tea created an enormous trade imbalance with China, because the Chinese did not import any British goods in return. Instead, the tea had to be paid for in gold and silver. Seeking to address this trade deficit, the East India Company started shipping opium from India to China, selling the opium through its so-called factories in Guangzhou and sending its clippers back to Britain full of Chinese tea. By 1839 the Chinese consumption of opium had increased dramatically, so that they now imported some 240,000 kilograms of the drug, representing more than half of their total foreign imports. The trade imbalance had now swung in Britain's favor, and the British were able to use Chinese gold and silver to pay for their imperial ambitions in India.

Chinese protests against the opium trade resulted in a British declaration of war in 1839, the dispatch of an armed fleet, and open hostilities in 1840 that saw the Chinese roundly defeated by superior British firepower. The resulting Treaty of Nanjing in 1842 and the subsequent so-called unequal treaties signed with France, the United States, Germany, and Russia gave Western powers the right to establish settlements on the Chinese mainland under Western jurisdiction and to conduct trade with low fixed tariffs. The failure of the Qing court to ratify a subsequent unequal treaty known as the Treaty of Tianjin in 1858 led to a joint invasion by British and French forces, the burning of the imperial summer palace, and still further concessions wrought at the barrel of a gun. These included the right of missionaries to travel freely in China's interior with a kind of diplomatic immunity that put them entirely above Chinese law. The missionaries were instrumental in bringing European thought to China and establishing colleges and universities. Several of China's revolutionary leaders studied in those institutions; many studied abroad, and some were even Christians. As Francis Ching-Wah Yip points out in Chapter 8, there is no doubt that the Christian missionaries directly contributed to the adoption of Western thinking and European values that we see in such revolutionaries as Chen Duxiu. Ironically, however, they were tainted by their association with European colonialism and the unequal treaties and were regarded as part of the problem that modernization would seek to eliminate.

One of the most devastating consequences of this missionary activity, however, was the millenarian religious movement known as the Way of Great Peace (Taiping dao), which fused together Christian and Chinese religious ideas and spread like wildfire among the Hakka ethnic minority community in southern China. The leader of the Taipings, Hong Xiuquan (1812–1864), believed himself to be the younger brother of Jesus and preached a revolutionary gospel of gender equality, abstention from drugs, and the coming of the Kingdom of God on earth. He organized his followers into communes, armed them with weapons and an apocalyptic faith, and took over much of southern China between 1850 and 1864, destroying local temples and the instruments of Qing authority. The Taiping rebellion was put down only when the court assigned a high degree of military autonomy to its elite officials. The sheer scale of death, estimated at between 10 and 40 million persons, was a significant factor in the ultimate weakening of the court and the dissolution of the empire.

From the end of the Taiping rebellion to the mid-1890s, China's relations with the Western powers were relatively stable, but the court was increasingly weakened by internal dissent. The Muslim rebellions (1855–1873) in China's northwest provinces, for example, were put down only at horrific cost in terms of human lives. China's intellectual leaders aimed at strengthening the administration and the economy through an emphasis on traditional values rather than reform and "modernization." Their efforts at "self-strengthening" are generally described as conservative, in that they tried to preserve the existing system of government rather than reform or overthrow it. But in 1894 Japan invaded Korea on the pretext of putting down a rebellion, defeating the Chinese armies there and, under the terms of the Treaty of Shimonoseki in 1895, obtaining the island of Taiwan and the Liaoning peninsula on China's mainland. Thus humiliated by a remote island nation, China had no choice but to submit to the demands of Russia, France, and Germany to let them put together a force to expel Japan from China's mainland. This intervention, though successful, was paid for by the exacting of yet further territorial concessions from China. To many Chinese intellectuals this proved that the existing political order was no longer capable of guaranteeing China's harmonious prosperity. It was not that what was required was a change of leadership, but rather an entirely new political worldview.

A compromise vision was proposed by two reformist intellectuals, Kang Youwei (1858–1927) and Liang Qichao (1873–1929), and was implemented in a brief "hundred days' reform" authorized by the court in 1898. Kang promoted a quasi-religious utopian vision of an Era of Great Peace that would be a constitutional monarchy with Confucianism as its state religion, gender equality, and even gay rights. Kang's and Liang's reforms were quickly shut down by conservative forces, and they fled for their lives to Japan. The Dowager Empress Cixi (1835–1908) reassumed power and covertly supported a popular antiforeign uprising known as the Boxer Movement, which lasted from 1897 to 1901. During that uprising, Christian churches in particular were destroyed because they concretely symbolized the new foreign worldview, and Chinese converts to Christianity were executed on sight. This movement was deemed a rebellion by the foreign powers when it reached its height in 1899–1900; it was put down by allied Western armies that exacted severe economic reparations from China as well as the end of the traditional Confucian examination system, which had provided the civil service with its administrators. By 1905 many Chinese in-

HISTORICAL BACKGROUND | 35

tellectuals argued that the Qing dynasty was doomed. Sun Yat-sen (1866–1925), typifying a new breed of revolutionary, established a Revolutionary Alliance or "United League," which advocated nationalism, democracy, and "people's livelihood," a type of socialist land reform. In 1911 the empire came to an abrupt and anticlimactic end as provinces in swift succession declared their independence from Beijing.

Sun Yat-sen, who was abroad at the time, hurried back to China, and in 1912 he was proclaimed provisional president of the Republic of China; Pu Yi, the last emperor of the Qing dynasty, was forced to abdicate the dragon throne. For political reasons, however, Sun Yat-sen stood aside and permitted the military commander Yuan Shikai (1859–1916) to be formally elected as the republic's first president. Sun headed the Guomindang (Kuomintang), or republican party, organized in 1912 to succeed the Revolutionary Alliance. Inasmuch as the disintegration of the Qing dynasty had been obtained by brokering deals with the many regional factions and warlords, such as Yuan Shikai, Sun had not succeeded in creating a stable government system to replace the imperial system. To all intents and purposes, the Republic of China was a unified country in name only, and the first half of the twentieth century, though economically more stable and prosperous, was just as bad for China politically as the second half of the nineteenth.

In 1915, Yuan installed himself as the constitutional monarch, so as to shore up central control over the still disintegrating country, and acceded to a series of twenty-one demands presented by Japan, conceding territory and trading rights in an effort to stave off a war that he was in no position to win. After Yuan's death in 1916, China effectively fell under the control of a group of regional warlords, each vying for control of his own territory. This period of political chaos, however, sparked one of the most intense phases of intellectual vibrancy in China's history. The time between 1915 and 1922, known as the May Fourth era, or the New Culture Movement, is commonly described as a transition to a completely new way of thinking about the world and a rejection of traditional values. This intellectual movement takes its name from a mass protest by college students in Beijing on May 4, 1919, against the Treaty of Versailles, which ended World War I and in which Chinese territory was given away in secret deals between Japan and its European allies. During the seven-year period, symbolized by the May 4 protest, China's intellectuals drank freely from the fountain of modernity and became intoxicated with science, democracy, Darwinism, and Marxism. Unremarked upon

Chiang Kai-shek (Jiang Jieshi) during the attempt to organize war against Japan, ca. 1936. (Bettman/Corbis)

at this time, but subsequently significant, was the founding of the Chinese Communist Party in 1921 by Chen Duxiu and his friend Li Dazhao (1889–1927).

On the advice of Moscow, the newly established communists entered into a United Front with the nationalists in 1924, but in 1927 the nationalist leader Chiang Kai-shek (1887–1975) broke the agreement with a murderous purge of communists that took place just as Chiang assumed control over Shanghai and its wealth. From that period on, the Communist Party became increasingly based in rural areas and fell increasingly under the dominance of Mao Zedong (1893–1976), the eventual leader of Communist China. Mao developed his political ideology in reference to China's agricultural heartland, as opposed to Marx's more urban experiences of industrial capitalism.

With the communists severely weakened and relegated to remote areas, Chiang Kai-shek strengthened his hold over China. Although himself sympathetic to Christianity, Chiang and his wife, May-ling, promoted a New Life Movement that advocated Confucianism as a national code. This state-led moral reform movement provided a guide for disciplined life that blended traditional values with modern notions of citizenship and nationalism. At the same time that he promoted this code, Chiang also undertook to exterminate the communists with an army recently invigorated by German training. Mao's communists and their army escaped only after the legendary 6,000-mile Long March from their southern base to China's remote northeast. Fewer than 10 percent survived, but at their new base at Yan'an in Shaanxi province they were able to regroup and finally implement the policies of land reform that they had been developing.

In 1937, Japan again invaded China, bringing about an uneasy truce between the communists and the nationalists as they temporarily joined forces to defeat the invaders. During the period between 1937 and 1945, however, the nationalists and their army gradually came to be hated by the peasantry, whereas the communists gradually won a large following with the land reforms they undertook in areas under their control. The defeat of Japan in 1945 did not immediately bring about a communist victory in China, but World War II certainly ruined the nationalists. The civil war resumed in 1946 and culminated in the battle of Huaihai, in which Chiang ordered the air force to bomb his own troops, lest their weapons fall into communist hands. When in 1949 communist victory was ensured, Chiang and the nationalists fled to the island of Taiwan, recently liberated from Japanese occupation, carrying with them the country's massive gold reserves and important art treasures. The Republic of China continues to this day in Taiwan, supported militarily by the United States. Its separation from the mainland remains a thorny diplomatic and military issue.

On October 1, 1949, Chairman Mao Zedong proclaimed the liberation of the Chinese people and the establishment of the People's Republic of China in Tian'anmen Square, Beijing, bounded to the north by the Forbidden City, the walled-off section of the capital that housed the imperial palaces and courts. As their grip on the nation strengthened between 1947 and 1952, the communists undertook land redistribution, as well as the purging of the gentry and the bourgeoisie. During the first Five Year Plan (1952–1957), these reforms continued with the collectivization of agriculture in a largely successful attempt to turn China back into a stable country that was able to feed itself. Mao put his distinctive stamp on Chinese communist ideology, however, with the disastrous Great Leap Forward that began in 1958. Overthrowing traditional Marxist economics and party bureaucrats, he calculated that China could become a major industrial power through an effort of collective will. The rural population was organized into communes intended to achieve economies of scale in agriculture, and the entire country set up backyard furnaces to produce steel. Within two years it was clear that Mao's plan had been a disastrous failure, and he was sidelined by other party leaders who installed Liu Shaoqi as head of state.

By 1965, Mao had become so thoroughly dissatisfied with the centrist policies Liu had put in place that he launched what he termed a Cultural Revolution to revitalize the country and restore the party's ideological purity. The

Cultural Revolution officially lasted from 1966 until Mao's death in 1976; in its first three years, it was a period of terror and anarchy during which young Red Guards overthrew the existing authorities, imprisoned or killed those deemed ideologically suspect, and unleashed havoc and destruction on anything associated with "old China"—including its temples and cultural treasures. As Mao's health declined in the 1970s, the Cultural Revolution came increasingly under the control of a so-called Gang of Four headed by Mao's wife, Jiang Qing. After Mao's death, the reformist wing of the party wrestled back control and put the Gang of Four on trial. By 1978, Deng Xiaoping, a pragmatist rather than an ideologue, became recognized as the country's paramount leader. He put China on a path toward economic reform and liberalization that led to the country's extraordinary economic growth in the last two decades of the twentieth century. Calls for China's political modernization, however, have been consistently repressed, most tragically in the massacre of prodemocracy students that were demonstrating in Tian'anmen Square on June 4, 1989. Since then the party has maintained its authority chiefly by delivering a steady diet of economic progress and nationalist propaganda to China's 1.3 billion people.

Having briefly surveyed the main facts of China's modern political history, it is time to examine more closely the ideology of modernity that China's revolutionaries embraced, and its effect upon China's religions. To do so we will return to Chen Duxiu's four characteristics of the new Chinese leader.

Independent, Not Servile

The first characteristic that Chen Duxiu advocated was independence, not servility. In his essay he argued that "all men are equal. Each has his right to be independent," and he went on to describe modern European history as a history of emancipation, which

> means freeing oneself from the bondage of slavery and achieving a completely independent and free personality. . . . [T]here is no reason why one should blindly follow others. On the other hand loyalty, filial piety, chastity and righteousness are a slavish morality (quoted in Lawrance 2004, 2).

Here Chen is distinguishing two senses of self-identity. The one he advocates, that of freedom and independence, can be traced back to the ideology of the European Enlightenment, and in particular to the concept of the autonomous rational self, which was most famously summed up in the maxim by Immanuel Kant (1724–1804), "Dare to think."

Kant's view was the culmination of a tradition of doubt and skepticism begun by Descartes, who declared that the only safe starting place for any philosophy was the one thing of which one could be absolutely certain. For Descartes the only true source of intellectual authority could be oneself as a thinking person: "I think, therefore I am." The authority of tradition, history, and even sensory experience had the potential to be deceptive and was to be distrusted. This epistemological breakthrough also entailed a set of moral and political consequences. If individuals were autonomous and rational, there could be no reason in principle why they should be subject to the authority of others except by free, rational choice. There could be no "divine right of kings" whereby monarchs claimed the privilege of power by appeal to the will of an invisible deity. Nor could there be any justification for slavery or oppression. The ethical obligations that one owed to a fellow human being were to be grounded not in the fear of divine judgment but rather in the rights and freedoms that are vested equally in all autonomous rational beings.

The view that Chen denigrates, however, is a sense of self that is defined first and foremost by one's obligation to others. Loyalty, filial piety, chastity, and righteousness are forms of relationship that are most clearly associated with Confucianism. In the Confucian view human self-identity is not grounded in some ultimate freedom or individual autonomy but rather by the quality of relationships that one engages in with others. One must treat others well because one's relationships constitute one's own integrity and identity.

Since both the European Enlightenment and Confucian thinking result in a reasonable and frankly attractive set of ethical principles that are not based on fear of supernatural punishment, it is necessary to ask why Chen considered the former so attractive and the latter so repulsive. What was so wrong with Confucian loyalty or respect for one's parents?

There are at least two answers to this question. The first is that Confucianism was despised because it represented the ideological orthodoxy adopted by the Qing dynasty, which was (it must be remembered) of Manchu ethnic origin. Confucian thinking was therefore tainted by its association with the subjugation of Chinese people to the foreign yoke, whether Manchu, Japanese, or

Western. Paradoxically, the quintessential Chinese philosophy of deference and piety was associated with national humiliation; the quintessential European philosophy of autonomy and self-determination thus became the vehicle for national pride.

The second answer is that the Confucian virtues of loyalty and filial piety have at their core a conservative or retrospective element. Loyalty means acting in the present on the basis of a relationship established in the past. Because of this prior relationship one is obliged to act in a certain way in the present. In effect it is a means for the past to gain control over the present. Similarly, the concept of respect for one's parents and ancestors vests authority in age, and it entails a deference on the part of the young. Kant's philosophy did not make any claim that elders are wiser than youth. Rather he held that the truth is radically free—it belongs to no one save those who have the audacity to think it for themselves.

In an article written the year after his *Call to Youth,* Chen Duxiu places "the way of Confucius" in direct opposition to "modern life." He argues that Confucianism is holding the country back because it does not allow for individual autonomy. He writes of Confucian values:

> Sons and wives possess neither personal individuality nor personal property. Fathers and elder brothers bring up their sons and younger brothers and are in turn supported by them. . . . This is absolutely not the way to personal independence (quoted in de Bary and Lufrano 2000, 353).

Chen thus associates Confucianism with tradition, and he views traditional culture as a set of unreasonable bonds that are preventing China's liberation. In particular he goes on to attack the social conventions associated with Confucianism that restrict the liberty of women and uphold the patriarchal control of husbands and fathers. Traditional culture and religion were thus held to be a burden or obligation restricting China's economic and social freedom.

It should be noted that although Chen is attacking the specifics of the traditional way of life, his attack serves also to undermine the notion of traditional society itself. As Prasenjit Duara (1991, 69) has observed, in traditional societies people do not recognize that there can be valid alternatives to the values that their society espouses. In modern societies, individuals feel free to choose their value systems. In that sense, therefore, it was not merely Confucianism that was the object of the modernizer's hatred, but rather the whole concept of tradition, in whose unflinching grip most people's minds, they believed, were imprisoned. Chen Duxiu's *Call to Youth* was an attempt to wake people up from the slumber of tradition to the liberating power of individual freedom.

There is here an intriguing parallel with Buddhist philosophy. The Buddha viewed the path to enlightenment as a personal quest to eliminate the root causes of suffering—though the Buddha saw those causes as psychological, not social. Moreover, one of the reasons that Zen Buddhism has become so popular in the West is that it espouses a philosophy of radical, individual enlightenment that in effect transcends the institutional and doctrinal walls of traditional Buddhist religion. Modern Buddhist reformers have consistently emphasized the values of personal enlightenment and the compatibility of Buddhism and scientific ways of thinking, so much so that one famous expositor of Buddhism famously declared that "Buddhism is not a religion" (Rahula 1959). By this statement he meant to imply that Buddhism is compatible with the sort of modern values that Chen espoused—"freeing oneself from the bondage of slavery and achieving a completely independent and free personality"—and is opposed to the "slavish morality" of blindly following others. Although Buddhist reformers in China were actively contemplating the compatibility of Buddhism with the politics of freedom and the rationality of science, such ideas had not yet filtered into the popular cultural imagination. Buddhism, like Confucianism, Daoism, and local religions, was regarded as promoting habits and customs of the past that were part of the false ideological framework deemed responsible for China's humiliation at the hands of foreigners. As much as Chen and his ideological heirs valued freedom, they despised religion.

Progressive, Not Conservative

It can readily be seen, therefore, that the logic of autonomous rationality entails a progressive historical momentum. Truth is not located in the past, in some revealed wisdom recorded in the books of prophets and seers; rather, in Kant's terms, it is to be *dared*. Thinking the truth is an audacious act that involves the risk of rejecting conventional wisdom and leaving behind the safe comforts of tradition to make a leap into the unknown. In short, it is intrinsically revolutionary, overturning the worldviews and ideas of the past. And as the histories of France, the United States, Russia, and China have all testified, that revolution is not merely an intellectual revolution but a political one, too.

The history of China's transition from dynastic imperialism to communism can thus be looked at in terms of how the cultural leaders of the time saw themselves in relation to history. The progressive reformer Kang Youwei was inspired by European science but used language adopted from Chinese classics to create a vision of progress that was both modern and Confucian. He did not advocate revolution but instead the notion that as history progresses, so also must the thinking of the people and the instruments of government. He wrote in 1898 that "[it] is a principle of things that the new is strong but the old weak; that new things are fresh but old things rotten; that new things are active but old things static" (quoted in de Bary and Lufrano 2000, 269). Kang's vision of progress was grounded not in the idea of change for change's sake but in a utopian vision of "grand commonality" (*datong*) in which all discriminations would be abolished, including those of race, class, sex, and even species. Kang's hundred days reform was, as we know, stamped out by conservatives at the court. What he praised as innovative, others condemned as thoughtlessly radical. Intellectual debate was so consumed with the question of modernity versus tradition that a 1901 imperial edict vowed to "suppress vigorously the use of the terms *new* and *old*" (quoted in ibid., 286).

The wishes of the court evidently went unheard, and the terms "progressive" and "conservative" became the rhetorical means for attacking one's opponents. But the terms "new" and "old" were more than simple rhetoric: they carried with them heavy ideological weight based on Darwin's theory of evolution and Marx's theory of history. Both Marx and Darwin were seen as advocating a view of history that came to be constitutive of the very sense of modernity. According to that view, history is not an eternal cycle or steady decline into chaos, views common in Buddhist or Daoist theology, but in fact linear and progressive, steadily advancing toward a goal. When Chen named progress as an important value in 1915, he was not simply attacking his opponents as backward; he was also accepting the view of history as progress that was common to both Marx and Darwin.

In terms of Darwin's theory of evolution, it was the sociobiological interpretation of Herbert Spencer (1820–1903) that caught the attention of Chinese intellectuals who wanted to understand why white European culture and technology were "superior" to those of the Chinese. Chen Duxiu argued that China's achievements compared unfavorably with the achievements of the "white race," and that he would "rather see the past culture of our nation disappear than see our race die out now because of its unfitness for living in the modern world" (quoted in Lawrance 2004, 2). Here he was espousing the racialist theory of cultural evolution that was popular currency at the dawn of the twentieth century. That some cultures were more evolved than others was held to be evidence of their superior adaptation to their environment. Races would compete with each other for environmental resources, and the ones that prevailed would propagate their success in future generations. Chen was eager that the "yellow race" would prove strong enough to resist the imperialist advances of the "white race."

Unlike Spencer's sociobiological view of progress, Marx held the cause of this progress to be a dialectical struggle between the ruling class and the oppressed. Such a struggle did not result in genetic warfare, but rather in a synthesis that caused history to progress to a new, more evolved form. In a dialectical system such as Marxism, therefore, what drives progress is conflict. What Chen was articulating in the set of four dichotomies we are currently discussing was not just the superiority of A over B, but rather the view that A and B must inevitably clash, that such a clash is desirable, and that out of the clash progress will be won.

Chen's rhetoric, therefore, can be accurately described as revolutionary—that is, deliberately designed to provoke a conflict. It stands in contrast to the views of harmony, tradition, and peace generally espoused by Buddhists, Confucians, and Daoists. Their conservative views were grounded in Confucian notions of restoring harmony in social relations, Daoist theories of the eternal cycle of yin and yang, or Buddhist views of the imprisonment of history in the captivating chains of karma. In order for Chen to liberate his fellow countrymen from the hands of imperialist foreigners, it was necessary for him to define his own cultural history in terms of the logic of tradition and modernity, with religion clearly belonging to the past. By asserting the opposition of progress to conservatism, science to religion, and modernity to tradition, Chen and similar-minded revolutionaries were not merely providing their perspective on history but actively provoking conflict designed to spur history forward.

The logic of progress versus conservatism and modernity versus tradition was so powerful that it was largely accepted by modernist historical scholarship both within China and without. To the extent that we too affirm this binary view of history, we are also affirming the dialectic advanced by Marx and Hegel. We are asserting that history has a goal and that it advances toward this goal by sloughing off that which is traditional in favor of that which is modern. The history of the twentieth century is largely a testament to the brutal violence of the modern, and the romantic idealization of the past, that this view of history alternately entails.

Aggressive, Not Retiring

Since conflict was at the heart of progress, it was only inevitable that modernization would be accompanied by iconoclasm, the destruction of the symbols of the past. Again it must be emphasized that the iconoclastic tendency of modernist thought does not necessarily imply needless destruction or wanton anarchy, but rather a catharsis in which culture is liberated from the vise of history and set free to embrace the future. Such a view necessarily values action over passivity and favors an outlook on life in which the solution to suffering is changing the conditions of existence rather than accommodating oneself to them. Chen, for instance, denigrates those aspects of religion that involve withdrawal to hermitages and monasteries (ibid., 3). There is no time for contemplation when people are struggling for their very survival. Chen writes that "it is our natural obligation in life to advance in spite of numerous difficulties" (quoted in ibid.).

In this context it is useful to think about Marx's famous definition of religion as the opium of the people. Marx said:

> Religious suffering is at one and the same time the expression of real suffering and a protest against real suffering. Religion is the sigh of the oppressed creature, the heart of a heartless world, and the soul of soulless conditions. It is the *opium* of the people.
>
> The abolition of religion as the *illusory* happiness of the people is the demand for their *real* happiness. To call on them to give up their illusions about their condition is to *call on them to give up a condition that requires illusions*. The criticism of religion is therefore in *embryo* the *criticism of that vale of tears* of which religion is the *halo* (quoted in Raines 2002, 171).

In this complex and poetic statement, Marx sees religion as a genuine expression of people's suffering but also as an illusory consolation for that suffering. The Marxist criticism of religion is that religious people make the mistake of choosing the illusory, supernatural happiness of some mythical world to come over a real, actual happiness grounded in social and economic fact. Religion is thereby seen as part of an addictive illusion from which humans must free themselves if they are to reach enlightenment and emancipation. But this struggle for liberation is not merely the struggle to replace illusion with reality. It is also a struggle simply to act. The effect of religion as an opiate, in Marx's terms, is that it prevents people from being stirred to action. It is a reactionary force because only if people can be awakened to the true conditions of their existence can they be forced to do something about it. Instead, people seek illusory consolations for their suffering and remain in a state of passivity.

Marxist theory generally regards religion as a by-product of social inequality. To the extent that people are oppressed, there will be religion. But Chen and many of China's modernizers viewed religion not just as a by-product of suffering but also as an active force holding back progress toward liberation. Instead of acting to free people from suffering and watch religion wither, China's modernizers thought it was necessary to free people from religion and watch suffering wither. In effect they stood classical Marxist theory on its head. The history of Chinese modernization can thus be read as a history of destructive action against traditional culture and religion, which were seen as a reactionary force that impeded China's yearning to belong to the future. The cultural and religious iconoclasm was physical, economic, and ideological. Religious institutions and buildings were torn down in waves of attacks that took place throughout the twentieth century, before and after the communist revolution. Part of this animus was directed, as in the Boxer Movement, against foreign religions as symbols of foreign occupation. Part, on the other hand, was directed against China's own religious elite where they were seen to be aligned with the class interests of the gentry and the bourgeoisie. According to Marxist economic theory, religion was to be repudiated not only because it was illusory but also because it was an economic and ideological instrument of the ruling classes. But perhaps the physical and economic destruction of China's traditional religions can be read simply as the outcome of a dialectical movement in which traditional ways of thinking were seen as absolutely incompatible with freedom and modernity.

The most compelling argument for this view is that traditional religion declined throughout the twentieth century, and not just at the hands of the communists. The military commander Yuan Shikai, for instance, though in some ways a reactionary figure in the first two decades of the twentieth century, was nevertheless committed to dismantling the "institutional foundations of popular religion" because he saw popular religion as incompatible with his goal of rebuilding China as a modern society (Duara 1991, 76). Moreover, although popular cults and local religions had previously been regarded with disdain by elite religious leaders as heterodox (*xie*), they were now increasingly categorized as superstition (*mixin*), which, as Duara notes, placed them more squarely in opposition to the values of science and progress (ibid.).

Here we see the convergence of a theory of progress with the emergence of a positivistic, atheistic scientism that advocated the rejection of all things supernatural in favor of a deliberate focus on what could be empirically seen and verified. Wu Zhihui (1865–1953) was an influential advocate of progress and science and an iconoclast who advocated throwing the classics down the toilet (de Bary and Lufrano 2000, 374). In his famous personal creed he asked, "What is the need of any spiritual element or the so-called soul, which never meets any real need anyway?" The answer to all of life's problems was to be found in science, through which "all things in the universe can be explained" (ibid., 375). One did not have to be a Marxist to be a scientist, but there was certainly a strong overlap between the two when it came to the emphasis on material reality over speculative metaphysics, and demonstrable activity over quietistic passivity.

Modernizers thus attacked not only China's patriarchal traditions but also its traditional knowledge systems, such as astrology, *fengshui*, or physiognomy, all of which were deemed superstition and incompatible with modern science. The fact that modern China saw the need to regulate religion and prohibit superstition demonstrates clearly the self-identity of the "new China" was founded on an absolute disjunction between tradition and modernity.

Cosmopolitan, Not Isolationist

Chen Duxiu's fourth characteristic of the future leaders of China is perhaps the one that has been most ambivalently embraced, precisely because the struggle for China's modernization was forged out of the conflict between China and foreign imperialist powers. The paradox already noted is that Chen advocated China's strengthening not by a reassertion of its tradition and culture but by an embrace of progress, which effectively meant an embrace of the West. To embrace the future meant to embrace the world: "When its citizens lack knowledge of the world, how can a nation expect to survive in it?" (quoted in Lawrance 2004, 3). This indicates that although Chen was actively in favor of what we would now call globalization, it was chiefly for the purpose of strengthening China.

But in advocating cosmopolitanism over isolationism Chen was making a specific attack on the cosmology that had underpinned traditional Chinese society. In this traditional worldview, as discussed in Chapter 1, China saw itself as the middle country, at the center of the world, and with a hierarchical power structure conceived of as concentric circles radiating out from the capital where the emperor, as the father of the people and the son of heaven, held court.

It is this "geography of power" that has remained most clearly in place in the transition to the new China. When Chairman Mao declared the establish-

Chinese soldiers walk beneath a portrait of Mao Zedong between Tian'anmen Square and the Forbidden City, Beijing. (Steven Harris/Newsmakers/Getty Images)

ment of the People's Republic he did so in front of the Forbidden City in Beijing, where his portrait hangs to this day. Mao's picture was also hung in homes where family shrines had formerly been located. He was deified as the "great helmsman" who would chart China's course into the future. To a large degree the communists completely reinvented Chinese economics, gender relations, education, and medicine. But they did not reinvent the reverence for authority vested in the country's leaders or the power of a small number of men in Beijing over the whole country.

The hierarchy of power in traditional China thus continued into the twentieth century, with the Communist Party replacing the Confucian elite as the small number of people who effectively wielded power. Although Chen advocated the overthrow of China's traditional vision of itself, it seems doubtful that he advocated anything like a cosmopolitan society such as is found in the United States or Canada. China remains largely racially homogenous, and Chinese people, even if citizens of the United States or some other country, frequently label their non-Chinese compatriots as "foreigners."

China's integration into global society was first undertaken economically and culturally in the twentieth century. China's economic system has been opened up, and China joined the World Trade Organization in 2001. The inhabitants of China's cities now shop at Wal-Mart, as do Americans. Further, because of the relaxation of immigration rules in the United States and Canada in the 1960s, there has been a steady stream of immigrants from China to North America—so much so that, for example, mainland Chinese immigrants now represent the single largest segment of new Canadians. The combination of immigration and economic globalization has led to the strengthening of economic and cultural ties, the results of which we will discover only in the next few decades.

Paradoxically, however, this embrace of globalization has occurred at the same time as a renewed interest in China's traditional cultures and religions. Most significantly, this resurgence of interest in Confucianism, Buddhism, and Daoism indicates a broad questioning of the dialectical paradigm of tradition versus modernity that so clearly characterized the ideology of China's revolutionaries in the twentieth century.

Questioning Modernity

The status of Chinese religions in the twentieth century stands as a testament to the failure of China's revolutionaries to frame religion definitively within the construct of tradition versus modernity. One of the most important reasons for this is that religious institutions proved resourceful in adapting themselves to the cultural situation of modernity, both before and after the communist liberation of 1949. That is to say, religions have resisted being framed as "tradition" where that is taken to mean something dead and buried. Rather, the notion of tradition, as discussed in Chapter 1, speaks to the continuous handing forward of historical beliefs and values and their subsequent transformation and adaptation to the contemporary situation.

Yes, religions are traditions, but that does not necessarily mean they are imprisoned by the past. Chinese religions in the twentieth century thus sought to engage the prevailing cultural milieu through engaging in a process of reform and modernization.

The status of Christianity was particularly problematical because of its association with foreign imperialism. To avoid being framed in this way, Protestant Christian leaders developed the so-called Three-Self principles of self-administration, self-support, and self-propagation. Their intention was to cut the link between Chinese Christians and foreign missionaries so as to propagate an entirely indigenous, thoroughly Chinese Christianity that was compatible with the demands of nationalism and independence. The founding group of the Three-Self Movement issued a manifesto in 1950 "to heighten our vigilance against imperialism, to make known the clear political stand of Christians in New China, to hasten the building of a Chinese church whose affairs are managed by the Chinese themselves, and to indicate the responsibilities that should be taken up by Christians throughout the whole country in national reconstruction in New China" (quoted in de Bary and Lufrano 2000, 539–540). By placing Christianity unequivocally on the side of New China, Christians carved out a niche for themselves within the ideology of communism, but because of the history of Christianity in China they had to do so by cutting the umbilical cord to their overseas spiritual parents. Although that was relatively easy for Protestant Christians, it caused a split in the Catholic Church between those Catholics who wished to maintain an allegiance to Rome and those who, like the communist rulers, saw such an allegiance as incompatible with the spirit of modernity and nationalism.

The task that faced Buddhists was not so drastic, because even though Buddhism too was a foreign religion, it had been in China for so long that it had become to all intents and purposes thoroughly sinified. Buddhists, however, faced two quite different problems. On the one hand Buddhism had become associated with the ruling classes, because Buddhist monasteries owned vast tracts of land that they rented out to peasants. The solution to the problem of association with the gentry was effectively forced on the Buddhist clergy in the land reforms of 1950. Those reforms called for the "confiscation of land of temples, churches, schools, and collective units in the countryside and other public land" (Luo 1991, 66). In effect, then, Buddhist monks were no longer on a par with the aristocracy—though that, of course, dealt a crushing financial blow to Buddhism, the consequences of which are discussed in Chapter 4. Internally, however, Buddhists had initiated a process of reform long before such drastic measures were imposed upon them. In the Republican period Buddhist reformers such as Taixu (1890–1947) had established universities in Shanghai, Wuchang, Ningbo, and Xiamen, where Buddhist education could be modernized and reformed (Pittman 2001, 56). Reformers were concerned not only with the status of Buddhism and the appropriation of Buddhist lands by both Christian republicans and atheist communists but also—and more deeply— with the response of Buddhism to science and democracy. Buddhists were grappling with and responding to the worldview put forward by the modernist revolutionaries and were not content to accept their obsolescence. On the contrary, as early as 1935, Taixu saw a dark side to science and technology and feared the day when "consumer desires" would erupt into global conflict (ibid., 160). This suggests that he foresaw a need for the Buddhist critique of desire in an economic system founded upon the gratification of desire. Perhaps that is one reason for the interest in Buddhism in an age of global consumerism.

The official history of Daoism in the twentieth century, like that of other religions in China, has consisted of the construction of bureaucratic frameworks by which to manage the relationship between church and state. In late imperial China there was little centralized religious hierarchy but rather various lineages of priests, local temples, and monasteries. Of the various forms of Daoist expression, the easiest to bring under bureaucratic control were the monasteries. In April 1957 the first meeting of the Chinese Daoist Association was convened in Beijing. That organization was meant to represent all varieties of Daoist religion at a national level. In fact, as the fieldwork of Tam Wai Lun demonstrates in the next chapter, local forms of religious expression were never really brought under any sort of centralized control. The character of priestly, communal Daoism was such that it was frequently difficult to distinguish it from local religious cults and traditions; thus it did not really rise to the level of national political consciousness.

The history of religions in modern China has demonstrated that, although religions have been controlled, suppressed, and attacked, they have not been obliterated. After the collapse of the Cultural Revolution, with its iconoclastic destruction of China's religious heritage, the Chinese Communist Party has had to confront anew the question of religions. It is worth considering the ways in which religions have survived. To begin with, Chinese scholars have offered a standard Marxist explanation that religion is the product of suffering, and that so long as China has not achieved the communist utopian dream, religion is bound to persist. Therefore the attitude toward religion since 1979 has been one of regulation and toleration. So long as religions conform to the patriotic norms of building the new China, there is no valid reason for suppressing them. Religions have formed national associations that report to the government's Religious Affairs Bureau and have thus allied themselves with a patriotic agenda of promoting the welfare of the motherland.

Secondly, scholars have also offered a psychological-existential explanation of why, for instance, an "intellectual with a brilliant professional career could not stand the loneliness [after] his beloved wife died, so he went to a Christian pastor to learn about the church's teachings on immortality of the soul" (Luo 1991, 103). Although religion may be an illusory consolation for human suffering, people still find it useful at times of personal crisis.

Thirdly, local religious expression has varied so much and is so decentralized that it thrives in a relatively uncontrolled and uncontrollable form, especially in rural areas. Whereas urban religion or national shrines can relatively easily be brought under the oversight of central religious authorities, popular local religion is much harder to regulate.

But from the perspective of political ideology evident in the Third Plenary Session of the Eleventh Party Congress, which restored freedom of religion after the Cultural Revolution, perhaps the most important reason for the survival and even resurgence of religion in contemporary China is the way in which religion has been formally distinguished from superstition. At the Eleventh Party Congress in 1979, five religions were recognized: Buddhism, Catholicism, Daoism, Islam, and Protestantism. Confucianism was not considered a religion. All other forms of traditional religious culture were deemed superstition.

Just as the early modernizers had legitimated science and democracy by defining them in contrast to tradition and religion, so communist policy in 1979 legitimated religion by differentiating it from superstition:

> By superstition we generally mean activities conducted by shamans, and sorcerers, such as magic medicine, magic water, divination, fortune telling, avoiding disasters, praying for rain, praying for pregnancy, exorcising demons, telling fortunes by physiognomy, locating house or tomb sites by geomancy and so forth. They are all absurd and ridiculous. Anyone possessing rudimentary knowledge will not believe in them (Document 3 from *Selected Documents of the Third Plenary Session of the Eleventh Party Congress, 1979;* quoted in MacInnis 1989, 33–34).

Labeling such activities as superstition was useful both to the religious and political elite. Religious leaders were able to carve a niche for themselves within a modern socialist state by creating forms of religion that disassociated themselves from the prohibited activities listed above; political leaders were able to rationalize the toleration of religion while still maintaining the ideology of science and progress. The statement bears witness to the continuing desire in the late twentieth century to regulate religion through a process of ideological definition and bureaucratic control. It demonstrates the persistence of the notion that religion is ultimately incompatible with progress, science, and modernity. But it also grants religion a legitimate place within the ideology of modern China.

Contemporary Chinese Religions

The following chapters in this book forcefully demonstrate the ways in which religion has survived and evolved into the twenty-first century in Chinese communities throughout the world. In so doing they also demonstrate the limitations of the dialectical framework of tradition versus modernity so beloved of China's twentieth-century revolutionaries, and they aspire toward new perspectives for interpreting Chinese religions in contemporary societies. In fact, the latest set of regulations governing religion in China, published in 2004, recognize the new reality of Chinese religions and demonstrate a clear shift away from considering religion in the context of political ideology. The new regulations do not deal with thorny theoretical questions, such as the definition of religion, or the relationship between religion, superstition, and scientific belief. Rather, they tend to focus on more bureaucratic questions, such as which government agency is the competent authority for dealing with various types of religious issues, or economic questions such as the relationship between religious pilgrimage and secular tourism.

Article 18 of the new regulations, for example, governs the management of religious sites and well typifies the new direction in communist policy toward religion:

> A site for religious activities shall strengthen internal management, and, in accordance with the provisions of the relevant laws, regulations and rules, establish and improve the management systems for personnel, finance, accounting, security, fire control, cultural relics protection, sanitation and epidemic prevention, etc., and accept the guidance, supervision and in-

spection by the relevant departments of the local people's government (State Council of the People's Republic of China 2004).

As this regulation indicates, the overall goal now is to promote the smooth management of religions in such a way that they do not disrupt social harmony or pose a threat to the authority of the government. It seems that party officials are no longer concerned with understanding the nature of religion in terms of political theory, but only with managing its social and economic functioning. In contrast to the divisive ideological debates of the May Fourth and early communist era over secularization, tradition, and modernity, the contemporary framework for understanding the relationship between religion and society emphasizes economics, management, and social harmony. The CCP no longer seems intent on attempting to control the religious beliefs of Chinese citizens, but rather on ensuring that religious organizations, whatever they believe, work to support the nation and its economy.

A second aspect of the new regulations also bears consideration, and that concerns the relations between Chinese and foreign religious organizations. In the early communist period, religious organizations were organized into patriotic associations. Christian missionaries were expelled, and Christian organizations, in particular, were nationalized in a way that they had never been previously under the Three-Self framework of self-propagation, self-administration, and self-support. In an interview given in 1980, Bishop K. H. Ting emphasized the importance of these principles for the Protestant church after the re-establishment of religious freedoms:

> We cannot return to the old situations representing a "foreign religion." Following the ten-year catastrophe [of the Cultural Revolution], we are returning to our guiding principle of the fifties, not that of the forties. It is wrong for those people outside China who long for a return to the past to think that we are returning to the forties. A return to the forties would mean discarding Three-Self, again making Christianity a "foreign religion" (quoted in MacInnis 1989, 65).

The regulations of 2004 continue to stress the necessity of the independence of China's religious organizations:

> All religions shall adhere to the principle of independence and self-governance. Religious bodies, sites for religious activities and religious affairs are not subject to any foreign domination (State Council 2004, Article 4).

This regulation goes on to state, however, that:

> Religious bodies, sites for religious activities and religious personnel may develop external exchange on the basis of friendship and equality; all other organizations or individuals shall not accept any religious conditions in external cooperation or exchange in economic, cultural or other fields (ibid.).

Article 10, moreover, recognizes the necessity of international exchanges for religious educational purposes:

> In light of the need of the religion concerned, a national religious body may, in accordance with the relevant provisions, select and send people for religious studies abroad, or accept foreigners for religious studies in China (ibid., Article 10).

Articles 4 and 10 thus seem to recognize that religions are transnational cultural organizations and that this global aspect of religions is legitimate and necessary for their development. Article 35, moreover, explicitly permits religious organizations and sites to receive donations from overseas. Together, these new articles accept that religions can operate at an international level provided that those relationships are conducted on an equal footing. The official recognition of this global aspect of religion represents at the very least a change in tone from the earlier emphasis on self-reliance.

What are we to make of these two apparent shifts in policy emphasis, one away from the ideological categories of religion and superstition, the other offering a more pragmatic view of the globalization of religions? It would be wrong to think that these shifts mean that China's leaders have discarded their modernist ideology of progress with regard to religion. Rather, it seems that the contemporary ideology of the progress is now denominated principally in terms of national development and global economics. The CCP now seems to recognize that religions are a social fact, and, as such, have a role to play in contemporary China's economic development. Many religions are, moreover, global in nature, operating in conjunction with Chinese communities throughout the world, or in dialogue with coreligionists from non-Chinese ethnic and cultural backgrounds. As such they are potentially useful in forging positive links between China and the rest of the world. The following chapters demonstrate the way in which these global links are currently operating and the way in which religions in mainland China are dealing with their newfound freedoms.

References

Cohen, Paul A. 1984. *Discovering History in China: American Historical Writing on the Recent Chinese Past.* New York: Columbia University Press.

de Bary, William Theodore, and Richard Lufrano. 2000. *Sources of Chinese Tradition.* Vol. 2, 2d ed. New York: Columbia University Press.

Duara, Prasenjit. 1991. "Knowledge and Power in the Discourse of Modernity: The Campaigns against Popular Religion in Early Twentieth-Century China." *Journal of Asian Studies* 50.1: 67–83.

Lawrance, Alan, ed. 2004. *China since 1919: Revolution and Reform. A Sourcebook.* New York: Routledge.

Luo Zhufeng, ed. 1991. *Religion under Socialism in China.* Armonk, NY: M. E. Sharpe.

MacInnis, Donald, ed. 1989. *Religion in China Today: Policy and Practice.* Maryknoll, NY: Orbis.

Mungello, David E. 1999. *The Great Encounter of China and the West, 1500–1800.* Lanham, MD: Rowman and Littlefield.

Pittman, Don A. 2001. *Toward a Modern Chinese Buddhism: Taixu's Reforms.* Honolulu: University of Hawai'i Press.

Rahula, Walpole. 1959. *What the Buddha Taught.* New York: Grove.

Raines, John, ed. 2002. *Marx on Religion.* Philadelphia: Temple University Press.

State Council of the People's Republic of China. 2004. *Decree no. 426: Regulations on Religious Affairs.* Adopted at the 57th Executive Meeting of the State Council on July 7, 2004, promulgated November 30, 2004, effective as of March 1, 2005.

3

Local Religion in Contemporary China

TAM WAI LUN

Introduction

Chinese religion has long been understood in terms of the so-called Three Religions: Confucianism, Daoism, and Buddhism. Formal members of those traditions, however, do not constitute a majority of the Chinese people. According to a white paper on religious freedom in China published by the Beijing government in October 1997, there were 10 million believers of all faiths out of 1.2 billion people. Those figures include the five officially recognized religions—namely, Buddhism, Daoism, Catholicism, Protestantism, and Islam. They would seem to lead to the conclusion that most mainland Chinese are irreligious. But such a conclusion contradicts observable reality—the presence of temples in every village and the prominence of ritual events in rural China. Except during the turmoil years of the Cultural Revolution (1966–1976), countless people have continued to visit local temples that cannot readily be classified under the category of the Three Religions. Villagers participate in numerous religious festivals and ritual events on the village level. Those activities are, of course, not "religious" according to the official ideology, but rather "superstitious" and "feudal." There are two obvious problems of definition here. One has to do with the official ideology of limiting religion to only the five established institutional religions, for the purpose of easier control and regulation. The other lies in referring to Chinese religion as Three Religions. Both concepts are flawed, in that they leave out the faith of the common people, who constitute the majority of the population.

The earliest reference to the idea of three teachings is attributed to Li Shiqian, a prominent Chinese scholar of the sixth century, who wrote: "Buddhism is the sun, Taoism the moon, and Confucianism the five planets" (Teiser 1996, 3). To represent Chinese religion as the Three Religions is, however, Western inspired. There is no traditional Chinese linguistic equivalent for the word "religion." The modern standard Chinese translation for the English term "religion," *zongjiao,* was borrowed from the nineteenth-century Japanese translation by Christian missionaries at the beginning of the twentieth century. Late-sixteenth- and seventeenth-century Jesuit missionaries created an image of Chinese religion based on the concept of three teachings, an idea that has since dominated the Western perception of Chinese religion. As noted by Paper, a deeper implication of representing Chinese religion as the Three Religions is that it is compatible with the Western model of religion and is readily interpreted from a Eurocentric Christian perspective; thus it serves to perpetuate Eurocentric values. That includes giving priority to canonical texts, a focus on faith, an understanding that the goal of religion is transcendence, and an emphasis on intellectual activities such as philosophy (Paper 1991, 76–77). Proceeding from such a normative European Christian viewpoint will lead to a mistaken understanding of non-Western religions—including Chinese religions. An alternative way to study Chinese religion in its own context and apart from the framework of the Three Religions is, hence, called for.

The contemporary scholar of religion Gavin Flood observes that religion cannot be abstracted from its cultural matrices; the academic study of religion needs to examine religions within their political, cultural, and social contexts (Flood 1999, 2–3). Recognizing the contextualized nature of all cultural practices including religion, this chapter examines Chinese religion in its local and rural setting. Inasmuch as 95 percent of the Chinese population have traditionally lived in villages—a figure that, in spite of rapid urbanization, still hovers around 70 percent—it is clear that any examination of Chinese religion sensitive to its context can lead us only to the countryside (Lagerwey 1966, 2–3).

Outline of the Religious Scene in South China Villages

In Chinese religion, as in many other Asian religions, the dividing line between religion, custom, or culture is at times not obvious. The lion dance and dragon parade, for instance, are two well-known Chinese customs. Their seemingly secular ceremonial use in modern cities sometimes has blurred their original "religious" bearings, which are closely related to exorcism. Both the lion and the dragon are auspicious mythical animals persistently appearing in Chinese symbolism. What follows will demonstrate that in dealing with Chinese religion, we have to expand our conception of religion to include many of the customary practices like the lion dance and the dragon parade. Our discussion begins first by giving a general picture of religion in rural China before proceeding to more concrete examples.

Lineage Activities and Temple Festivals

Francis Hsü aptly described life in south China as being lived "under the ancestors' shadow" (Hsü 1967). His argument is that family lineages constitute the essential social fabric of China. Lineage activity—that is, rituals concerning the family and the ancestors, being closely related to what is sometimes called "ancestor worship"—is still an important aspect of Chinese religion.

There is, however, another aspect of Chinese society that is highlighted by considering the Chinese word *shehui*, which is equivalent to the English word "society." The term originally meant the "festival of the god of the soil," and it is no accident that the Chinese adopted a term referring to such festivals for the modern word "society." The most elaborate type of religious activity in traditional Chinese society was, in fact, the welcoming and parading of gods during temple festivals, usually an occasion on which to celebrate the god's birthday. These activities were highly structured and organized. Thus, in addition to the system of ancestral lineages noted by Francis Hsü, temple festivals were also an important means by which local society was organized in traditional China. The contemporary scholar John Lagerwey is right, then, in claiming that if the people lived "under the ancestors' shadow," the ancestors, in turn, lived "in the shadow of the gods." These traditional Chinese gods represented a public dimension of life that circumscribed and transcended the private life of the lineage (Lagerwey 2000, 4–5). Hence, to represent the religion of the common people in China, it is important to consider both private lineage activities and the public ritual events surrounding local temples. Those two aspects of local religion in China are perhaps better characterized as "customary forms of life" or "customary religion" than as "religion" in the

Dragon parade. (Courtesy Tam Wai Lun)

normative Western sense of the word, institutional in character and Protestant in aspiration.

Variation and Diversity

Within this framework of lineage activity and temple festivals, it is necessary to note the enormous and endless variation in local religion in China. China is an immensely varied subcontinent marked by significant geographic diversity, and it is well known for the multitude of its dialects, cuisines, and ethnic groups. These great disparities and divergences have prevented scholars from establishing any simple monolithic conceptualization of China. However, a major theme in Chinese history over the past millennium or so has been the gradual shift of the center of human activity from the interior to the southern coastal area (Yang and Zheng 2001, 33). There were two great migrations to the south, the result of wars in Chinese history. One was in the fifth century, during the Six Dynasties period; the other was in the tenth century, or southern Song dynasty. The Pearl River Delta in Guangdong and the Yangzi River Delta in Shanghai have now become major economic powerhouses, with Hong Kong and Shanghai serving as the anchor and engine for those areas of the Chinese economy. This recent development has enlarged economic inequalities and widened the cultural differences between coastal and interior China. Since it is impossible to give a general description of all of China's local religious activity, this chapter concentrates on south China, with special reference to two southeast coastal provinces—Guangdong and Fujian. They are two of the most dynamic areas in contemporary China.

Continuities and Discontinuities of Traditions

Before we move on, we must deal with the issue of changes in rural China—the result not only of economic development but also political movements in modern times. Changes started with the various antireligious campaigns between the years 1900 and 1930, during which time temples were turned into schools and temple land confiscated to provide funding for education. The first phase, from 1900 to 1915, was associated with the warlord Yuan Shikai in north China who, as a promoter of modernizing reform, was determined to eradicate so-called superstition and establish a modern society by appropriating temples and temple property. The second phase, from 1915 to 1930, was initiated by the Nationalist Party, which subsequently retreated to Taiwan. During that period there was a vigorous antisuperstition drive in the lower Yangtze provinces to arrest temple priests and appropriate their lands (Duara 1991).

The next tide of the antireligious movement was launched by the communists after 1949. The history of contemporary China could be divided into two broad periods: a period of revolution, from 1949 to 1976, and a period of reform and modernization from 1976 onward (Mackerras 2001, 3). Land reform during the first period from 1950 to 1953 aimed at the elimination of wealthy peasants through the establishment of cooperatives and the collectivization of private estates. All lineage and temple lands were redistributed to landless peasants. There was also a suppression of all forms of organized gambling, a major source of finance for public worship in villages. These changes went further in the Great Leap Forward campaign (1958–1961), a mass movement initiated by Mao Zedong to step up the socialization of the economy (a move that brought about the institution of large-scale communes) and to tear apart old social structures in favor of collective organizations. During this period, peasants pooled all their land, animals, and pieces of large equipment under common ownership; a cooperative committee managed production in accordance with quotas issued by the government. In this period, a commune consisted of as many as sixty thousand households and incorporated many natural villages. Temple rituals were brought almost to a full stop in a so-called Anti-Fours campaign, and religious "superstition" was considered one of the four evils that hindered socialist development in China.

Repression of local religion was intensified during the Great Proletarian Cultural Revolution (1966–1976), launched by Mao Zedong as his second major attempt at radicalization of the Chinese revolution. Temples were desecrated and ancestral halls demolished by the Red Guards, who were young students answering Mao's call for a radicalization of the Chinese revolution. Very often, however, instead of being completely destroyed, temples and lineage halls were converted into workshops, storage areas, or factories. In the case of destruction, though, the original sites of demolished temples, shrines, and ancestral halls were left unoccupied as empty lots. Stories of divine retributive punishment inflicted on people involved in temple destruction circulated widely in the villages and helped indirectly to preserve the empty lots, which made later rebuilding possible. Statues of deities and the tablets of ancestors were often hidden in private houses.

The fall of the Gang of Four (four influential supporters of the Cultural Revolution) in October 1976 symbolized the end of the Cultural Revolution. A new era opened during the period of reform and modernization that began in 1976. The ideology of Deng Xiaoping, entitled "socialism with Chinese characteristics," promoted modernization. Production contracting was introduced in 1978. Reform abolished the commune system in 1983, allowing the re-establishment of a more traditional structure. A responsibility system was adopted, whereby the household was taken as the productive unit again (Aijmer and Ho 2000, 21). Land was given to individual households on short- or long-term contracts, and patches of land were assigned to peasant families on household-by-household contracts. The household would supply a specified amount of grain and other products to the state, keeping the rest for itself.

Decline of centralized power and collectivism thus led to a new situation, in which families had to build up their own networks of relations, revive old-time alliances, and establish new ones.

This new economic and political situation gave rise to a resurgence of traditional communal ritual activities, such as the temple festivals. Ritual paraphernalia including incense and paper money for worship once again became available in the markets. The situation went even further in the four special economic zones established in Guangdong and Fujian provinces in 1979. That was followed by the designation of fourteen coastal cities deemed open for foreign investment in 1984, and of coastal economic development zones in 1985. In 1990, Shanghai was given approval to launch the development of the Pudong, a new area in east Shanghai (Yang and Zheng 2001, 35). The Pearl River Delta and the Yangzi River Delta became major economic power-houses. The resurgence of tradition in those areas was enormous. Temples and lineage halls were rebuilt on the original sites with the financial support of former villagers now living in Hong Kong and Macau. Very often, however, people had to improvise, and perform the ritual events in an ad hoc manner or in an experimental fashion, so much having been forgotten in the intervening years. Temple cults as they are performed today, consequently, are patchworks of old tradition intermingled with new innovations (Aijmer and Ho 2000, 202). The traditions have thus been reinvented, reinterpreted, and restored in an integrated way, so much so that some scholars call this resurgence of traditional activity the construction of a neotradition (ibid., 203).

Villages and Lineages in South China

Two kinds of village can be distinguished in rural China today. Administrative villages, designated by the modern Chinese government, are generally composed of two or more natural villages—that is, villages that developed naturally over history. Each natural village may consist of one or more lineages or extended families usually sharing the same surname. In the past, a group of villages formed a circumscription (*bao*) that sometimes corresponds to today's administrative village; all these terms have changed many times over history. Nonetheless, the basic unit is a group of natural villages that usually occupies a valley. At the confluence of the streams at the valley's exit there is often an earth god mound or a temple guarding the exit of the water. As a rule, all lineages in the villages of south China are migrants from the

Worshipping at the lineage hall of the Li family. (Courtesy Tam Wai Lun)

north. Most claim to have arrived in the Song dynasty, during the southern migration of the tenth century, but their lineage genealogy records usually trace them back only to the Ming dynasty of the thirteenth century.

Each lineage also possesses a mythological account or legend of how the village was founded. These legends typically follow a pattern involving geomancy (*fengshui*) of the local geography. In some legends, the first settler of the lineage, usually a scholarly official, passed by the area sometime during an official trip to the south and, attracted by the good geomancy, decided to settle. In other legends, a carrying pole broke when the migrating lineage entered the area, and that was taken as an auspicious sign of where to settle. In still other cases, the founder of the lineage received instructions in a dream from the local deity to settle there. Foundation legends of lineages arriving after others have settled usually take the form of herding ducks. A lineage founder could be a servant of the already settled lineage who, led by the prodigious laying of eggs by the ducks (an indication of good geomancy) built the first hut on the site, from where the lineage developed. That site might also later become the ancestral hall for the lineage. Another often encountered story recounts how the founder of the lineage came as an indentured servant on whom a geomancer took pity because a wealthy employer had slighted him, the geomancer telling the founder the best site on which to build his first hut; the lineage later became strong and prosperous because of good geomancy. The ancestral hall built for the lineage founder and other ancestors is thus an important focus of religious culture in Chinese villages.

Village Gods

When we come to the religion of the village, local gods dominate the scene (see Shahar and Weller 1996). Based on field observation, Lagerwey classifies village gods in south China hierarchically into three groups: (a) those with neither open air altar nor temple; (b) those with an open air altar; and (c) those with a temple (Lagerwey 1997, 7). Deities of rocks, fields, trees, or bridges belong to the first kind. Sons and daughters with bad health may be "sold" contractually to these tree or stone gods (some may even be given names with the character of "trees" or "stones"). Elsewhere, sons and daughters are contracted out to Guanyin, the Buddhist bodhisattva of compassion, or other local deities. The contracts in those cases are written on red paper and are still commonly found sticking to the walls of local temples. Parents of such children usually have to worship annually the divine foster parents of the child and "ransom" the child when he or she reaches the age of sixteen.

Gods with open air altars are usually called Duke King (*Gongwang*) or Big King (*Dawang*). Very often they are the protectors of a village, with their altar situated at and guarding the water exit. At the start of the new year, villagers pray for good fortune. At the winter solstice, they thank the god. Children are contracted to him, and there may be a medium, called the "lad," who is possessed by him.

Gods with a temple are, generally speaking, higher-level gods. There are two main categories for temples: altars and temples (*tan miao*), and cloisters and monasteries (*si guan*). Different places use slightly different terms, but the broad division remains the same. The different terms for "temple" illustrate well the interpenetrating of the Three Religions and the local cults in China. In local gazetteers, for instance, there are usually sections on altars and temples, and on cloisters and monasteries. The first category, altars and temples, consists of three types: altars (*tan*), temples (*miao*), and shrines (*ci*). *Tan* are altars for local gods. The *miao* are temples for gods like the City God, the renowned Empress of Heaven (Tianhou), and King Guan (Guandi). These temples of higher-level gods are likely to be found in townships rather than villages. The *ci* are shrines for historical worthies and meritorious officials reflecting the Confucian ideology of righteousness and state loyalty.

The second category, cloisters and monasteries, generally refers to Daoist cloisters and Buddhist monasteries. They are frequently established in the surrounding hills and are normally occupied by monks, nuns, or the *zhaima* (a group of old vegetarian women). They perform both village funerals and communal sacrifices called *jiao* rituals. More often, another group of ritual specialists or local Daoists, who remain at home, perform the *jiao* ritual. The *jiao,* one of the most important and elaborate religious activities in Chinese villages, is analyzed in some detail later in this chapter.

Ghosts

The account of village gods would be incomplete without mentioning their spiritual opposites: ghosts (*gui*), a term also translated as "demons." Although gods occupy various vital points in the villages, ghosts, their opposites, are not tied to a single spot. They wander about and make unwanted appearances in solitary places. By definition, ghosts are the spirits of those who are not the ancestors. They either do not have any offspring or, because of violent death, they are unable to receive offerings from their descendants (Yu 1990; Wolf 1974). One of the main purposes of *jiao* ritual is precisely to subdue wandering ghosts in the area. A sacrifice is first offered, followed by the driving away of any uncooperative ghosts.

Interconnection between Villages

Although the Chinese peasant can be said to live in a self-contained world, that world extends beyond the borders of the village and can be said to include the standard marketing community, that is, the broader market within which the peasant exchanges goods and services (Skinner 1964, 32). Skinner's insight of taking the standard marketing community rather than the village as the "self-contained world," or "social field," of the Chinese peasant is revealing. The social world of the Chinese peasant appears, however, to be much larger than Skinner's standard market town. Local society in China was not a closed society, but rather "a society on the move," with basic goods and sometimes people traveling astounding distances between markets along ancient paths and rivers. That is especially evident in the coastal area of southeast China, where such trading took place well before the advance of modern globalization. Boatmen, log rafters, cart pushers, and seasonal laborers were all constantly on the move, and with them traveled news and tales of all kinds, including tales about local gods and the rites related to them (Lagerwey 2002, 42–43).

This situation reminds us of the need to cover a broader area in our study of Chinese local religion, but the vast area and enormous diversity of culture in China simply prevent us from studying the whole of the country. However, to get a sense of this diversity, it is worth considering a smaller scale study—of the traditional minority Hakka society in southeast China—designed by John Lagerwey and in which I participated. What follows below is based on four fieldwork surveys covering two lineage activities, one temple festival, and one *jiao* ritual in Guangdong and Fujian provinces. Although they cannot be considered representative of the whole of rural Chinese religion, they do illustrate important aspects of contemporary religion in rural China.

Contemporary Situation

Lion Dance and Lineage Activities in Northwest Guangdong

On April 24, 2002, we attended a spring offering at Li's ancestral hall in Yangshan. It was organized by the Li lineage. According to a recent survey, the Li is the largest lineage in China. The lineage activity of the Li lineage centered on its lineage hall in Libu township, which was rebuilt in the 1990s. The main organizer was a retired cadre; his son is a cadre in the county government. That proved to be an added value to his prestige as a lineage leader. To ensure the anonymity of our informant, we simply called him Ligong, literally "old man Li." Ligong's basic strategy was to differentiate lineage activities from temple activities. He regarded temple activities as belonging to the category of "superstition" according to official ideology, but he carefully excluded lineage activities from that class. What he was doing, Li argued, was promoting filial piety, which in turn brings about order in families. (Order and stability, basic for the development of the economy, are the current key values in official ideology.) Ligong particularly emphasized that he never invited Daoists to perform a ritual in his lineage hall, and that it is therefore free of "superstitious" activities. This did not mean, however, that Ligong was hostile toward temple worship. In fact, Ligong was one of our main local guides, those guides who showed us major local temples in the area when we were in Yangshan. He personally attended some of the ritual events in these local temples.

The organizing committee for the lineage activity consisted of retired men in the lineage. Different segments of the lineage—living in different parts of the county and the neighboring three counties—came in groups to visit the lineage hall. We learned that it was a new arrangement to involve so many groups. Before 1949 it had been common to involve the descendants of a first settler in a region, but the detailed lineage register was lost in the Cultural Revolution. Without the written record to trace their common ancestor, the Lis had no choice but to rely on oral tradition—and hence there was plenty of room for reinventing the tradition. The Lis claim to be descendants of an official in Fujian called Huode Gong (1206–1292), who loosely connects all Lis from four counties. The most interesting group is an ethnic minority group, the Yao people, who claim to be descendants of a Li who married into the Yao tribe. Building up solidarity between the minority Yao and the majority Han was in fact one of the slogans used by the Li to win the support, or rather the silence, of the local government concerning their lineage activities. An effort was also made to include another minority group, the Zhuang people, who also claim to be the descendants of a Li man who married into the Zhuang tribe. We were told that in 2003 there would be a Zhuang group coming for the autumn worship.

All groups, except the Yao group, came with a lion dance troupe, a revival of an old-time tradition. It had been a long tradition for lineages in Guangdong to gather their youngsters during low farming season from about the eleventh month of the lunar year until the fourth month of the lunar year (roughly corresponding to the winter and the springtime) in the lineage hall at night to learn martial arts from seniors. There would be a separate altar set up for the members of the troupe worshiping the god Huaguang. Each group, usually consisting of a segment of a lineage, carried a hall name. The main program was to learn the lion dance. The whole activity was known as "eating the late night porridge," as all participants would be served rice porridge after nighttime practice. It had the double function of training a security force for the lineage in case of a lineage feud, and training a lion dance troupe for festival activities. Nighttime martial practice has now become weekend practice. The key person of each lion dance troupe was the leader, dancing with a wooden box containing a red piece of paper on which are written auspicious sayings and the hall name of the troupe. The red paper would be affixed to the wall of the main lineage hall after the performance of the lion dance.

The lion could be danced by a single person (as in this case) or by two persons. The dress of the lion also differed from group to group. The troupe would be accompanied by a percussion team playing big drums, cymbals, and gongs. Each group arriving performed a dance before the ancestors, led by the man with the box. The climax of the dance was for the lion to "grasp the greens" (*caiqing*), an object made of lettuce. Hidden in it was some money put in a red envelope. It would be hung high, testing the skill of the troupe. After grasping the greens, the lion could take the red envelope and the money inside while spitting out the greens, and firecrackers would be set off. The leader of the troupe would then recite improvised poems to praise the events. In the past, this could be turned into a competition between different troupes or between the troupe and the host. Sometimes the poem competition would turn into or be followed by a martial arts competition. Nowadays such martial competition is forbidden by the local government, and only a handful of troupes recited poems after the dance we witnessed.

Representatives of each group would then come forward to present incense, wine, pork, and fruits to the altar. In the old times, when lion troupes met each other, there could be a ritualized fight if the leaders, those holding the boxes, so chose. A big group offering took place before noon, by which time most of the groups had arrived. A memorial written in red paper stating the purpose of the event was read and burned, and then groups lined up to come forward to present incense and wine again. The Yao group was the last group to come forward. They do not have a lion troupe, and they all dressed in their traditional clothing, accompanied by a dancing team of two people dancing with their typical long drums slung around their necks. The event was concluded by releasing three long lines of firecrackers, followed by a big meal for all in the lineage hall. People were so numerous that they had to take turns eating.

We found that, despite the stripping of land from lineages, lineage activities have been revived in contemporary China. Republishing their lineage registers and making annual offerings to their ancestors are two main lineage activities found in most of the places in south rural China that we visited.

Dragon Parade and Lineage Activities in Western Fujian

Lineage activities in the Gutian township in Liancheng county in western Fujian province take the form of a dragon parade. Between February 24 and 27, 2002, we attended a dragon parade there that lasted for two days. It is performed annually on the fifteenth day of the first month in the lunar calendar. Now it alternates between two lineages, the Huas and the Jiangs. In the past, many small lineages joined together, so that there were as many as ten dragons performing each year. The Hua is a large local lineage, and more than a thousand members participated in the dragon parade of 2002. Each household of the lineage was responsible for making a section of the dragon from bamboo sticks and colored paper in an omega shape. It was about five meters long and took two men to hold it up with a long stick. As the event went on for two days, the holding of each section of the dragon required five to six men taking turns. The dragon's head was prepared and stored in the lineage hall.

The event began with a sacrifice at the lineage hall. A pig was killed and its blood used to "animate" the dragon. The local god Dongshan fuzhu (Lord of Happiness of the Eastern Hill) had to be carried on a sedan chair on parade around the township before reaching the lineage hall, where he was worshiped prior to the dragon parade. This provided us with a unique insight into the relationships between the lineages and the gods in local society. The god came from a village in the Longyan city to which Liancheng county also belongs. According to legend, the emperor was said to have secretly visited the village sometime between 1505 and 1521 and was met by robbers. It was this god who protected the emperor and escorted him back to the palace, where he bestowed an imperial title, Dongshan fuzhu, on the local god. The parade of the god is played down today by allowing teenagers and children to do the job. Apparently this was a local strategy to fade out the religious content of the dragon parade, which was presented as a local tourist attraction by the local government.

The whole of the lineage was divided into ten segments of the dragon. It was decided by lot who would be in charge of the dragon's head and tail, the most prestigious positions. When the god Dongshan fuzhu arrived in the lineage hall, he was put inside and worshiped by representatives of the lineage. The dragon's head was then carried out to the open courtyard of the lineage hall, where a simple altar was set up and a worship ceremony performed. A pig was killed to animate the dragon and a memorial read and burned, followed by the offering of incense and wine by the three eldest lineage members. At about three o'clock in the afternoon, the dragon's head was carried to the nearby hill, where all the other sections of the dragon were linked together. According to the principles of local *fengshui,* performing the dragon dance on that hill had the function of rejuvenating the cosmic force (*qi*) flowing from the mountain along what was known as the dragon meridian (*longmai*) of the village. A spectacular parade of the dragon by more than a thousand people then began. There were 236 sections of the dragon. In front of the dragon, there were 250 dragon eggs made from bamboo sticks and paper, carried by the children of the lineage under fifteen years of age. Together they spoke for the prosperity of the lineage.

The parade continued until dark, when candles were put inside each section of the dragon, turning them all into lanterns. The climax took place in front of the local government office building of the township. Firecrackers and fireworks were set off continually. The original plan was to let the dragon coil up in front of the government building, but the lack of space made it impossible; so the dragon just passed by the building before the sections separated and the people carrying them went home.

The parade started again at nine o'clock the next morning, in front of the Jiang family lineage hall after a small act of worship. The whole dragon was then paraded to the temple of the local god, Dongshan fuzhu. The dragon first coiled up in front of the temple, and when the dragon's head re-emerged, its body was broken up and thrown in a heap. After all the parts were completely demolished, they were burned in front of the temple.

The dragon parade in Liancheng attracts hundreds of local tourists each year, many of whom are relatives and friends of the Huas and Jiangs. That was also an important reason the local people in Gutian gave to argue for a revival of the event. While it was hard to calculate how many people actually came to the township to watch the event, we did find that it was impossible to use a cellular phone all night long—the network was overloaded.

The Temple Festival of the Five Old Buddhas

On July 4, 2002, we attended a temple festival in Yangmei township of Yangshan county in Qingyuan city, northwest Guangdong. Again the main organizer was a retired cadre, this time being seventy-four years old and with the family name of Wen. The festival took place at the top of a mountain. Had a road not recently been built, we would have had to spend two and a half hours climbing to the top of the mountain to reach to the temple. In the past, it had been a pilgrimage experience to go to the temple. The main gods in the temple were known as the Five Old Buddhas (Wugong fo). The temple was rebuilt in 1986 but was closed down by government officials in 1988 and the statues confiscated. No public worship was allowed to take place until 1991, when the statues were returned to the temple and a big *jiao* ritual was performed. A road was built to the top of the mountain in 2002. It was decided that a temple festival would be held annually on the birthday of the gods. The Five Old Buddhas were known as Zhigong, Langgong, Kanggong, Baogong, and Huagong.

According to legend, the Five Old Buddhas appeared on Mt. Jinji in the years between 1875 to 1909. Villagers saw five men dressed in white, each with a paper fan in hand, but found no one upon arrival at the mountain. Later they decided to build a temple, which turned out to be very efficacious, on the mountain. Its name quickly spread around the nearby counties including Huaji, Qingyuan, and Guangning. There was a scripture, of which a 1913 version survives, believed to be narrated by the Five Old Buddhas on the famous Mt. Tiantai in Zhejiang, which included eighty talismans found at the back of the scripture. The scripture predicts an age of catastrophe approaching, and it recommends that people write the talismans as recorded in the scripture, adopt a vegetarian diet, burn incense to the gods, and recite the scripture daily. Later on, the scripture recommends the worship of Guanyin, the recitation of the scripture seven times in the morning, the use of fruits, tea, and incense as offerings, and the recitation of the names of the gods or bodhisattvas. It also recommends that the faithful carry the talismans and recite the names of the Buddha (*nianfo*). We have not confirmed whether these private practices have been carried out uninterruptedly, but public worship in the form of temple festivals has been carried out annually since 1991. The Five Old Buddhas were renowned for bestowing sons on the family, and the incense ash from their temple was known to have a healing effect. Six Daoists were invited to perform the ritual to celebrate the birthday of the gods in 2002.

Female spirit mediums were found to attend the festivals. These were housewives who came at night after regular housework. They sang and danced during the intermission of the Daoist rituals. They also shared their possession experiences among themselves and discussed their dances and songs. They were possessed when they danced, and their dances sometimes continued and went side by side with the Daoist rituals. We could not confirm whether that also happened prior to 1949. When possession went on too long, other mediums would come out and interfere by burning incense and paper money to ask the spirits to let the medium take a break. On one occasion, the Daoists had to ask the spirits to leave by simply yelling to the medium, so that they could continue with their ritual.

Individuals came and went during the two-day event and generally would not stay longer than an hour. They came to present incense and offerings carried in a traditional basket and to release firecrackers. Some also performed divination by shaking the bamboo container holding a hundred numbered bamboo sticks. They shook the container until one rose above the others and finally fell to the ground. Moon-blocks, semicircular wooden blocks with one flat and one convex surface, would be thrown to confirm that the right stick had been drawn. This was indicated by one flat side and one convex side down. A man was ready to interpret the result for a small fee. Others might also go to a side altar to beg for the "white flower," which locally means to ask for a son. A Daoist would perform a simple ritual that simply announces the wish of the petitioners, most of whom were women, by singing with cymbals. Women presented "red pocket money" (money in red envelopes) and promised a gift should a son be bestowed on them. The request would be checked by throwing moon-blocks. Should the answer be negative, the petitioner would increase her promised gift and also the red pocket money, until a positive answer was acquired.

Worshipers might come in a large group, sometimes accompanied by a small troupe of musicians. They usually were members of a village. Among their offerings would be two large pieces of incense, three to four feet long.

Daoists offered an entire program of ritual that lasted for two days. Most people did not understand their program and would participate only in some of it. They might come and go, but most of the time there would be participants or onlookers. The organizing committee would take turns participating.

The *Jiao* Ritual in Qigong, Northwest Guangdong

One of the most important local religious activities in China is no doubt the *jiao* ritual. The Chinese word *jiao* means offering, but it is used specifically as the technical term for the large-scale ceremonies, lasting several days, performed by Daoist priests in Chinese communities on behalf of the people of those communities. Andersen (1995, 187) calls it a "definitional ceremony." It is the means by which a Chinese community defines itself on the religious level and renews its contract with the gods. It also serves as a periodic restatement of the identity of a community.

A classical *jiao* is considered to be a Daoist ritual that originated at the foot of Mt. Longhu in Jiangxi province. It is presided over by a Daoist priest of the Orthodox Unity (Zhengyi) tradition who is hired for the occasion (Lagerwey 1987, passim; Schipper 1995). The field studies that we conducted in a village called Heshang of Qigong township in Yangshan county in northwest Guangdong challenge that view. Rather than being a purely Daoist ritual, the *jiao* that we observed was a local ritual interpenetrated by both Buddhist and Daoist traditions.

From October 30 until November 3, 2003, we attended a five-day *jiao* ritual in Heshang village. The Flying Phoenix temple was named after the small hill on which it is situated; it was built by four villages: Dandu, Shangong, Yangpi, and Heshang. About a thousand donors from the four villages had contributed to support the ritual event. The main gods of the temple are the Five Old Buddhas, and it was believed that the incense burner had flown by itself to this mountain from Nanyue Mountain in Fujian with the word "Five Old Buddhas" written on it. A temple was built later, in 1940. It was decided to hold a *jiao* every other year, but the practice was stopped during the Cultural Revolution and was resumed partially in the 1990s. It was not until 2003 that the four villages were able to organize a *jiao* ritual that involved a Daoist "climbing the sword ladder." The Daoist performing the ritual was called Li, and he lived in the Xinshu village. He had a helper, Qiu, and two young disciples, Huangs, who were in their thirties. There was another group of Buddhist ritual specialists headed by Xie, who was seventy-six years old, and two collaborators, Tangs, also in their seventies. Three huts were built in front of the temple. The middle one was for the statues of the gods, which were moved out for the ritual. The left hut was for the Daoist altar and the right for the performance of operas. The Buddhist altar was set up inside the empty temple. There was an office to the right and a kitchen to the left.

Day One. The ritual began at night. The focus of the first night was to invite the gods to attend the ritual and to perform the consecration or animation of the statues. Both the Buddhists and the Daoists tied candles onto long sticks for waving in front of the statues. The Daoists' dances involved horn blowing and many body movements, and part of the dances was a re-enactment of the story of the matriarchs of the Lushan school of Daoism, the three ladies Chan, Lin, and Li. Lady Chan had decided to go to learn magic to fight off a malevolent local god. She met Ladies Lin and Li on her way, and they became sworn sisters. They eventually went together to Mt. Lu to learn magic. After learning the magic successfully, they used it first to resurrect a dead person but were accused of causing the person to die in the first place. On another occasion, the three ladies used their magic to help resuscitate a dying dog. The dog, however, once it was resuscitated, out of its terror tried to bite the three. Thereupon the three ladies decided never again to work on the dead with their magic. This story explains the division of labor between the Buddhist and the Daoist ritual specialists in the village. The local word for Daoist means one who "*diao*-s" the ghosts. *Diao* literally means to tease, to settle, or to discipline. The Daoists never perform death rituals, which are reserved for the Buddhists. Hence there was a saying that Buddhists deal with the dead (funerals) and the Daoists with the living (exorcism).

During their dances, one of the Daoists had to dress himself in women's clothes and to role play the story of the three ladies. This sometimes turned the ritual into a cultural performance, or even an amusing comedy. When the Daoist acted as a woman it attracted onlookers, mostly children and old people. The Buddhists performed mostly singing and scripture recitation accompanied by percussion instruments, and they failed to attract onlookers most of the time.

Also important in the first day's ritual was the announcement of the names of the donors. They were written on a large red paper attached to the outside wall of the temple.

Day Two. The second day began with a presentation of memorials announcing the *jiao* event to the heavens. A ritual to bless the published list announcing the names of donors was also performed. Another important program on the second day was to enlist divine soldiers for the gods. This involved many dances with two small triangular flags. The focus of the second day, however, was on the preparation for the sword ladder, a ritual known as "sealing the swords." This was accomplished by the Daoist spitting holy water on each sword and writing virtual talismans on them in the air using a wooden gavel

Climbing the sword ladder. (Courtesy Tam Wai Lun)

similar to the one used by a traditional Chinese judge in court. Paper talismans were also prepared, to be attached to the swords. The Daoist wore a red turban and used his ritual knife while performing these ceremonies. At the Buddhist altar a ritual of penance was performed simultaneously, but it attracted almost no onlookers. Devotions to the flag, set up at the outskirts of the temple, and to the deity to guard the ghost known as Shandaren were performed daily. These rituals were performed by the Daoists and Buddhists side by side. At night the Daoists performed comedies by making fun of some religious terms and ritual instruments first, and then afterward explaining their meaning to the laughing audience. This obviously had a religious educational value. The Daoists used a moon-block frequently to check that everything they did was done correctly.

Day Three. The focus of the third day was on constructing the sword ladder by the villagers, in cooperation with the Daoist priest. This had not been done since 1949. A tree trunk about twenty feet in length was made to rest on a flat piece on wood and fixed in place by four strong ropes, tied at four points by hammering a large wooden block into the ground. Swords were then hammered into the trunk to make a ladder leading from the bottom to the top. A small platform consisting of two six-foot-long rods was constructed near the top of the trunk. The Daoist priest, wearing both his red turban and girdle, climbed carefully up to the platform of the sword ladder. A table was set up near the foot of the sword ladder for the performance of a ritual called "breaking the six pieces of armor," a ritual meant to exorcize or expel the evil that might threaten the children. Two female mediums came to help with the ritual. A pack of children's clothes was brought, and one was taken out with which to wrap an egg. After waving it a few times over the candle and incense fire, the egg would be taken out and cracked with a ritual knife. The pack of clothes would then be stamped with the magic stamp of the Daoist priest. The whole pack of clothes would then be pulled up by a pulley to the top of the sword ladder. The Daoist priest, after blowing his horn at the top of the sword ladder, would then send the clothes back down.

More than a thousand people paid to sponsor this long-missed ritual, but only two hundred showed up to witness it. We were told that this was because many family members had moved out of the village to work in the Pearl Delta area. Also, the Daoist stayed on the sword ladder for only half an hour. Children's clothes were continually pulled up the sword ladder, however, even without the Daoist to perform the ritual at the top. That, we learned, would not have happened in the past. The Daoist, instead of staying on the sword ladder, came down to help with the "breaking-six-armor" ritual with the mediums.

At the Buddhist altar, the Buddhists performed the worshiping of the twenty-four heavenly kings. At night the sacrifice to the five malefactor gods, Wushang, was performed by the Daoists. We understood that this had been an important exorcistic ritual in the past but was done this time on a much-reduced scale, apparently because the aged Daoist priest needed rest, and because his young disciples were not ready to handle the rituals on their own.

Day Four. The fourth day was a repetition of the second. The ritual of "breaking the six pieces of armor" was performed, and the children's clothing was pulled up the sword ladder. In the Buddhist altar, presentation of ten offerings to the gods was performed. The focus of the afternoon, however, was the ritual called "opening of the gate of Heaven" performed by the Buddhists. Opening up the gate of heaven means the delivery of an important memorial requesting the blessing from heaven to the villagers. A special altar was set up by putting a small table on a big one. One of the Five Old Buddhas was taken out from the shack and put on the top of the table. A Buddhist climbed up and knelt on the first table before the god and performed the ritual. The whole crowd then moved to the riverside to perform the releasing of water lanterns, together with both the Daoists and Buddhists. This is a ritual to help with the delivery of wandering ghosts drowned in water. At night, the Daoists performed the ritual of paying a salary to the divine soldiers of the gods.

Day Five. On the final day was the farewell and the escorting of the gods back to their temple. A pig was killed and distributed to the participants, its head being placed in front of the altar of the gods. All programs finished before noon, at which time the villagers went back home.

Concluding Remarks

Life in south China villages follows an agricultural cycle that repeats twice a year: rice transplantation in the paddy field is done in spring and harvested in early summer, immediately followed by the second rice transplantation, with another harvest in early winter. This means that winter is the farmers' time for a break. Therefore, almost all temple festivals or *jiao* rituals were held in the winter. The overall rhythms of traditional Chinese life were thus marked by customs that divided the year into "ordinary time," when economic production and exchange were central, and "festival time," when social exchange was fundamental. Unlike the division of "sacred" and "profane" in the West, ordinary time was never conceived of as less important than festive time in China, and the Chinese have never placed priority on one over the other.

Festival time performs multiple functions, and Wu lists five aspects of temple festivals: the political, social, economic, cultural, and religious (Wu 1988). Festival time is, first of all, a time of freedom from work and for enjoying leisure, but it is also a time for religious activities. To put it another way, religious festivals in China always have a dimension of leisure time enjoyment.

Therefore, a *jiao* always has a theater performance for the enjoyment of both gods and people. Many rituals have an amusing aspect, as was seen above.

This dimension of ritual has a long history in China. Confucius speaks of the philosophy of "strung and unstrung" in the *Book of Rites*. When his disciple Zigong went to see the agricultural sacrifice at the end of the year, Confucius asked him whether it gave him pleasure. Zigong answered that "the people of the whole state appeared to be mad; I do not know in what I could find pleasure." Confucius answered, "For their hundred days' labor in the field, [the husbandmen] receive this one day's enjoyment. . . . [Sage kings] Wen and Wu could not keep a bow [in good condition], if it were always drawn and never relaxed; nor did they leave it always relaxed and never drawn. To keep it now strung and now unstrung was the way of Wan and Wu" (Legge 1967, 167).

Festival time is, therefore, the time to relax and "keep the bow unstrung." One scholar has even termed the religious festival in China a "mad-with-joy culture" (Li 1993). Chinese festivals involve competitive activities like the lion dance, which brings excitement to the participants. It is a break from farmwork and provides a relaxing and amusing time for villagers. It is also a safety valve for the stern, restraining, and manipulative official Confucian culture (ibid., 141). Being a communal event, a Chinese festival also reinforces community spirit (Zhao 2002, 135).

This chapter has discussed local Chinese festival times in terms of two basic communal events: lineage activities and communal temple rituals. The examples we have given above are not isolated cases. Fieldwork conducted in southeast China in the past decade confirms that there has been a general resurgence of similar activities in southeastern rural China since the period of reform and modernization (*gaige kaifang*) in the early 1980s. The frequency of activities is inversely proportional to the proximity to local government offices. The rule of thumb has now become that as long as there is no disorder or fighting, and there are no fire accidents, communal activities like lineage worship and temple festivals in remote places will be tolerated. The Chinese government's policy on traditional ritual events seems to be strict in cities and counties but comparatively loose in townships and villages. Rebuilding a lineage hall or temple in a county seat or township is very difficult if not impossible, with the exception of renowned historic temples that have proven to attract tourists. Rebuilding local temples and lineage halls in relatively inconspicuous places in the villages outside the county and township government office, however, is now being tolerated. Lineage halls in many cases are concurrently used as a community hall, senior center, or as the office for local cultural affairs (*wenhua zhan*).

Lineage activities and temple ritual events are presented as cultural traditions. Villagers justify their ritual activities either as tourist attractions or as the restoration of old cultural traditions. The lion dance we witnessed in Guangdong and the dragon parade in Fujian illustrate that religious activities cannot be separated from other customary practices in China. The blurring of the distinction between customary practices and religious activities does not come just from a strategy of survival in communist ideology. For the villagers, dancing the lion is a solemn way of worshiping the deities and the ancestors. Parading the dragon is related to a rejuvenation of unseen forces.

It is at times difficult to get a contemporary native interpretation of ritual events. There is an inconsistency between public and private discourse (Aijmer and Ho 2000, 239). People display agnosticism or antireligious stances in public as a strategy to avoid accusations of traditionalism and feudalism, and their public stance therefore cannot be taken at face value; it must be carefully checked against their actual private behavior. In a post-Mao era, despite the repeated campaigns in the 1980s for a socialist spiritual civilization to combat spiritual pollution or bourgeois liberalization, most people experienced a cynicism and a loss of faith in official ideology and communist tenets (Brugger 2001, 15).

Following an era of collectivization, people are looking for ways in which to orientate themselves in their social lives. A resurgence of ritual activities at times signals a search for alternatives or even a vague resistance to communist ideals. The time lag since rituals were previously performed, however, has meant that villages have forgotten exactly what they were like, and that has forced them to develop syncretistic strategies that are free to synthesize or borrow from different religious systems and local cults (Aijmer and Ho 2000, 244). Aijmer calls it an ad hoc approach to their religion (ibid., 246). That, however, is not exclusively a feature of the post-Mao era. Cooperation between Daoists, Buddhists, and spirit mediums that challenges our preconceptions of the sharp distinction between Buddhism and Daoism is by no means new. The misunderstanding of the *jiao* as a Daoist ritual while neglecting its Buddhist and local cultic elements, for instance, comes about because of limited and insufficient fieldwork (Lagerwey 1998, 38). If there is an ad hoc approach to their religion, it must be a long-standing tradition. Instead of calling it an ad hoc approach, however, a more appropriate metaphor is, perhaps, that of the traditional Chinese pharmacist, who takes herbs from different jars to mix them into a new medicine. He never rejects any potential herbs, and there is always a great degree of flexibility in what is used and in what quantities. This does not mean that he doing as he pleases, or working in a random manner.

Re-emerged traditions, however, are different in many ways from the old ones. They have to be reconstructed from fragments and recollections from the past, owing to the time lag. Helen Siu claims that resurgent rituals appear in a transformed state and represent cultural fragments recycled under new circumstances. They are new reconstitutions of traditions (Siu 1989, 123, 134). Local temples and lineage halls today have neither landholdings nor financial assets; all activities now rely upon donations. Overseas Chinese are an important financial source, but not all local temples, especially the small ones, have access to that resource. Local contributions remain important. Income and expenditures for every ritual event are now announced on red papers attached to the walls of the lineage hall and local temples.

It is indeed a miracle that, despite a century of systematic destruction, local religion still exists. The time has come, perhaps, for us to change our perception of local religion in China—not as a feudal superstition that hinders economic development but rather as an important cultural resource of indigenous traditions (Dean 2003, 353) without which we would have nothing to resist globalization, modernization, and capitalism.

References

Aijmer, Goran, and Virgil Ho. 2000. *Cantonese Society in a Time of Change.* Hong Kong: Chinese University Press.

Andersen, Poul. 1995. "The Transformation of the Body in Taoist Ritual." Pp. 168–208 in *Religious Reflections on the Human Body.* Edited by Jane Marie Law. Bloomington and Indianapolis: Indiana University Press.

Brugger, Bill. 2001. "Ideology: Radicalism and Reform." Pp. 13–16 in *Dictionary of the Politics of the People's Republic of China.* Edited by Colin Mackerras, Donald H. McMillen, and Andrew Watson. London and New York: Routledge.

Dean, Kenneth. 2003. "Local Communal Religion in Contemporary South-east China." *China Quarterly* 174 (June): 338–358.

DeGroot, Jan J. M. 1910. *The Religion of the Chinese.* New York: Macmillan.

Duara, Prasenjit. 1991. "Knowledge and Power in the Discourse of Modernity: The Campaigns against Popular Religion in Early Twentieth-Century China." *Journal of Asian Studies* 50.1: 67–83.

Flood, Gavin. 1999. *Beyond Phenomenology: Rethinking the Study of Religion.* London and New York: Cassell.

Hsü, Francis L. K. (1967/1948). *Under the Ancestors' Shadow: Kinship, Personality and Social Mobility in China.* Stanford: Stanford University Press.

Lagerwey, John. 1966. "Preface." Pp. 1–14 in *Meizhou diqu de miaohui yu zongzu* [Temple festivals and lineages in Meizhou]. Edited by Fang Xuejia. Hong Kong: International Hakka Studies Association, Overseas Chinese Archives and École française d'Extrême-Orient.

———. 1987. *Taoist Ritual in Chinese Society and History.* New York: Macmillan.

———. 1997. "The Rational Character of Chinese Religion." Public lecture on Chinese Religion, organized by the Centre for the Study of Religion and Chinese Society, Chung Chi College, Chinese University of Hong Kong, September 19.

———. 1998. "Introduction." Pp. 1–41 in *Tingzhou fu di zongzu miaohui yu jingji* [Lineage, festivals, and the economy in Tingzhou Prefecture]. Edited by Yang Yanjie. Hong Kong: International Hakka Studies Association, Overseas Chinese Archives and École française d'Extrême-Orient.

———. 2000. "The Structure and Dynamics of Chinese Rural Society." Pp. 1–43 in *History and Socio-economy: Proceedings of International Conference on Hakkaology.* Edited by Cheng-Kuang Hsu. Taipei: Institute of Ethnology, Academia Sinica.

———. 2002. "Introduction." Pp. 1–45 in *Changting xian di zongzu jingji yu minxu* [Lineage, the economy, and customs in Changting County]. Edited by Yang Yanjie. Hong Kong: International Hakka Studies Association, Overseas Chinese Archives and École française d'Extrême-Orient.

Legge, James, trans. 1967. *Li Chi: Book of Rites.* Vol. 2. Edited by Ch'u chai and Winberg Chai. New York: University Books.

Li, Fengmai. 1993. "You chang ru feichang: zhongguo jieri qingdian zhong di kuang wenhua" [Entering the abnormality from normality: On the mad with joy culture in the celebration of Chinese festivals]. *Chung Wai Literary Monthly* 22.3: 117–150.

Mackerras, Colin. 2001. "Overview History of the People's Republic of China." Pp. 1–8 in *Dictionary of the Politics of the People's Republic of China.* Edited by Colin Mackerras, Donald H. McMillen, and Andrew Watson. London and New York: Routledge.

Paper, Jordan. 1991. "Religious Studies: Time to Move from a Eurocentric Bias?" Pp. 75–84 in *Religious Studies: Issues, Prospects and Proposals.* Edited by Klaus K. Klostermaier and Larry W. Hurtado. Atlanta, GA: Scholars Press.

Schipper, Kristofer M. 1995. "An Outline of Taoist Ritual." Pp. 97–126 in *Essais sur le Rituel III.* Edited by Anne-Marie Blondeau and Kristofer Schipper. Louvain-Paris: Peeters.

Shahar, Meir, and Robert P. Weller. 1996. *Unruly Gods: Divinity and Society in China.* Honolulu: University of Hawai'i Press.

Siu, Helen F. 1989. "Recycling Rituals: Politics and Popular Culture in Contemporary Rural China." Pp. 121–137 in *Unofficial China: Popular Culture and Thought in the People's Republic.* Edited by Perry Link, Richard Madsen, and Paul Pickowicz. Boulder, CO: Westview.

Skinner, G. William. 1964. "Marketing and Social Structure in Rural China, Part I." *Journal of Asian Studies* 24.1: 32–42.

Teiser, Stephen F. 1996. "The Spirits of Chinese Religion." Pp. 3–37 in *Religions of China in Practice.* Edited by Donald Lopez, Jr. Princeton: Princeton University Press.

Wolf, Arthur. 1974. "God, Ghosts and Ancestors." Pp. 131–182 in *Religion and Ritual in Chinese Society.* Edited by Arthur P. Wolf. Stanford: Stanford University Press.

Wu, Chenghan. 1988. "The Temple Fairs in Late Imperial China." Ph.D. diss., Princeton University.

Yang, Dali L., and Zheng Yongnian. 2001. "Regional China." Pp. 33–37 in *Dictionary of the Politics of the People's Republic of China.* Edited by Colin Mackerras, Donald H. McMillen, and Andrew Watson. London and New York: Routledge.

Yu, Kuang-hong. 1990. "Making a Malefactor a Benefactor: Ghost Worship in Taiwan." *Bulletin of the Institute of Ethnology Academia Sinica* 70: 39–65.

Zhao, Shiyu. 2002. *Kuanghuan yu richang: mingqing yilai di miaohui yu minjian shehui* [Mad with joy and ordinary time: Temple festivals and popular society since the Ming and Qing period]. Beijing: Sanlian shudian.

4

Buddhism and Economic Reform in Mainland China

VEN. JING YIN

Introduction

During the Great Proletarian Cultural Revolution (1966–1976), Buddhism in China experienced a total catastrophe. Monasteries were destroyed, their lands were expropriated, and monks and nuns were sent to work in the fields. In 1979, however, Deng Xiaoping instituted a policy of economic reform and modernization, opening China's door to the world—a policy that led to China's rapid rise as a world economic power and its eventual entry to the World Trade Organization in 2001. During that period of market reform, Buddhism underwent a distinct revival. According to rough estimates, by the end of 2003 more than 13,000 monasteries had been put back into operation. The Chinese Buddhist Association (CBA) estimates that there are now some 180,000 monks and nuns in China (CBA 2003, 199). Of those, 120,000 belong to Tibetan Buddhist orders and are located mostly in Tibet, as well as in the Tibetan regions of Sichuan and Qinghai provinces. China also counts some 8,000 Theravada monks, mostly in the southern province of Yunnan. The majority of the 50,000 Han Chinese monastics belong to Chinese Mahayana traditions throughout China. Of the thirty-four Buddhist schools, twenty-six are associated with Chinese Mahayana traditions, six belong to Tibetan orders, and two follow the Theravada tradition (ibid., 238). Hardline atheist policy on religion seems gradually to be diminishing, and Buddhists are experiencing an inspiring period of revival and restoration.

Although the political situation faced by Chinese Buddhists has eased considerably in the last twenty years, Chinese Buddhist associations are now facing severe challenges entailed by market reforms, modernization, and economic openness. From an external perspective, it would seem that monasteries now function as "money-making machines" and compete in the public and private sectors to earn the revenue necessary to continue their operations. From an insider Buddhist perspective, it has been argued that many monks and nuns put too much time and energy into moneymaking and have little or no time to practice and teach Buddhist dharma. According to Zhao Puchu, the former chairman of the CBA:

> Some people are not firm with their faith and are relaxed in precepts and practices. These people are chasing after money and fame, living a luxurious and corrupt lifestyle. If this goes on unchecked, it may seriously imperil Buddhism's future (quoted in CBA 1993, 12).

During the Cultural Revolution, Buddhist followers were inspired to defend their religion against repressive government crackdowns. However, Zhao argues, the current incentive to make money has the potential to breed corruption and cause damage that will last for generations.

Given the scenario depicted above, Chinese Buddhists are currently grappling with four key questions: Where is Buddhism in China going? How can Buddhists resist corruption from materialism? How can Buddhists defend the purity and sanctity of Buddhism and maintain its traditions? and How can Buddhists spread the teaching of the Buddha and be of benefit to society? This chapter explains the background and function of the market economy in China and its impact on Chinese Buddhism. It explores the direction of Buddhism in China and some practical solutions that Buddhists are currently debating.

The Economic Situation of Chinese Buddhist Monasteries

Traditionally, monasteries have derived their income from four principal sources: leasing land; leasing buildings and properties owned by monasteries; income from rituals, ceremonies, dharma teaching, and other religious services; and donations from followers. In prerevolutionary times, the principal source of income for many Buddhist institutions that were not major sites of tourism was their landholdings. As Holmes Welch (1967, 219) notes, from the time of the first antireligious protests in 1922 it became increasingly difficult for monasteries to collect rents, as tenants were unwilling or unable to pay. He concludes that the economic status of most monasteries in the first half of the twentieth century declined considerably as Qing dynasty laws that favored landlords gradually tilted in favor of tenants, under the reforms of the Republican period. This forced monasteries to look to lay Buddhist movements for alternative sources of income (ibid., 243).

During the early communist land reforms of the 1950s, land owned by monasteries was expropriated by the state. During the early 1980s, when the state began to restore property to Buddhist associations, very little of the original land was in fact returned; in most cases, only buildings and their immediate grounds were restored. This means that present-day opportunities for monasteries to derive income from real estate are strictly limited. Moreover, because of the long-term impact of atheistic policies, the lay Buddhist movement has dwindled, and comparatively few people openly admit to being Buddhists. Consequently, income from rituals, ceremonies, and dharma teachings is also limited. A third problem is that the Chinese monastic community is forbidden from going out in public to seek alms or beg for food from followers, as was traditionally the case in Theravada Buddhist countries such as Sri Lanka and Thailand. The good news is that Buddhists today have buildings to operate and services to perform; the bad news is that they have almost no money with which to work. Therefore the urgent priority for nearly every monastery is to find a way to generate revenue. Monasteries are thus trying to become economically independent and to minimize their dependence on state government. The problem is how to do that while at the same time maintaining their distinctive Buddhist character and authentic Buddhist identity.

On the occasion of the thirtieth anniversary of the Chinese Buddhist Association, Zhao Puchu, the CBA's former chairman, advocated that monasteries maintain a balance of "Chan [Zen; meditation] practice and agricultural activity" so as to promote economic independence. He defined Chan practice broadly, so as to include Buddhist studies, practices, and teachings, and agricultural activity as any production or service activity beneficial to society (see Zhao 1983). After the Cultural Revolution, that proved to be an efficient way for monasteries to recover under the new economic regime. Monasteries thus developed their own economic systems, referred to as the "monastery economy."

Chinese worshippers offer coins for prosperity while praying at Longhua Temple to greet the lunar new year in Shanghai on February 9, 2005. Tens of thousands of worshippers visited the ancient temple in China's business capital to welcome in the Year of the Rooster. (Claro Cortes IV/Reuters/Corbis)

At present, most monasteries located in major cities and tourist sites are themselves centers for tourist activity. Many monasteries, such as the Fayuan Monastery in Beijing, have the advantage of a thousand years of history; others, such as the Baogong Monastery in Sichuan or the Potala Palace in Tibet, possess extensive collections of precious historical artifacts. Still others, such as the monasteries located on Emei Mountain, enjoy stunning scenery that attracts millions of tourists each year. Monasteries also function as the ancestral shines of the various schools and sects that have played important roles in Buddhist history—for example, the Qixia Monastery in Nanjing, which is the ancestral shine of the Three-Treatise school. All these monasteries are internationally famous and attract significant numbers of tourists, as well as being important religious sites. Many monasteries open themselves to tourists as

Buddhist attractions in order to generate revenue and to support the development of the local economy.

In response to increasing numbers of tourists, however, monasteries have initiated ancillary economic services (known as "tertiary industrial activities"). These include vegetarian restaurants, exhibition halls, souvenir stores, tea houses, food stands, photo shops, and even hotels. As a result, the income of monasteries has increased steadily each year since the policies of economic and religious freedom were implemented. In 1985, for instance, the Xiyuan Jiezhong Monastery in Suzhou made more than 1 million RMB from its economic activities, which included a vegetarian restaurant, incense stalls, and a souvenir shop. To give another example, the total annual income of the monastery on Mt. Jiuhua in Anhui province rose from less than 100,000 RMB in 1979 to nearly 10 million RMB in 1992 (CBA 2003, 122).

Monasteries in remote areas have also joined the ranks of the moneymakers. Their so-called tertiary industrial activities include planting trees and forests, printing and selling sutras and books, gardening, animal husbandry, setting up medical clinics, running groceries and other stores, and operating transportation and other kinds of services. Take, for example, the Zhonghua Shanxinghai Monastery in Lianchang, Fujian province, which is a small monastery with about fifty monks. Starting in 1981 it contracted out more than 3,000 hectares of land for farming, of which 9 were for growing grain, 120 for trees, 6 for tea, and the rest for fruit. By 1985 it was generating revenue from 7,500 kilograms of grain, 300 kilograms of tea, and 15,000 kilograms of fruit. It subsequently expanded its operations to include a sewing workshop, store, clinic, and brick factory. Within a few years the monastery achieved great wealth. As a result, it was able to construct a large dharma hall, a parking lot, a sutra chamber, and sangha chambers, all equipped with electricity, telephones, and running water (CBA 1993, 78).

This rapid economic development has enabled most monasteries not only to become financially self-sufficient but also to initiate a wide range of social welfare projects. For instance, Buddhist monasteries in Guangdong province spent more than 118 million RMB on social welfare between 1993 and 2002. Outstanding among them, Nanputou Monastery in Xiamen contributed a massive 17,426,315 RMB to those in need between 1994 and 2002 (CBA 2003, 328).

The flourishing of monastic economies and the relative economic independence of monasteries have contributed much to their development over the last quarter-century. Economic independence has improved the standard of living of the sangha, helping to renovate monasteries and to contribute to the general welfare of Chinese society. However, becoming rich has also brought with it problems that challenge the very survival of Buddhism in China.

The Impact of the Market Economy on Buddhism

Problems associated with the impact of the market economy on Buddhism can be divided into two categories. The first can be broadly termed external problems that arise when government officials—particularly low-ranking local ones—infringe upon the rights and interests of the monastery. The more wealthy monasteries become, the more frequently that occurs, and it constitutes a rather serious problem in some areas. As to the second category of problems, they are associated with internal disputes that arose when the state returned property to the monasteries following the implementation of the policy of religious freedom in 1979.

Take, for example, the case of the Great Xiangguo Monastery in Kaifeng, Henan province. One of China's ten most famous Buddhist monasteries, it has long been known as "the most magnificent under heaven." It was first built in 555 C.E. and, at the height of its prosperity in the Northern Song dynasty (960–1126), the monastery covered an area of about 34 hectares, containing sixty-four meditation and Vinaya halls. It has had contact with Japan since ancient times. After the Cultural Revolution, Jing Yan (1892–1991), president of the Henan Province Buddhist Association, appealed to the relevant government organizations for its renovation. His efforts, however, were in vain. In 1991 he passed away at the age of ninety-nine in a poor farmer's house.

When Japanese Buddhist delegations wanted to visit Xiangguo Monastery in 1988, a local official sent a telegram saying, "You are welcome to visit the Great Xiangguo Monastery as sightseers, but not as Buddhist pilgrims, for religious activities are not allowed there" (CBA 1988.1, 4). This caused a very bad impression abroad, which put pressure on those in power. Later, Zhao Puchu, former president of the CBA, appealed to Jiang Zeming, then president of the PRC, for the renovation of the Great Xiangguo Monastery. It was eventually returned to the sangha in 1992 (CBA 1992.3, 20–28). The reason for the delay had to do with the enormous sums of money generated by selling entrance tickets. That is precisely the reason why many ancient monasteries, some more than a thousand years old, are turned into tourist attractions. Many monasteries in Beijing are in that category, such as the Jietai Monastery, the Wofo Monastery, and the Biyuan Monastery. Some monasteries have still not been returned to the hands of Buddhists, despite the fact that the number of Buddhists in China is growing rapidly and the venues for Buddhist activity are few and far between.

Another problematic situation occurs with some monasteries that are returned to Buddhist organizations. In these cases some monasteries are still being treated as tourist attractions and moneymaking machines. Certain individuals seem to be running the monasteries chiefly for economic purposes, causing difficulties for Buddhists who have a genuine religious desire to visit. To give an example from my own experience, in June 1993 I visited the ancestral shine of Chan Buddhism, the Shaolin Temple on Mt. Song. At the foot of Mt. Song, long before I could see Shaolin Temple, I was asked to buy a ticket at a booth. I attempted to ask for a waiver because I am a monk. The man was very impatient and said, "You must pay to enter, no matter who you are. That is the regulation." I considered it a great pity that a monk has to buy a ticket to return to his own ancestral shine.

Another example is Mt. Putuo Monastery in Zhejiang province, which is on another famous Chinese mountain. Its fame derives from its Buddhist heritage and also the fact that it is a world-renowned scenic attraction. However, most of the income generated by selling entrance tickets goes to the government officials who administer the scenic area. Similar situations are occurring in many other areas in China (see ibid., 4).

From a Buddhist perspective, one can say that the one-sided economic development in many monasteries has made them lose their distinctively Buddhist characteristics. I have accompanied many overseas Buddhist delegates on visits to monasteries in China. In my experience, visitors often feel that despite the proliferation of monasteries, there is a lack of character here. Monasteries commonly operate vegetarian restaurants, guest houses, souvenir shops, and food and drink booths. Some even go to the extreme of running factories and operating companies. The long-term effect is that the market economy is seriously hurting the religious nature of the monasteries. Once monasteries become large-scale enterprises, it is difficult for them to back out. And when monasteries become principally tourist attractions, the danger is that the energy of the monks becomes devoted chiefly to receiving tourists, leaving no time for the sangha or to engage in Buddhist practice.

More and more foreigners are visiting China as a result of recent internal reforms and the country's increasing openness to the outside world. Moreover, many Chinese people can now afford to travel, because the standard of living in China has improved dramatically. Many people are now visiting famous monasteries and ancestral shines in the scenic mountains during their holidays. Mt. Wutai, for example, is a famous Buddhist mountain that has attracted many Chinese and international visitors and pilgrims. The number of Chinese visitors from Hong Kong, Macau, and Taiwan rose from 1,200 in 1985 to 1,600 in 1986, and to 1,900 in 1987; the number of domestic visitors increased at about the same rate, from 200,000 in 1985 to 240,000 in 1986, and 330,000 in 1987. At that latter time the monastery was staffed by some 160 elderly monks. After devoting their time and energy to receiving visitors, they had no time left to practice Buddhism (CBA 1988.4, 7).

Fang Litian has observed:

> First of all, since both monks and nuns have to participate in labor activities, this is going to bring objective changes to their lifestyle. Secondly, Buddhist activities have had to be reduced in frequency and scale. For example, in Tibetan monasteries, there used to be more than thirty Buddhist activities every year, each lasting about seven days. Now, these have been reduced to about two or three per year, each lasting about five days. Economic reforms in China have also brought about a similar situation among lay Buddhist followers. Occupied with economic production and business, lay Buddhists have no time to participate in Buddhist activities and have become very weak in their faith (1990, 98).

The most serious problem has to do with monks whose aim is to perform rituals in order to make money. In some places, people send their children to join the sangha for the sole purpose of learning rituals as a skill or trade, in order to make money. Informal interviews suggest that some young monks consider going into Buddhist studies to be a waste of time. They consider learning the business of rituals, however, to be far more practical. This adds to the existing problem of a shortage of manpower in Buddhism.

The strong emphasis on developing the economy of the monasteries has had a tremendous impact on Buddhism in China. On the one hand, it has brought improvements to infrastructure and income to the monasteries, as well as raising the social status and value of the sangha. On the other, it facilitates a certain decay in Buddhism by directing the attention of monastics away from their Buddhist practices and toward the mundane business of making money. This is a severe challenge, which Chinese Buddhists are currently wrestling with. Responses to this challenge fall into three categories: reforming Buddhism, reforming the sangha, and reforming monasteries.

Reforming Buddhist Studies in China

Historically in China, the way Buddhism has been presented has varied in content and method during different historical periods. The Buddha is said to have attained enlightenment under the Bodhi tree with the realization of the "marvelous mind of Nirvana" that has no form. Buddhist teaching, consequently, surpasses the limitation of thinking, words, forms, and worldly description: it cannot be captured with words or easily be transmitted to ordinary minds that are full of illusion, greed, desire, and negative cravings. The Buddha started teaching the dharma only after repeated requests to relieve the suffering of sentient beings, and thus the original intention of this teaching was to liberate people from the cycle of birth, aging, death, and suffering. Therefore, a major characteristic of Buddha's early teaching was an emphasis on the analysis of existential phenomena and practical methods for the elimination of suffering, instead of abstract philosophical studies. The goal was to help people to recognize the true nature of suffering, and the necessity and feasibility of liberation from that suffering. One can make the argument, therefore, that Buddhists ought to be predisposed toward practical applications and not theoretical studies.

However, the historical situation of Buddhism in China has been marked by the transmission of sutras and the establishment of schools centered on lineages of teachers who specialized in certain sutras and the theories they transmitted. That may well have been simply a matter of convenience for transmitting the teachings to beginners. However, the transmission of Buddhist dharma came to be marked by a highly scholastic process of writing commentaries, interpretations, and footnotes, analyzing terminology, and compiling detailed rules and regulations for engaging in spiritual practice.

It is in this context that the work of Hui Neng (638–713), the sixth Chan patriarch, stands out. He advocated "not relying on words or letters, a special transmission apart from the scripture, directly pointing to the human mind, awakening one's own true nature and [thus] attaining Buddhahood." Hui

People praying before monk, Yunnan province. (Michael S. Yamashita/Corbis)

Neng believed that one who searched for truth should make use of words and letters, but should not become attached to them. If people become attached to words, those words will become obstacles that will restrict them from understanding the truth of liberation. Therefore he emphasized a process of self-understanding according to which the truth lies fundamentally within one's own mind: it can be attained only through experiencing life. As a result, he used the concept of "the special transmission apart from the scripture" and "mind to mind transmission" to rectify what he considered to be the failings of previous Buddhist teachings (see Yampolsky 1977).

The sectarian teachings, methods, and practices taught by the various grand masters and patriarchs were indeed based on what the Buddha taught, tailored to the needs of different individuals in different historical periods. That is the origin of the variety of teachings practiced during particular periods of history. Each sect has its own unique expression, geared to the needs of the time, and each gradually becomes a tradition. However, any claim by a particular sect to the absolute, universal, and permanent truth is a distortion of the Buddha's original insight: that teachings must be flexible and geared to different needs and different levels.

Contemporary Chinese Buddhists live in the shadow of these debates. Their task is to sort through the vast legacy of the various schools of Chinese Buddhism in such a way as to renovate Buddhism and integrate it with the rapid pace of social development. That is a complicated and important task. Buddhism can serve the society only after positioning itself by integrating its strength with everyday worldly activities. Buddhism cannot survive and consolidate itself without social recognition and respect. Buddhism needs to be applicable to all sectors in the society, in order to liberate individuals and the world. How then are Buddhists engaging the contemporary Chinese religious scene?

In China today, it is a commonplace that materialism is emphasized and spirituality is scarce. In China's urban centers Wal-Mart is king, and as the shelves of Chinese bookstores testify, people are searching for a spiritual direction in life. Popular author John Naisbitt argued in his best-seller *Megatrends* (1982) that spiritual growth is not just a trendy New Age business; it is an education craved by today's society in order to balance out the alienation that people suffer as a result of overdevelopment in high technology and automation (see also Carrette and King 2004). Books written by Western authors on the topics of spiritual growth and awakening are now best-sellers in the Chinese market. These include Daniel Goleman's *Emotional Intelligence* (1995), the *Chicken Soup* series (Canfield and Hansen 1993), and the work of James Redfield (1993 et al.). This is not merely a trend within popular culture; it is also a trend that is gaining recognition among Buddhists. Through translations of these popular Western books, Chinese people are now rediscovering aspects of traditional Buddhist teaching such as mindfulness, breathing exercises, acceptance, compassion, and wisdom. Moreover, major universities and medical centers in Europe and North America are actively pursuing research into the topic of Buddhist meditation, psychotherapy, and neurobiology. Ironically it is through the West's adaptation of Buddhist meditation practices that Chinese people are now coming to terms with their own religious history. This renewed emphasis on practical, socially engaged Buddhism seeks to apply Buddhism to everyday life and to solve the real problems of today's Chinese people.

The emphasis on social and psychological well-being is currently receiving the favor of the Chinese government. Chairman Jiang Zemin has advocated the use of morality (*de*) as a political tool, and Buddhists have a long history of advocating Buddhist virtues to cure social illness and to nurture a happy and healthy life. The task for contemporary Buddhists is to develop a new mode of morality to serve the modern world, and they are currently looking for answers to the host of social problems that have emerged as a side effect of China's rapid economic expansion. How do Buddhists look at wealth? How can one balance economic gain and spiritual growth? What is the Buddhist position on war and peace during this time of terrorism and chaos? In short, Buddhists are seeking to renovate their teachings by serving the people.

The Sangha in Chinese Society

The parlous economic state of China's monastic communities has required many members of the sangha to devote their energies toward economic gain in order to generate revenue for the monasteries. Little time has been spent on teaching and meditation, to the extent that the core religious functions of monasteries are in danger of becoming merely decorative. In fact, the question of the appropriate relationship between the Buddhist monastic community and the wider society is not new; it has been subject to debate throughout Buddhist history. In terms of Chinese Buddhism, the phrase that came to summarize the correct functioning of monastic communities is "balance agriculture and meditation," which goes back to the Tang dynasty Buddhist master Mazu (700–788). Mazu initiated the concept of balancing agricultural activities with Chan meditation while setting up monasteries in the forests. His disciple Baizhang (720–814) supplemented that concept with the well-known Buddhist maxim, "Every day that you do not work, you shall not eat" (see Welch 1967, 216).

The concept that physical labor—in addition to meditation practice—is a necessary tool for tuning the mind and body is not, therefore, new to Buddhism in the modern period. However, it could be argued that the contemporary practice of "balancing agriculture with meditation" has deviated from its original purpose of helping to set up a better environment in the monasteries in which to teach the dharma. Unfortunately, it is clear that some communities today emphasize agriculture and income over practice and meditation. Monasteries are now becoming active participants in the process of commodification that characterizes contemporary Chinese economic life, a phenomenon that is equally familiar to North American society (see Carrette and

King 2004). Needless to say, this commodification runs the risk of impairing the ability of Buddhists to concentrate on their fundamental work, which is, in Buddhist terms, to liberate sentient beings from suffering and to propagate the dharma.

One significant result of the transformation of Buddhism in the last fifteen years has been the increase in the number of monastics, the most recent estimate being some 180,000. However, the development of lay Buddhism in China has not been as successful. There are very few lay Buddhist organizations and few people who openly identify themselves as Buddhist followers, except in the areas dominated by minority nationalities. Lay organizations rarely organize Buddhist lectures, seminars, or talks by famous masters, and there is a lack of mutual support and collaboration between monastic and lay Buddhists. In fact, one reason why monastics have been forced into economic enterprises is that they receive little support from lay Buddhist followers. Consequently, monks and nuns are frequently unable to make a contribution to lay Buddhist life in the form of teaching and organization. This lack of integration between lay and monastic Buddhists is one of the most serious problems facing Chinese Buddhists today. In a few monasteries, a minority of the community has gone so far as to commit crimes and violate laws, which seriously damaged the reputation of Buddhism and stifled its growth. Chinese Buddhists are now faced with the task of strengthening ties between lay and monastic Buddhism, as is the case in Thailand and Sri Lanka, and setting clear standards for those who want to join the monasteries.

Buddhism and Globalization

Since the time Buddhism entered China during the first century of the Common Era, Buddhism has developed through a process of international exchange. The translation of the *Sutra in Forty-Two Verses* marked the beginning of Buddhism in China, and that process of translation and internationalization resulted in the spread of Buddhism to Korea, Japan, and the West. The Sui and Tang dynasties were the golden era of Buddhism in China, in part because of frequent international travel and exchanges: Chinese scholars traveled west to India to search for dharma, and Japanese Buddhists came to China to seek dharma. International exchange between Buddhists was at its peak. The postcolonial period in Chinese history has, however, been particularly grim. During the civil war between the communists and the Nationalists, monasteries were occupied, land was expropriated, and monks were chased out or even executed. The great reformer Taixu (1890–1947) sought to revitalize Chinese Buddhism by creating new institutional forms (see Pittman 2001). He established new Buddhist institutions and encouraged monastics to study abroad, as they had done more than a thousand years earlier. During the twenty years between 1921 and 1941, more than thirty Chinese monks were sent to study abroad. The ones who studied in Tibet, India, and Sri Lanka achieved the best results. The outcome of this international training was that a generation of Chinese Buddhist teaching was preserved at a time when it was difficult for it to prosper in China.

Today, Buddhism faces a similar need for international training. Not many Buddhist masters survived the Cultural Revolution, and those that did are passing away. Modern Chinese Buddhism has consistently faced the problem of a lack of teachers and educational resources. Two strategies are currently emerging for the future success of Buddhism. On the one hand, contributions have been raised to establish Buddhist schools in China. A system of Buddhist education has now been established at the advanced, middle, and elementary levels. So far, three advanced-level institutions have been created, and twenty medium-level institutions. On the other hand, as before, Buddhists are being encouraged to travel overseas and study abroad. This is seen as a quick and efficient solution, one that will help Chinese Buddhism keep pace with global Buddhist standards and practices.

In 1982, the Buddhist leader Zhao Puchu sent many Buddhists abroad to study in Japan, Sri Lanka, Thailand, England, and Burma. I myself happened to be one of them; I studied in Sri Lanka from 1986 until 1995. In my experience Sri Lanka turned out to be an ideal place to study Theravada Buddhism. Formerly known as Ceylon, Sri Lanka was under British colonial rule for almost three hundred years prior to its independence in 1948, and therefore English is well understood. The dominance of English as a global second language, a by-product of colonialism, meant that Sri Lanka has proven an excellent location for Chinese scholars with a good command of English to learn Pali and study Theravada Buddhism. Moreover, after independence, the Sri Lankan government made use of Buddhist teachings and institutions to advance its anticolonialist agenda; thus Buddhism remains well integrated into the social fabric. During the 1950s, Buddhism was a popular subject for young people, and many young Sri Lankan Buddhists studied abroad. Those

Buddhists are now actively involved in Buddhist studies and are playing a key role in the development of Chinese Buddhism; more than forty Chinese Buddhist monks are studying in Sri Lanka today. Chinese Buddhism developed out of the interaction between Indian monks and Chinese culture. There is every reason to suppose that its future strength lies not only in economic prosperity but also in the international ties that for centuries have been one of the hallmarks of one of the world's truly global religions.

References

Canfield, Jack, and Mark Victor Hansen, eds. 1993. *Chicken Soup for the Soul*. Deerfield Beach, FL: Health Communications.

Carrette, Jeremy, and Richard King. 2004. *Selling Spirituality*. New York: Routledge.

Chinese Buddhist Association (CBA). 1993. *Zhongguo fojiao xiehui chengli sishi zhou nian jinian wenji* [Collected works in commemoration of the fortieth anniversary of the founding of the Chinese Buddhist Association]. Beijing: Chinese Buddhist Association.

———. 2003. *Zhongguo fojiao xiehui wushi nian* [Fifty years of the Chinese Buddhist Association]. Beijing: Chinese Buddhist Association.

Fang Litian. 1990. "Zhongguo fojiao sishi nian" [Forty years of Chinese Buddhism]. *Shijie zongjiao yanjiu* [Studies in world religions]: 2.

Goleman, Daniel. 1995. *Emotional Intelligence*. New York: Bantam.

Naisbitt, John. 1982. *Megatrends: Ten New Directions Transforming Our Lives*. New York: Warner.

Pittman, Don A. 2001. *Towards a Modern Chinese Buddhism: Taixu's Reforms*. Honolulu: University of Hawai'i Press.

Redfield, James. 1993. *The Celestine Prophecy*. New York: Warner.

Welch, Holmes. 1967. *The Practice of Chinese Buddhism 1900–1950*. Vol. 1. Cambridge: Harvard University Press.

Yampolsky, Philip. 1977. *The Platform Sutra of the Sixth Patriarch*. New York. Columbia University Press.

Zhao Puchu. 1983. *Zhongguo fojiao sanshi nian* [Thirty years of the Chinese Buddhist Association]. Beijing: Chinese Buddhist Association.

5

Daoist Monasticism in Contemporary China

KIM SUNG-HAE

Historical Background

Contemporary Chinese Daoism has two main branches with distinct characteristics. One is the Orthodox Unity (Zhengyi) sect, which began in the year 142 as a popular movement known as the Way of the Celestial Masters (*Tianshi dao*) or the Way of the Five Pecks of Rice (*Wudoumi dao*). This movement was begun by Zhang Ling (respectfully referred to as Zhang Daoling) during the political disintegration of the Later Han dynasty. In 748 the Zhang family line reclaimed its leadership, and in 1304 it changed the official name to the Way of Orthodox Unity (*Zhengyi dao*). The Orthodox Unity sect focuses on ritual practices and continues its popular character as folk-oriented priests who are usually married and live among the people. Its main center has been at Dragon and Tiger Mountain (Longhu shan) in Jiangxi province, and it continues to exercise influence in the southern part of China. Although from the time of the Ming period (1368–1644) the Orthodox Unity sect has been in charge of official ordination certificates for all Daoist masters, its leadership was put into question when the sixty-third Celestial Master, Zhang Enpu, fled to Taiwan in 1949. The sixty-fifth generation of the Zhang family, Zhang Jiyu, currently resides at the White Cloud Monastery (Baiyun guan) in Beijing and is vice president of Chinese Daoist Association.

The other branch of Chinese Daoism, which began in the twelfth century but is presently exercising the role of leadership in the People's Republic of China, is the Order of Complete Perfection (Quanzhen jiao). It is a monastic form of Daoism with a strictly celibate life and communal lifestyle based on a monastic code known as "pure rules" (*qinggui*). It was founded by Wang Chongyang (also known as Wang Zhe), who encountered two famous Daoist immortals, Lü Dongbin and Zhongli Quan, in 1160 and underwent a period of intense training. He and his seven disciples went through several years of self-cultivation and finally succeeded in the total transformation of body, mind, and spirit, which they called inner alchemy (*neidan*). Present-day Daoist monasticism is based on the Way of Complete Perfection established during the Yuan period and favored by the Mongol emperors as well as by ordinary people, who were grateful for the Quanzhen masters' active participation whenever misfortune such as famine, fire, disease, or war occurred. Its main center is the White Cloud Monastery in Beijing, and its influence has been predominant in the northern part of China.

The origins of Daoist monasticism can be traced to the fifth century during the Six Dynasties period, when interaction between Buddhism and Daoism increased. According to Kobayashi Masayoshi (1998, 142–150), the first Daoist monastery was the Monastery of Venerating Emptiness (Chongxu guan), which the Emperor Ming built for the Daoist master Lu Xiujing (406–477). Stephan Peter Bumbacher traces a slightly earlier establishment at Mt. Mao (Maoshan), the founding mountain of the Highest Clarity (Shangqing) movement. He states that Daoist female masters at Mt. Mao started a celibate community in 420 and received imperial recognition in 480 (Bumbacher 2000). Monasteries grew steadily during the Six Dynasties period through the generous donations of emperors and nobility, but it was not until the Tang dynasty that monasticism began to occupy a central position in Daoism (Kobayashi 2003, 1, 56). What the relatively late Way of Complete Perfection contributed to Daoist monasticism were the obligatory requirements of celibacy and strict self-cultivation for all Complete Perfection masters, male and female. As a result of this requirement, all the Daoist temples where Complete Perfection masters resided became monasteries— sacred spaces in which the dual dimensions of self-cultivation (the practice of inner alchemy and external works of compassion) complemented each other.

According to 1992 government statistics, there are 12,000 Daoist masters living in monasteries and some 50,000 Orthodox Unity priests scattered throughout China (see Li 1993). However, according to Wang and Chen (1999, 206–208), Quanzhen monasteries constituted two-thirds of all Daoist temples in 1985, and 88 out of 111 representatives gathered for the fifth

Daoist Congress of 1992 in Beijing were Complete Perfection masters. Li Yangzheng (1993, 107) has also noted that, of the Daoist masters attending the Chinese Daoist Academy in 1990, 70 percent were Complete Perfection masters and 30 percent Orthodox Unity. This suggests that although there may be more Orthodox Unity masters in China, it is Complete Perfection Daoism that holds sway at the official level. Field visits to the Daoist temples in China that are open to outsiders further reveal that more than two-thirds currently belong to the Way of Complete Perfection. Even the monastery at Mt. Heming in Sichuan province, the birthplace of the Orthodox Unity sect, is presently occupied by the Complete Perfection masters who see themselves as encompassing all the Daoist sects and orders (Kim 1996).

When I visited the monastery on Mt. Heming on January 23, 1995, the chief Daoist master, Yang Mingyi, was building the monastery gateway at the foot of mountain and repairing the main temple. The monastery had been damaged in the late 1960s during the Cultural Revolution and turned into a dormitory for laborers, a warehouse, and finally a primary school (Wei 1992). It was restored in 1987, and in 1995 nine female and six male masters were living there. Master Yang told me that Taiwanese Orthodox Unity masters had visited the birthplace of their religion the year before and had donated 10 percent toward the total expense of construction. During the interview I asked what his goal was in life, and he said without hesitation that the first goal was to become an immortal and the second the preservation of the Daoist monastery. When I probed further concerning the method of inner alchemy (*neidan*), he answered simply that one has to lessen one's desires, refrain from evil, and follow the direction of the *Daoist Commentary to the Book of Changes.*

When I visited the Mt. Heming monastery again on July 4, 2001, the mountain gate was finished, the temple buildings were repaired, and Master Yang's face was shining with energy and tranquillity. He was teaching younger nuns, of whom the bright ones were sent to the White Cloud Monastery in Beijing. A larger number of lay people were around him, and we enjoyed his hospitality in the form of a delicious vegetarian lunch. A Daoist master who survived imprisonment during the Cultural Revolution (1966–1976), Master Yang is now the teacher of inner alchemy to younger Daoist masters and the preserver of the temple and its cultural tradition. I observed in him the intriguing combination of reserved withdrawal and inwardly shining energy that I have encountered many times in Daoist masters. Moreover, Master

Yang has a special vocation to rebuild Daoism and overcome its sectarian divisions at the holy place from which Daoist religious communities sprang two thousand years ago.

Mt. Qingcheng in Sichuan province is located 25 kilometers from Mt. Heming. After the Cultural Revolution, the Mt. Qingcheng Daoist Association was re-established in 1979, and it is presently one of the most lively Daoist centers in China, with eleven monasteries and 140 Daoist masters (Zhang Ming 1989, 2). The monks and nuns are proud of its purely Daoist character—that is, that there are no Buddhist temples on the mountain. Mt. Qingcheng is currently a major site of Daoist cultivation and pilgrimage, as well as a tourist attraction visited by 1 million people every year, who come to see its natural beauty.

Mt. Qingcheng is a good example of the threefold function of a Daoist monastery. First of all, it is a sacred site where Daoist masters practice inner alchemy in order to become immortals; secondly, it is a center where lay believers and Daoist masters meet to celebrate rituals through the year, and where masters conduct counseling and healing activities; thirdly, it is a place of rest for Chinese and overseas tourists who appreciate the beauty of the Dao in nature. These three functions are shared by more than four hundred restored Daoist monasteries, and especially twenty-one central monasteries located on sacred mountains including Mt. Tai, Mt. Mao, and Mt. Wudang.

Kristofer Schipper commented that Daoism possesses two notions of body: one is the physical body, which consists of life energy and is related to the soteriological desire for long life and immortality found in the concept of the Dao as the wellspring of primordial energy; the other is the "social body," which deals with the liturgical structure of local communities, myths, and symbols such as the holy tree beside the local shrine, which is "useless" but vivifies the social life of the area (Schipper 1993, 33). The concept of social body implies a mystical unity with the Dao that is immanent within everything as the inner principle and life force of the myriad beings (*wanwu*). According to my research, while the process of transformation through inner alchemy is concerned with the physical bodies of individual Complete Perfection Daoist masters, their daily morning and evening services, recited in common, signify the continuous formation of social body in the process of communal cultivation. As a way to grasp one of the important principles of Daoist monasticism today, a principle that is embedded in its communal liturgy, I will introduce my analysis and interpretation of the

Complete Perfection prayer book, printed by the White Cloud Monastery in Beijing in 2000.

Daily Prayer in the Complete Perfection Order

During the summer of 2001, I directed a research tour of Daoist monasteries along with nine graduate students. The first monastery we visited was the White Cloud Monastery in Beijing, the center of the Order of Complete Perfection, where we attended the morning service (*gongke*), which lasted about forty minutes. They proudly presented us with a few copies of their prayer book, newly printed in January 2000 at the White Cloud Monastery. I was able to follow their prayers closely, and not only did I understand the general meaning of their service but, in addition, I was deeply moved by the fact that Daoist masters are praying every day for all those who are sick, troubled, and alienated. In fact, the scope of their prayers is so wide that it embraces the whole of humanity, and even the entire universe. While listening to the initially slow chanting accompanied by bronze and wooden gongs, which accelerated as the prayers progressed, I thought of the description of the Dao in the *Daode jing* as the "mother of the myriad things." I myself, a Catholic Sister who prays communally twice a day with a similar vision, was able to appreciate the importance of the Daoist daily prayer book. Thus I was not surprised when I learned that, according to their disciplinary code, absence from daily morning or evening prayers is the first infraction mentioned, punishable by kneeling until one incense stick has been consumed. (Other violations that receive the same punishment are disrespect during the liturgy, and fighting.)

Fortunately, during the same research tour, I was able to stay overnight in the Grotto of the Celestial Master (Tianshi dong) Monastery on Mt. Qingcheng in Sichuan province. About fifteen female Daoist masters finished their activities at sunset, donned red vestments, and lined up in the main hall. Early in the morning, before dawn, they did the same. Using the ritual prayer book that I had received as a gift at the White Cloud Monastery, I followed their evening and early-morning services, which lasted about a half-hour. When they saw my long yellow book, they informed me that they use the same book, as does all the Complete Perfection Order throughout China.

However, during another two-week research tour in the summer of 2002, I learned that the Daoist masters in Changsha, Hunan province, were using a

Daoist monks sing in Tianxin Guan temple, Anhui province. (Cancan Chu/Getty Images)

slightly different version of the prayer book. A Daoist master, Ma Yongqi, who represents the Daoist Association in that area, told me that the Daoist masters in the south are using the text printed in the monastery at Mt. Wudang. Cao and Pu (1992, 31) also state that they have seen two versions of the Complete Perfection communal liturgy. One was printed at the White Cloud Monastery in Beijing; the other, the *Supreme Complete Perfection Liturgy* (*Taishang Quanzhen gongke*), did not indicate details of its publication. According to Hammerstrom (2003, 4–9) there were two different kinds of liturgical texts as early as the Qing dynasty. Master Ma was very helpful in presenting to me the version they are using and in pointing out a few differences between the two texts. A close analysis reveals some variation of words and a few additions in the southern version, such as *Precious Teaching of the True Valiant One* (*Zhenwu gao*) and the *Precious Teaching of the Holy Emperor of the South Mountain* (*Nanyue shengdi gao*). It seems that it is in the area of the Precious Teachings of the immortals (*baogao*) that regional mythological and cultural differences enter into the communal prayer tradition of the Complete Perfection Daoists. I will discuss this further when I analyze the structure of the Daoist morning and evening communal prayers.

There are three important reasons for studying the liturgy of Complete Perfection Daoism. First of all, it is the officially recognized prayer book that is accepted and used daily by the largest Daoist order. This means that if we comprehend the content of this prayer book and its aspirations, we grasp the core of the Daoist spirituality as an officially sanctioned reality in contemporary mainland China. The preface to the White Cloud Monastery edition of the prayer book states that the morning and evening prayers are the door through which one enters the world of the Dao; they are the direct path to immortality, and the very steps by which one ascends to the realm of the immortals. Secondly, the liturgy displays the self-identity of Complete Perfection Daoism, which, from its inception, has emphasized both interior self-cultivation and external works of compassion. It has forged an ambitious synthesis of the best teachings of the Three Religions: Daoism, Confucianism, and Buddhism. This small prayer book of some seventy pages summarizes well the main insights and unique syntheses of this form of Daoism. Thirdly, this prayer book encapsulates the whole history of Daoism as a reservoir of ancient Chinese popular culture and mythic imagery. It uses the ancient imagery of "nine heavens," "nine-headed lions," "five colored clouds," and "sweet dew of the Western Mother," which were composed in the Warring States Period (403–221 B.C.E.) in classic texts of Chinese literature such as the *Songs of the South* (*Chuci*) and the *Classic of Mountains and Seas* (*Shanhai jing*). In addition to these ancient images, the text incorporates and reinterprets within its synthetic vision important cultivation methods of the Highest Clarity sect and the ritual symbols of the Orthodox Unity sect.

The history of the formation of this Complete Perfection liturgy is not found even in the official commentary (Min 2000) published by the Chinese Daoist Academy in October 2000. Only one page out of 267 is devoted to explaining the origins of the liturgy. Because of the scarcity of materials on the transmission of the morning and evening prayer liturgy, it is possible to draw only a general sketch of how the Daoist tradition of petitions and prayers of repentance has developed.

To trace the origin of the Complete Perfection daily prayer liturgy, it is necessary to go back to the rituals of confession in the Way of the Celestial Masters. This second- to third-century Daoist movement employed a ritual of confession that involved handwritten memorials to the offices of heaven, earth, and water (*sanguan shoushu;* see Zheng 2002, 253). We also know that such rituals of confession were important in the Way of Great Peace (*Taiping dao*) and that such rituals developed in the fifth and sixth centuries (Tsuchiya 2002). During the Six Dynasties period, Daoist ritual practices were reformulated under a Buddhist influence, adapting ancient Chinese fasting regulations into the formal structures of Buddhist liturgies (Cao and Pu 1992, 29). This liturgical structure included purification chanting, recitation of sutras, confessions, and petitions to the bodhisattvas (ibid., 327). In addition to those elements adapted from Buddhism, Daoist liturgies also incorporated the techniques of visual meditation on inner deities that were developed in the Way of Highest Clarity. Moreover, chanting the texts was regarded as the path of deliverance, not only for the practitioners themselves but also for their ancestors. In the Way of Complete Perfection, chanting a common liturgy is also central, but it is by no means the sole focus of monastic life. Both inner meditation and outer works of compassion are necessary.

It is generally recognized that it was during the Tang dynasty that Daoist morning and evening prayers formally took shape, incorporating Confucian sacrificial rites with music and regular Buddhist chanting. The Daoist master Du Guangting edited a ritual text called the *Supreme Yellow Register* (*Taishang huanglu zaiyi*) that was chanted three times a day: in the morning, during the day, and in the evening. It is also in the Tang period that celibate Daoist masters residing in monasteries began to occupy a central position in the transmission of Daoism (Kobayashi 2003, 1, 56). According to historical evidence from the Yuan dynasty, Complete Perfection masters began to recite daily prayers from the thirteenth century onward (Chen 1997, 48–51).

The Structure of the Daily Prayers

In order to explain the significance of the daily liturgy of the Complete Perfection Order, it is necessary first to analyze the basic structure of the morning and evening services. Then I will point out the fundamental similarities and some interesting differences between the morning and evening rites. These differences indicate a slight distinction in their function in the life of the monastery.

A comparison of the structure and content outlined in Table 1 reveals that the general sequence of the morning and evening services is the same, but the

TABLE 1. STRUCTURE OF MORNING AND EVENING PRAYERS

Morning Prayer

1. **Preparation**
   The ascent to the immortal world by "walking in the void" (*buxu*) and purifying of mind, mouth, body, heaven, and earth. Incense to the Heavenly Worthy of Purity and Stillness (*Qingjing tianzun*).

2. **Recitation of Scripture**
   Chanting of four canonical writings by the Three Pure Ones (*sanqing*), which teach how to cultivate the purity of heart and life energy, two dimensions of inner practice.

3. **Precious Teachings**
   Twelve precious teachings comprising admonitions by, and hymns to, the immortals; the Three Pure Ones; the stars; yin and yang; and the founders of the Complete Perfection Order.

4. **Petitions**
   The repentance of sins that Qiu Changchun made for disciples; and twenty-one or twelve petitions, which conclude with a vow to become an immortal.

5. **Closing**
   The morning service ends with the chant "taking refuge in the Three Pure Ones" in the form of the Dao, the scriptures, and the teacher. Some additional prayers for long life follow.

Evening Prayer

1. **Preparation**
   The ascent to the immortal world by "walking in the void" and request to the Heavenly Worthy of Deliverance from Suffering (*Jiuku tianzun*) on behalf of all the suffering lonely souls.

2. **Recitation of Scripture**
   Chanting of three canonical writings by the Three Pure Ones with an emphasis on delivering the dead from hell and driving away the evil energy from the body.

3. **Precious Teachings**
   Eleven precious teachings comprising admonitions by, and hymns to, the immortals; the Mother of the Dipper (*Doumu*); the three offices of heaven, earth, and water; the Pole Star; and the Deliverer of the Dead.

4. **Petitions**
   Twelve petitions and ten items of prayer for good weather, an end to famine, and the transfer of merit across the four seas.

5. **Closing**
   The evening service ends with the chant "taking refuge in the Three Pure Ones" and the offering of concluding prayers for the deliverance of all from suffering. A few additional prayers for ancestors and lonely souls.

central focus is different. While the morning prayers are for the living, the evening prayers are mainly for the dead. Every day Daoist masters in Complete Perfection monasteries pray for the well-being of all living and dead men, women, animals, plants, and forests (Baiyun guan 2000, B.50–51; Min 2000, 69–73).

Secondly, we can observe that even though the morning and evening services form complete and independent liturgical structures in and of themselves, they are designed to complement each other and create a continuous whole. In the morning the Daoist masters recite a purification incantation (*zhou*) for the mind, the mouth, the body, the land, and the entire universe. Then they read the first scripture, the Scripture of Purity and Stillness (*Qingjing jing*), which, according to the commentary, is traditionally ascribed to Laozi himself, being first transmitted orally by the Queen Mother of the West and written down by Ge Xuan (Min 2000, 42). The text is in fact anonymous and probably dates to the ninth century (see Kohn 1993, 24–29; Wong 1992). It embodies the notion of the Dao expressed in *Daode jing* 25: "It is capable of being the mother of the world, but I know not its name so I style it 'the Way.'" Its central themes also come from the *Daode jing*: "A person of the highest virtue does not cling to virtue" (ch. 38); and "The way of the sage does not contend" (ch. 81). Since the *Scripture of Purity and Stillness* teaches how purity and stillness gradually introduce a person into the path of true Dao, that scripture occupies the central position in the morning service. Of course purity of mind and stillness of physical energy have been the central themes of Complete Perfection Daoism from its inception in the twelfth century. Moreover, the daily prayer liturgy states that when one recites this text, the body and mind become transparent, and the immortals come to protect the reciter from all misfortunes.

If the scripture readings of the morning service focus on the inner self-cultivation (*neigong*) of Daoist masters in its dual aspects of spiritual practices (*xinggong*) and physical practices (*minggong*), the scriptures of the evening services center around outer practices (*waixing*), such as delivering all people from suffering and saving the lonely souls of the deceased. In the third scripture of the evening service, Laozi spreads out the light of primary energy to reveal the true nature of heaven and hell. Even though it is because of their own sins that they suffer in hell, Laozi has pity on the sinners and has provided this scripture for them. The scripture is like a boat of mercy in the ocean of life and death. The popular character of the evening service is fully demonstrated when we see the character of the immortals whose lives it narrates. First, the Mother of the Dipper delivers all the sentient beings from hardship; the Pole Star causes all the evil powers to surrender; the popular immortal Lü Dongbin drives away all the demons with his sword; the god of thunder (Leishen) brings down the rain and heals the sick with medicine.

In a word, the morning service takes care of inner cultivation, while the evening service concentrates on works of compassion as the outreach work of the Complete Perfection masters. The daily prayer liturgy, therefore, summarizes and represents the entire cultivation and orientation of the Way of Complete Perfection. The Daoist masters, men and women together, chant their morning liturgy in common as a symbol of their life as pilgrims who are continuously ascending to the realm of the immortals. After devoting the entire day to cultivation, they come together to chant the evening service so as to transfer all their merits to those who suffer, both living and dead.

The Daoist Synthesis of the Three Religions

Wang Chongyang, the founder of the Way of Complete Perfection, stated that his teaching unified basic elements of the three teachings of Buddhism, Confucianism, and Daoism (*sanjiao heyi*). He encouraged his followers to read not only Daoist texts such as the *Scripture of the Way and Its Power* and the *Scripture of Purity and Stillness* but also Buddhist texts such as the *Prajñaparamita Sutra* and the Confucian *Classic of Filial Piety* (*Xiaojing*). It is not surprising, therefore, to find various elements of the three teachings in this official prayer book of the Quanzhen Order. Complete Perfection Daoism borrows, without explanation, many technical terms from Buddhism, such as samsara, liberation from rebirth, the five aggregates, the six sense organs, Mara, mental afflictions, karma, and the transfer of merits. Such terms can be found throughout the daily prayer liturgy that is currently used by Complete Perfection Daoists in China. It is clear, however, that these Buddhist terms are incorporated to serve a Daoist end—namely, progress along the way of immortality toward ultimate unity with the Dao.

The importance of the thunder deity who is invoked in the morning service and the evening service may also show the influence of Buddhism. The thunder god was never prominent in ancient Chinese literature and was not included in the pantheon of nature deities in the ancient *Nine Songs* (*Jiu ge*). The *Nine Songs* honor the sun and the moon, the clouds, and the star deities

Homage to the First Principle, *ca. 1325. Painting of a procession of Chinese deities, including the Lord of the Southern Dipper, the Jade Emperor, and the Empress of Heaven. (Royal Ontario Museum/Corbis)*

who ride on the wind in the ritual hymns of ancient Chinese shamans. In a medieval Daoist text, the *Diagram of the Daoist Immortals* (*Zhenling weiye tu* by Tao Hongjing), the thunder deity is included among the pantheon of Daoist deities but is inconspicuously situated in the sixth heaven without any significant job. It seems that during the Tang dynasty, when Buddhism was most influential in China and mutual borrowing was active among the two religions, the thunder deity became prominent in Daoism. Indra, the Hindu thunder deity, was very popular as the guardian against evil powers and for removing obstacles. Within Chinese Buddhist circles, Indra was thought of as the highest Heavenly Emperor, who watched over all the transmigrating souls and thus was identified with the Lord on High (Shangdi) in ancient China. In the Daoist daily prayer liturgy, the ancestral deity of thunder (Leizu) is stationed under the command of the Three Pure Ones at the top of the ninth heaven. His duty is to conquer all the evil spirits. Thus the thunder deity with red face, mustache, and golden whip has become thoroughly integrated into the Daoist pantheon and has a prominent position in the contemporary Complete Perfection liturgy (Baiyun guan 2000, B.41; Min 2000, 245).

Both the Daoist morning and evening services finish with a threefold chanting of "Taking refuge in the Three Pure Ones" symbolized by the Dao, the scriptures, and the teacher. According to a contemporary Chinese Buddhist ritual collection, the Buddhist monastic community similarly completes their morning and evening rituals with the formula "taking refuge in the Buddha, the dharma, and the sangha," repeating it three times (Hunan sheng fojiao xiehui [n.d.] 28, 39, 58). The fact that the Daoist and Buddhist daily rituals conclude with a similar formula of taking refuge in the Three Pure Ones or the Three Jewels cannot be accidental. The founder of the Way of Complete Perfection made it a policy to combine the teachings from the Three Religions, and his adoption of a strictly celibate way of life for the Complete Perfection masters itself was probably also inspired by Buddhist counterparts. Once the celibate form of life and the consequential communal living in Daoist monasteries became obligatory for all Complete Perfection masters, daily communal services became indispensable. The daily communal liturgy is a public symbol of their cultivation practices, while the inner alchemy remains a private, hidden cultivation, even though its importance is greater because it causes the transformation of the human body into that which is immortal. Whenever I asked about the inner alchemy practice of Daoist masters, their answer was always the same: "It is done privately under the direction of a teacher."

Another Buddhist influence strongly felt in the evening service of the Way of Complete Perfection can be seen in two figures: one is the immortal who delivers the suffering souls from hell; the other is the immortal Lady, the Mother of the Dipper. The name of the first immortal in the White Cloud Monastery text is "the Great One, the Heavenly Worthy who Delivers from Suffering" (Taiyi jiuku tianzun); in the Mt. Wudang monastery text the title of his precious teaching is "the Precious Teaching of Azure Flower" (*Qinghua gao*). He is thus the immortal who presides over the east and symbolizes the life of the spring. This immortal acquired an immense capacity of compassion, comparable to that of the Buddhist bodhisattva Dizang. He is said to have vowed to deliver all the suffering dead, and so his manifold appearances can revive even the most desiccated bones (Baiyun guan 2000, B.45; Min 2000, 254). The Mother of the Dipper is comparable to the Buddhist Mother of the Seven Million Buddhas, Zhunti Bodhisattva, who takes away all sins. Chinese Buddhism and Daoism thus responded to popular religious desires, each within its own system.

The Confucian elements in the Daoist daily prayer liturgy are less conspicuous than the Buddhist ones. The Daoist masters' concern for those who suffer and for the dead is generally inclusive, but there is a special feeling of care for the well-being of ancestors. The eleventh precious teaching of the evening service is known as the "teaching of repaying the benefits" (*Bao'en gao*). Here the Daoist masters petition that the living parents may enjoy blessing and a long life, and that ancestors may quickly rise to the realm of the immortals. Concern for the salvation of ancestors is not unique to the Way of Complete Perfection. The *Perfect Scripture of the Great Grotto* (*Dadong zhenjing*), a major Six Dynasties text of the Way of Highest Clarity, states that if one recites the text ten thousand times, seven generations of ancestors will be delivered from hell. Like the Buddhist monks and nuns, Daoist masters reaffirmed the argument that the cultivation of a celibate way of life itself is the best form of filial piety (Baiyun guan 2000, B.11; Min 2000, 260). But the commonality with Confucianism is most clearly seen in the ethical consciousness that the Daoist masters exhibit in their petitions and lists of confessions.

The official daily prayer liturgy of the Way of Complete Perfection can be understood as the culmination and synthesis of the whole history of the Daoist spiritual tradition. Zhang Daoling, who began the first Daoist sect in the second century, is recognized as the ancestral heavenly master (*zu tianshi*). However, a recent study of an earlier version of the daily prayer liturgy makes no mention of the position of Zhang Daoling (Zhou 1999, 83). This means that the inclusion of the Precious Teaching of Zhang Daoling is quite recent, and that the Complete Perfection Order is now beginning to represent the whole of Daoism, including the Way of Orthodox Unity. The medieval Way of Numinous Treasure is similarly represented in the person of Ge Xuan (fl. 200 C.E.) and the *Heart Seal Scripture* (*Xinyin jing*), which occupy a notable position in the fourth scripture of the morning service (Baiyun guan 2000, A.21). The Way of Highest Clarity is represented in a visualizing meditation on the body gods, such as the mouth deity (*koushen*), the tongue deity (*sheshen*), the teeth deity (*chishen*), and the Nine Perfected Ones (*jiuzhen*) of the brain. The climax of this visual meditation, the "return of the whirlwind" (*huifeng*), is interpreted as the completion of physical practices (Min 2000, 87). The concept of Mara as the tempter or the barrier on the way of the immortal is also carried over from the Shangqing sect (Baiyun guan 2000, A.3, 36; Min 2000, 87).

The popular Daoist ethic that is represented in the *Treatise on Response and Retribution* (*Taishang ganying pian*) can be found in various parts of the morning and evening prayer liturgy. The importance of the order's founder and his seven disciples, the Seven Perfected, can be observed in the *Precious Teachings of the Seven Perfected* in the morning service and the short biographies presented at the end of the evening service in the White

Cloud Monastery text (Baiyun guan 2000, B.76–89). The Northern five ancestors (*bei wuzu*) and the Southern five ancestors (*nan wuzu*) are not forgotten, with a precious teaching from each in the morning service. Qiu Changchun, however, occupies a special place in the Complete Perfection daily prayer liturgy as the teacher of inner alchemy par excellence in the evening liturgy, and as the author of the morning confessions that begin "We repent:"

> We went against the wish of our parents and insulted them. We wrongly betrayed our rulers and teachers. We were disrespectful to Heaven, Earth and the Spirits. We blamed the wind and railed at the rain. We did not believe in sin, blessing and retribution. We clouded the right principle and deceived the mind. Finally we received the reward for them and transmigrated over and over, suffering afflictions unceasingly. All were derived from the error of one thought. . . . And so we are calming our thought and aspire for a clear pure heart. We return to the Holy True Ones and following them we truly beg to repent. Please pity our foolishness, forgive our sins and misgivings, release us from karmic misfortune and remove all of Mara's barriers. (Baiyun guan 2000, A.66–67)

The sins listed here are moral ones, such as avarice, jealousy, cursing, murder, sexual misconduct, violence toward parents and superiors, as well as religious ones including a lack of respect toward heaven and earth and the immortals, and cursing or laughing at the wind and rain. Many of these ideas are similar to those contained in the *Treatise on Response and Retribution* (Suzuki and Carus 1950, 60), but the aspirations of the Complete Perfection liturgy are clearly directed toward the attainment of immortality.

It is interesting that the *Edited Sayings of the Cinnabar Yang Perfected* (*Danyang zhenren yulu;* DZ 1057) reports that the founder Wang Chongyang was angered at his disciples on a few occasions. On one occasion a disciple said that he was not willing to go to his own village to beg. When Wang Chongyang realized that the disciple was still too proud to beg, he beat him so hard at night that the disciple even thought about leaving him. On another occasion, one disciple picked up a sales contract for a donkey that had been dropped on the road. When the teacher found this out, he was angry at his young disciple, who still had not given up the desire for worldly treasure, and slapped his face many times. Instances of this sort may have caused Qiu Changchun to compose a list of sins for confession that could be the forerunner of the present-day liturgy. The commentary on the liturgy explains that Qiu wrote such a list in order to warn his disciples, but there is no firm historical evidence for that contention.

Another list worth noting is the twenty-one petitions and the twelve further petitions of the morning service, as well as the list of ten petitions in the evening service. These formal petitions exhibit the general wishes and intentions toward life of the Daoist masters. We see the forerunner of these petitions in the so-called azure-paper prayers (*qingci*) of the ritual of renewal (*jiao*) in traditional Daoism (Schipper 1985, 46–48; Kim 1987). Just as the *qingci* summarized the intention of the ritual in the form of a memorial to the heavenly worthies written on blue paper, these lists of petitions directly show what the Daoist masters were asking through their daily common prayer. The petitions begin with a prayer for peace and prosperity for society in general and proceed to the well-being of all living beings—including animals, insects, forests, and the lonely souls of deceased men and women. The petitions end with a wish for the even distribution of benefits and the hope that the petitioners may attain the Dao through hearing the scriptures and may ascend to the realm of the immortals (Baiyun guan 2000, A.69–73). Such petitions depict a uniquely Daoist vision of salvation in terms of equality, freedom, and immortality.

The Daoist daily prayer liturgy symbolizes the unity of the Daoist masters with the Dao in the opening "walking in the void" melody (*buxu yun*), which accompanies the "walking in the void" (*buxu*), the well-known final ritual act of the Orthodox Unity Daoist masters during their several-day *jiao* ritual of renewal (Saso 1978, 223; see also Robinet 1993, 31 for an explanation of the efficacy of recitation). This performance of the ritual by walking around the main altar, as if the chief priest were walking up to the heavens through the empty cloud of the dipper, is the ritual climax showing the unity of the master with the Dao. It is interesting to note that the Complete Perfection masters chant this "walking in the void" at the beginning of the morning and evening services. They do not perform it, but simply chant along slowly with the melody named after the ritual. One possible interpretation is that the Complete Perfection masters start with the culminating ritual of the Orthodox Unity sect so as to present themselves immediately to the world of the immortals through the purifying invocations of their bodies, heaven, and earth. The Complete Perfection masters then communicate with the celestial world through the power of the scriptures and the precious teachings of the immortals on behalf of the whole of humanity and the universe.

Reinterpretation of Ancient Chinese Mythic Images

The Complete Perfection morning and evening prayers contain many colorful images, such as the body of an immortal flying up into purple clouds, five emperors riding a whirlwind, a nine-headed lion who sits beside the immortal delivering a precious speech, and the Prince of the East (Dongwang gong) and the Queen Mother of the West (Xiwang mu) (Baiyun guan 2000, A.3, 24, B.60, 64, 67). These images have a long history from the *Classic of Mountains and Seas* and the *Songs of the South* from the Warring States period. The commentary to the daily prayer acknowledges this fact, stating that in the *Classic of Mountains and Seas* "there is a god who has nine heads, a human face, and the body of a bird, and his name is called the nine-headed phoenix" (Min 2000, 153). The *Classic of Mountains and Seas* also contains mysterious depictions of the gods of the mountains in various combinations of human and animal forms. The high god (*di*), even though devoid of any particular form, had his city on Mt. Kunlun, surrounded by nine layers of boundaries. Both the heavens and the underworlds were divided into nine layers, and ordinary people could not approach those places because each gate was guarded by a fierce animal. In a word, the number nine was a symbol of mystery and perfection that one cannot reach without a special command from heaven. In the Daoist tradition the number nine has been interpreted as a symbol for the nine stages of transformation in becoming an immortal. It signified the completion of purification and fullness of life contained in the Dao. The Daoists, therefore, added two more invisible stars, to make the nine stars of the Big Dipper (Latin: *Ursa Major;* Chinese: *beidou*), which is believed to be the center of the universe.

At the beginning of the morning service the Complete Perfection masters offer incense to the Heavenly Worthy of Purity and Stillness and state their wish for total transformation.

> The highest medicine is the spirit, energy, and essence in the body.
>   Everyone is equipped with it; it is neither lacking nor full.
>   If you know the way to unify [all the differentiated parts] through the whirlwind,
>   The yellow sprout will grow daily in the golden furnace. (Baiyun guan 2000, A.5)

In this text the images of whirlwind, golden furnace, and yellow sprout are used to indicate the processes of inner alchemy within the human body.

Here the language and mythology of earlier Daoist traditions and ancient Chinese culture have been reinterpreted in an interiorized form. This interiorization is one of the general characteristics of the reinterpretation of earlier traditions undertaken by the Complete Perfection masters, a process of reinterpretation that involves a dramatic shift in meaning. In the earlier *Classic of Mountains and Seas* the shamans ascended to the heavens for short periods of time to obtain medicine, but in the Way of Complete Perfection, Daoist masters aspire to ascend to the realm of the immortals through the cultivation of the life energy in their own bodies. Moreover, the nine layers of heaven are not cut off from human experience but are accessible to the people through the revelation of scriptures by celestial immortals. In the *Songs of the South,* the Great One (Taiyi), whose ritual temple was located in the east, not only receives the sacrifices from the hands of the shaman but also orders the shaman to find the wandering souls of the dead by the ritual of "calling back the soul" (*zhao hun*). The overall religious purpose of the *Nine Songs* and the ritual of "calling back of the soul" is to bring peace and security to the deceased who have been killed in battle or in periods of unrest, or through some unhappy accident. There is a clear continuation of that theme from these ancient ritual songs to the Complete Perfection morning and evening chanting, but it has developed into the notion that the Daoist masters themselves benefit the lost souls though their inner and outer cultivation practices.

Actually, the recitation of morning and evening services is itself conceived of as an effective method of liberation. There is an intriguing combination of self-power (*zili*) and other-power (*tuoli*) here. In a way, the Daoist masters' prayer to the Three Pure Ones and other immortals for the liberation of the dead souls recognizes that they depend upon the unfathomable merits of all the heavenly worthies—but at the same time that it is they themselves who liberate the entire universe by their cultivation of their primordial energy. The effect of reciting the *Scripture of Purity and Stillness,* for example, is to invoke the protecting power of the immortals so as to dispel disasters; the body and mind are so spiritualized that the adept becomes one with the Dao and ascends to heaven (ibid., A.23–24). At the same time, during the inner visual meditation of the evening service, the commentary states that deliverance actually happens through one's own effort (ibid., B.191). Daoism thus maintains a creative tension between the personal and transpersonal aspects of the Dao, manifest as both personal deities and the nameless void. This duality is also evident in the internal Daoist dialogue concerning salvation through one's own efforts and salvation through the merits of others. The Complete Perfection daily prayer liturgy maintains a balance between those two aspects of liberation.

Conclusion

This chapter has attempted to show the basic structure of the daily common prayer of the Way of Complete Perfection, which is gradually assuming a dominant role in contemporary mainland Chinese Daoism. The structure as a whole includes primary scriptures that are recited daily, as well as historical figures of Daoist history who are remembered as models and spiritual masters for the present generation. Although the Complete Perfection liturgy consciously tries to encompass the whole history of Daoism, there is still a spiritual focus on the seven disciples of Wang Chongyang, and especially Qiu Changchun. When I first heard the liturgy chanted at the White Cloud Monastery in Beijing in the summer of 2001, it was chanted in the Hall of the Seven Perfected. Yoshitoyo Yoshioka mentions that he heard the morning service in the same Hall of the Seven Perfected in 1940 (Yoshitoyo 1979, 244). The fact that short biographies of Wang Chongyang and Qiu Changchun are printed at the back of the daily prayer book indicates that every Complete Perfection Daoist master aspires to become like them through inner and outer cultivation. When in an interview I asked a Daoist master of the Quanzhen Order, Ma Yongqi, "Do you want to be an immortal?" he answered without hesitation: "Yes, of course!" I felt that I had asked an unnecessary question, but as a scholar who is not of the tradition, I wanted to confirm what I had read in books.

At the beginning of their daily prayer, the Complete Perfection masters enter straight into the world of the immortals by chanting "walking in the void." Then they hear the sacred teachings of the Three Pure Ones and reflect on the holy lives of the immortals who have gone through human life as they themselves are doing now. After hearing the scriptures and the reflections on the immortals, the Daoist masters stand up to praise their worthy cultivations and vow to follow in their footsteps, trusting in their immeasurable merits. Their cultivation, however, includes not only themselves but also all living beings, the living and the dead.

The influence of other religions, especially Buddhism, is obvious, and it is so recognized by the Way of Complete Perfection's theory of the unity of the

Three Religions. It seems, however, that Buddhist influence on the Daoist daily morning and evening services lies more in the formal structure of the liturgy and on the level of providing inspiration (as in the case of "Taking refuge in the Three Pure Ones" and in the emphasis on the salvific power of the immortal who delivers all the suffering dead from hell). In their core aspirations and in their dual paths of inner and outer cultivation, Daoist masters follow Wang Chongyang and the Seven Perfected. Of course, one can argue that in their cultivation of nature (*xinggong*) the Buddhist influence is great, but the Daoist theorists of meditation are indebted to Buddhists more for their theoretical terminology than for actual practice. Moreover, Chan/ Zen Buddhist spiritual cultivation practices are also derived from Daoist practices, such as the "fasting of mind" (*xinzhai*) and "sitting in forgetfulness" (*zuowang*) that were first mentioned in the inner chapters of the *Zhuangzi* (Mair 1994). In other words, there has been a mutual learning and inspiration in the area of spiritual cultivation between the followers of Buddhism and the followers of Daoism in China. The relationship between the Complete Perfection Daoists and the Confucians is more subtle and interpenetrating because they share common ethical values, such as filial piety toward their ancestors, even though Daoism preserves more of the mythology and symbolism of ancient popular culture in combination with a wide concern for the entire universe and the souls of all the departed, irrespective of clan or lineage.

Finally, it is worth noting that the Daoist morning and evening services are official symbolic acts of cultivation, implying both aspects of inner and outer dimensions that the founders of the Way of Complete Perfection so clearly emphasized. The morning prayers signify the inner cultivation of the Daoist masters themselves, while the evening prayers are directed outward, toward liberating suffering beings from their agony. Through their daily petitions the Daoist masters embrace the whole world and bless it for its peace and well-being. They aim to ascend to the immortal realm of the Dao and to bring the entire universe with them. Through their common ritual prayer, Daoist masters manifest in public form the characteristics and aspirations of the internal private cultivation of inner alchemy.

References

Baiyun guan [White Cloud Monastery]. 2000. *Taishang xuanmen zaowantan gongkejing* [Supreme Mystery Gate morning and evening liturgy]. Beijing: Baiyun guan.

Bumbacher, Stephan Peter. 2000. "On Pre-Tang Daoist Monastic Establishments at Mao Shan according to the *Daoxue zhuan.*" *Journal of Chinese Religions* 28:148–215.

Cao Benye and Pu Tingqiang. 1992. *Wudangshan daojiao yinyue yanjiu* [A study of the Daoist music of Mt. Wudang]. Taipei: Taiwan shangwu yinshuguan.

Chen Yue. 1997. "Quanzhen Monastic Life in the Chin and Yuan Period." *Zongjiao lishi yanjiu* [Studies in the history of religion] 35: 8–51.

Hammerstrom, Erik J. 2003. "The Mysterious Gate: Daoist Monastic Liturgy in Late Imperial China." Master's thesis. Honolulu: University of Hawai'i.

Hunan sheng fojiao xiehui. N.d. *Fojiao niansong ji* [Collected Buddhist chants]. Changsha: Gulu shan si.

Kim Sung-Hae. 1987. "*Dongmun son* chorye chŏngsa e daehan jonggyohak jok kochal" [Writings on Daoist ritual in the *Dongmun son*]. Pp. 107–133 in *Dokyo wa hankuk sasang* [Daoism and Korean thought]. Edited by the Korean Association for the Study of Daoist Thought. Seoul: Bumyangsa.

———. 1996. "The Place and Characteristics of Sichuan Daoism." *East Asian Studies* 30: 89–121.

Kobayashi Masayoshi. 1998. *Chūgoku no dōkyō* [Chinese Daoism]. Tokyo: Sobunsha.

———. 2003. *Tōdai no dōkyō to tenshidō* [Tang dynasty Daoism and the Way of Celestial Masters]. Tokyo: Chisen shokan.

Kohn, Livia. 1993. *The Taoist Experience.* Albany: State University of New York Press.

Li Yangzheng. 1993. *Dangdai Zhongguo daojiao* [Contemporary Chinese Daoism]. Beijing: Zhongguo shehui kexueyuan chubanshe.

Mair, Victor. 1994. *Wandering on the Way: Early Tales and Parables of Chuang Tzu.* New York: Bantam.

Min Zhiting, ed. 2000. *Xuanmen risong zaowan gongke jingzhu* [Commentary on the Mystery Gate morning and evening liturgy for daily recitation]. Beijing: Zongjiao wenhua chubanshe.

Robinet, Isabelle. 1993. *Taoist Meditation.* Translated by Julian F. Pas and Norman J. Girardot. Albany: State University of New York Press.

Saso, Michael. 1978. *The Teaching of Taoist Master Chuang.* New Haven: Yale University Press.

Schipper, Kristofer M. 1985. "Vernacular and Classical Ritual in Taoism." *Journal of Asian Studies* 45.1: 21–57.

———. 1993. *The Taoist Body.* Translated by Karen C. Duval. Berkeley: University of California Press.

Suzuki, D. T., and Paul Carus, trans. 1950. *Treatise on Response and Retribution by Lao Tzu.* La Salle, IL: Open Court.

Tsuchiya Masaaki. 2002. "Confession of Sins and Awareness of Self in the *Taiping jing.*" Pp. 39–57 in *Daoist Identity: History, Lineage, and Ritual.* Edited by Livia Kohn and Harold D. Roth. Honolulu: University of Hawai'i Press.

Wang Xiping and Chen Fayong. 1999. *Chongyang gong yu quanzhen dao* [Chongyang palace and the Way of Complete Perfection]. Xi'an: Shaanxi renmin chubanshe.

Wei Fuhua. 1992. "Exploration on the History of the Taoist Monastery in Heming." *Zongjiao xue yanjiu* [Religious studies research] 21: 14–16.

Wong, Eva. 1992. *Cultivating Stillness: A Taoist Manual for Transforming Body and Mind.* Boston: Shambhala.

Yoshitoyo Yoshioka. 1979. "Taoist Monastic Life." Pp. 229–252 in *Facets of Taoism.* Edited by Holmes Welch and Anna Seidel. New Haven: Yale University Press.

Zhang Ming. 1989. "Daoism during the Ten Years of Reformation." *Studies on the History of Religions* 14.2.

Zheng Suchun. 2002. *Daojiao xinyang, shenxian yu yishi* [Daoist faith, immortals and rituals]. Taipei: Taiwan shangwu yinshuguan.

Zhou Gaode. 1999. *Daojiao wenhua yu shenghuo* [Daoist culture and life]. Beijing: Zongjiao wenhua chubanshe.

6

Shamanism in Contemporary Taiwan

ALISON MARSHALL

Introduction

The island of Taiwan, located southeast of the mainland Chinese coast, has a complex and varied cultural, social, and political history. It has been home to Polynesians and Austronesians, as well as the Dutch, Spanish, Japanese, and Chinese. At the end of World War II (1945), Taiwan returned to Chinese control when the Japanese surrendered, having been in control of the island for more than fifty years under the 1895 Treaty of Shimonoseki.

Within two years of Taiwan's return to China there occurred an uprising against the mainland Chinese takeover. This violent uprising became known as the 2–28 incident, occurring on February 28, 1947, and setting off a wave of protests and government killings for many months. Two years later, in 1949, the leader of the Chinese Nationalist Party, Chiang Kai-shek (Jiang Jieshi, 1887–1975), having been defeated by the communist forces after a civil war in China lasting twenty-two years, fled mainland China and set up the Nationalist government in Taiwan under the Nationalist Party (Guomindang, GMD; also called the Kuomintang, KMT). The year 1949 was also the year in which the Nationalist Party enacted martial law on Taiwan, which would last until 1987.

The United States has become Taiwan's greatest ally, providing military and economic aid. U.S. support dates back to the Korean War, when President Harry S. Truman sent U.S. Navy warships into the Strait of Taiwan to guard against potential Chinese attack. Today, Taiwan is not officially recognized by the United States (or most other countries) as an independent nation. Taiwan lost its status as an independent nation and as a member of the United Nations in 1971, when Beijing, China (not Taipei, Taiwan) became recognized as the official seat of China at the United Nations.

The Taiwanese cultural, social, and political landscape has experienced much change in the postwar period, not only because of its return to Chinese rule but also because of U.S. and Western influences. Taiwan has enjoyed economic success as one of Asia's strongest markets, and capitalism has flourished on the island—although some would say that this development has come at the expense of many Taiwanese traditions and customs. Since 1950, there has been increasing interest among the Taiwanese in learning English and sending their children to the United States and other Western nations for study.

Today, the relationship between China and Taiwan is tense. While China regards Taiwan as a province of "One China," many in Taiwan have called for greater independence from China and recognition of Taiwan as an independent nation. This tension has been exacerbated by the fact that, in 2000, the Nationalist Party was defeated (though narrowly) by Chen Shuibian of the Democratic Progressive Party, which is in favor of an independent Taiwan.

Shamanism on Taiwan manifests itself in many ways: through spirit medium practices of spirit writing, self-mortification, exorcism, healing, counseling, changing fate, and self-cultivation, as well as in pilgrimages and processions. Beliefs prominent in Taiwanese spirit mediumship derive from some of those shared by mediums on mainland China and in Singapore and Malaysia; there are also influences from the more traditional religions of Daoism and Buddhism, and to a lesser extent from Confucianism. The West has also had an impact of its own. Taiwanese shamans are now possessed by deities such as the Christian god and the Virgin Mary; mediums now speak English while they are possessed; and new doctrines have arisen about the cultivation of one's soul. Daniel Overmyer explains how today all forms of religious expression are thriving in contemporary Taiwan, creating new religions: "[N]ew freedom and economic resources have led to an increase of religious activities of all kinds including those of local temples, Buddhist monasteries, and charitable organizations, and a variety of new religious groups" (Overmyer 2003, 310).

This chapter initially examines Taiwanese identity through the worship of Mazu, an important deity discussed also in Chapter 10. Then we examine different understandings of shamanism, both inside and outside China. Before introducing the beliefs and practices of shamanism on Taiwan, however, we explore the phenomenon of procession performances, some but not all of whose influences are uniquely Chinese. The last part of the article focuses on the specific beliefs and practices of the Taiwanese shaman, offering examples of some of the most common types of mediums found on Taiwan today. While this chapter takes into consideration the impact of Chinese shamanism on Taiwanese beliefs and practices, it does not intend to make the narrow claim that Taiwanese religious identity can be understood by looking only to the Chinese legacy of shamanism—an assertion that takes us into an area of considerable debate. As Paul Katz notes, "Scholars who view Taiwanese popular religions as being linked to China's cultural heritage have been accused of legitimizing the Nationalist Party ideology, while those who emphasize the uniqueness of Taiwan's historical development have been scolded for kowtowing to local 'politically correct tenets'" (Katz 2003, 113–114). Taiwanese shamanism develops out of the richness of cultures and traditions that have been developing on Taiwan for hundreds, if not thousands, of years, and many of these cultures and traditions do not include those of the Han Chinese.

Taiwan and its people can be divided into four groups: first, the non-Chinese Austronesians, called Aborigines, who first came to the island roughly six thousand years ago; the second and third groups are the Hakka and the southern Min people, who came to Taiwan from Fujian and Guangdong provinces in the seventeenth century; and the fourth group is those who came from the mainland during and after the period of migration that followed World War II (1945–1949). Of these four groups only two, the early Chinese Hakka and southern Min migration, up to four hundred years ago, are known as native Taiwanese (*Taiwanren* or *bendiren*). Thus shamanism on Taiwan, like the worship of Mazu, has some elements that are native to Taiwan and many that are not.

Mazu and Han Taiwanese Identity

One of the most common ways to discuss the complex relationship between Chinese popular religion and Taiwanese popular religion—and more specifically shamanism and spirit mediumship—has been through the prism of Mazu temple processions. Mazu (also known as Tianshang shengmu and Tianhou) and her worship in southeastern China date back to the Song dynasty (960–1279 C.E.) and a story about a Buddhist woman of virtue named

Lin Moniang (960–987 C.E.). Steven Sangren summarizes the rendering of Mazu's early life in China:

> In brief, Ma Tsu [Mazu] is said to have been a shy, religiously inclined young woman who suffered an early death after saving her father and all but one of her brothers from drowning. After her death she continued her miraculous interventions [in] behalf of imperiled seafarers. Some versions credit her with subjugating demons who have great powers of sight and hearing and who now aid her in protecting seamen. Fishermen and sailors turn to Ma Tsu [Mazu] to allay anxieties associated with their profession, and the original Chinese settlers of Taiwan, faced with crossing the storm-ridden Taiwan Straits, also relied on her (Sangren 1983, 8).

The Mazu temple on the island of Meizhou, located off of Fujian province, is recognized as the place from which Moniang eventually ascended to heaven and gained her status as a popular goddess.

Taiwanese girl uses divining blocks in a Taiwanese Daoist temple. (Courtesy Alison Marshall)

Even though Mazu's nascent origins can be traced to southeastern China, she also has strong ties to southern Taiwan and to Taiwanese identity (Sangren 1988, 693). Each year, between 4 and 5 million pilgrims mark her birthday on the twenty-third of the lunar month by making a pilgrimage to the Mazu Beigang temple. In addition to this temple, there are more than three hundred temples on Taiwan dedicated to her. Her popularity on Taiwan and role in shaping Taiwanese identity dates back to the late sixteenth century, when she assisted the Chinese Koxinga (Zheng Chenggong 1624–1662) to defeat the Dutch occupants of Taiwan. Sangren explains:

> Koxinga, too, has a special meaning for Taiwanese. After all, it was Koxinga who freed

Taiwan from the rule of the barbarian Dutch, and Ma Tsu [Mazu] is venerated for having aided him in this endeavour. Moreover, at local Ma Tzu
[Mazu] temples in Taiwan, one frequently hears stories of how the goddess intervened to save people from the Japanese, head-hunting aborigines, floods and American bombs (ibid., 687).

As with the indigenization of Mazu, Taiwanese shamanism also has characteristics that reflect Taiwan's unique political, social, and cultural milieu.
Thus, to limit our discussion to the Chinese nature of Taiwanese shamanism
would be to overlook the rich history of traditions on Taiwan.

What Is Shamanism?

Before we discuss the specific beliefs and practices of shamanism on Taiwan
and its Chinese legacy, some time must be spent exploring the term "shamanism." The scholarly exploration of shamanism has become increasing popular
in recent years, with many new writings on Chinese and other forms of belief
and practice loosely defined under the rubric of "shamanism." Recent books
pertaining to Chinese or Taiwanese religion are likely to include a reference to
the shaman and sometimes also to the medium, but with no clear indication
of what distinguishes the two. Often the terms "shaman" and "spirit medium"
are used interchangeably to refer to individuals who perform exorcisms, who
heal, or who become possessed by demigods. However, as I will show, there
are many types of shamanism, including that of the traditional shamans of
Siberia, whose beliefs and customs provided the standard against which other
similar traditions have been measured. There are also the so-called techno-
shamans—who experience trances induced by music, dancing, and drugs at
raves—and neo-shamans, who display the influence of New Age beliefs. In
order to portray the origin of such new types of shamanism accurately, as
well as the West's fascination with terms such as "ecstasy" and "trance" and
with altered states of consciousness, some people refer to this burgeoning
class of shamans as "modern Western shamans" (von Stuckrad 2002, 774;
Høst 2001).

The term "shaman" originated in Siberia to describe the religious functionaries there. In the 1900s, however, early ethnographers in Europe began to
extend the term elsewhere. The Siberian shaman retains control of his body
and mind, being a master of the spirits who is able to engage them in discourse
and to take spirit journeys with them. So-called shamans elsewhere, however,

are not so rigidly defined. The absence of exact definitions for non-Siberian shamans has been owing in part to Mircea Eliade's extremely popular work on the subject, written in 1951. There, Eliade began a trend to refer to many kinds of religious specialists all over the world as shamans (von Stuckrad 2002; Hamayon 1998).

It is the rare author who takes the time to sort through all of the arguments about the defining characteristics for a shaman. In an attempt to avoid the problem, some scholars have started to use the term "ecstatic" to describe the unique talents of the religious functionary most often associated with mediumship and healing. But even the term "ecstatic" has its own problems. Whereas the word "shaman" is indigenous to Siberia, the English word "ecstatic" is derived from the Greek word *ekstasis,* meaning "to stand outside oneself." Roberte Hamayon has remarked that the term "ecstasy" as a means to describe the religious experience of a so-called shaman appeals to Westerners because they see in it an explicit reference to Christian ideas and spirituality (Hamayon 1998).

In China and on Taiwan, shamans or mediums are known as *jitong, wupo, huat-su, ang-yi, zhencai, lingji, lingmei, lingxiu,* and by many other names. It is still not wholly agreed upon as to what defines a spirit medium. Are mediums fully possessed by spirits, or only partially possessed? Do they become puppets of the gods, or are they able to exert some measure of control over the possession experience? In this article, the words "shaman" and "shamanism" refer to nontraditional shamans who are spirit mediums outside of the Siberian cultural sphere. For the most part, spirit mediums on Taiwan do not belong to any tribe or clan, and they have not inherited the profession from a parent; rather, they have come to be mediums through a spiritual calling or the recognition that they are fated to live shorter lives because of the year, month, day, and hour in which they were born—an eight-character (*bazi*) destiny that is sometimes called a light destiny (Berthier 1987). This *bazi,* or light destiny, causes them to be more susceptible to possession. Moreover, while these mediums are not masters of the gods they serve, nor are they mere puppets of the gods, with many mediums (including one in the second case study of possession, below) resisting the call to become a medium (Clart 2003; Jordan 1972). They are possessed to varying degrees, with some being more in control of their faculties during possession and others less so.

A man performs a dance to drive away evil spirits at a Buddhist temple during a festival in Taipei, Taiwan. (Eddie Shih/AP Photo)

The Legacy of Chinese Shamanism

The legacy of shamanism in popular religion on Taiwan extends back to Chinese antiquity and the first records of shamans or mediums in the Shang dynasty (ca. 1766–1122 B.C.E.), who were concerned with maintaining harmony between the heavenly and earthly realms. Chen Mengjia, K. C. Chang, and Julia Ching have all written works espousing the theory that the kings of the Shang dynasty were shamans, or individuals with a special talent for communicating with the spirit world during trance. Chen Mengjia and K. C. Chang looked to oracle bones and to animal-like images in bronze, jade, lacquer, and wood to prove their theories that the rulers of the Shang had shamanic powers and entered trance (Chen 1936; Chang 1983). Ching took a different tack, however, focusing instead on the inherent ecstatic powers of the ancient sages who became models for later rulers in Chinese history. In particular, Ching pointed out that the Chinese character for "sage" comprises the components for ear, mouth, and ruler. When the components of that character are understood collectively, they are seen to refer to an individual who can hear what the divine has spoken and communicate it to the people; because of that power, the ruler ensured harmony by providing the vertical link joining the realms of heaven, earth, and man (Ching 1997, 54–55). In recent years, however, there have been many scholars, including David Keightley, who have disputed the theory that the kings of the Shang dynasty were shaman kings, noting that there is too little evidence to show that Shang dynasty kings entered into trance or took spirit journeys (Keightley 1983).

Evidence of shamanism or mediumship in China is much more prolific for the periods following the Shang dynasty, when the position of shaman in Chinese society was declining. In the Zhou dynasty (1122–221 B.C.E.), both male and female mediums named *wu* (as well as other names, such as the *shi* or ancestral host, and the *zhuzi*) were part of an idealized bureaucracy recorded in the *Rites of Zhou* (*Zhouli*). There, a few male *wu* are low-ranking officials charged with training the other mediums in the rain dances and rituals. Unlike the rest of the *wu*, they did not go into trance. Those *wu* who did go into trance performed many court functions, such as accompanying the emperor or his consort in funeral processions, performing seasonal exorcisms, dancing for rain, and healing horses.

Exorcism of malevolent forces (seen as impediments to peace and harmony) was an especially important part of the Chinese shaman's duties, as evidenced by passages in the *Rites of Zhou.* Qitao Guo notes that exorcisms were performed regularly throughout the year: "During the Zhou, exorcism was performed three times every year, in late spring, mid autumn and late winter" (Guo 2003, 23). These shamans used spells (*zhou*), weapons, dances, and later talismans (*fu*) in rituals to get rid of malevolent forces such as demons, and illnesses such as the plague. The *Rites of Zhou* also tells of exorcists who, as part of funeral processions, wore animal skins and used weapons to ward off demons at grave sites.

The Han dynasty was also a significant period in the development of Chinese shamanism because with it came a new and youthful class of mediums who performed the rain dances formerly done by women (Marshall 2003a) and who became noteworthy exorcists (Guo 2003, 24). The other roles of mediums—as court advisors and ritual performers—declined during the latter part of the Han dynasty. Youth became an important way to define the power, purity, and inherent virtue of a medium. The popularity of youths as mediums continued into the Tang (618–907) and Song dynasties (960–1279), and it continues to the present day in China and on Taiwan (Davis 2001, 148). Although the contemporary medium on Taiwan is normally not younger than eighteen years of age, he or she is thought to be symbolically youthful as a child of the god the medium serves.

The last century saw many changes to Taiwanese shamanism, with the Japanese occupation of Taiwan from 1895 to 1945 (under the Treaty of Shimonoseki, after the Sino-Japanese War); the enactment of martial law in the aftermath of the 2–28 incident in 1947, lasting until 1987; and, most recently, the post–martial law period, during which time Taiwan enjoyed its first democratic election. Charles Jones divides the duration of Japanese colonization into three periods in which the government's attitude toward local religion changed and Chinese influences were curtailed. In the first period (1895–1915), religion—and, specifically, local religion—was regarded as a way to distract the people from rebelling against the new Japanese regime. Japanese investigation into Taiwanese local religious life grew during the second period (1915–1937), as officials sought to document temple activities and public involvement in them. The third period (1937–1945) was marked by the "Japanization movement," in which the Taiwanese were encouraged to adopt Japanese names, while Chinese dialects and some aspects of Chinese culture were prohibited. During this latter period there was a large-scale attempt to reform traditional Taiwanese religious life. Temples, deity images, and records were destroyed, and customs associated with shamanism—such as divination and consultations with spirit mediums—were banned in temples (Jones 2003, 19–28).

Following the 2–28 incident and the enactment of martial law, Taiwan experienced authoritarian rule under the Nationalist Party, the ruling party associated with mainland Chinese tradition and culture. It became the mission of the Nationalist Party (which had close associations with the mainland), and Chiang Kai-shek as its leader, "to educate all citizens, despite [their] origin, and to instill [in them a sense of] loyalty. . . . Mandarin and the reinvoking of traditional values and Confucianism became the dominant civic virtues" (Mau-Kuei Gang, as cited in Chang 2003, 47). Taiwanese popular religion, and traditions such as spirit mediumships, were now perceived as superstitions that would upset orderly Confucian society.

In the post–martial law period, Taiwan has experienced new religious freedom, with an explosion in temple membership and temple construction, new religions, and new mediums. Today, mediums on Taiwan are frequented by politicians at all levels of government. It is not unusual to enter a local temple and see pictures of a local mayor with the temple shaman, or to hear stories about the shaman's contribution to a politician's popularity and success.

Taiwanese Shamanism and Performance

Taiwanese shamanism is most obvious to the visitor to Taiwan in procession performances. Weekend processions, in particular on Sundays, to the large Wangye temples at Madou and Nankunshan attract large crowds, ranging from the hundreds to the thousands. Processions represent much organizational work and capital, and they require long hours from the many performers who make up the procession. To the outsider, the procession—with its loud music, constant explosions of firecrackers, and costumed dances—might seem to be theater put on for the amusement of the audience, but nothing could be further from the truth. Processions serve important religious functions in Taiwanese society, recognizing the power of gods, maintaining links between neighboring temples and religious communities, and facilitating the flow of magical efficacy (*ling*) from the originating temple to the host temple (Sangren 1991, 69–72). Processions include some kind of music, usually consisting of a band composed of members of the temple community playing drums, cymbals, and tambourines, as well as stringed instruments and occasionally winds.

Some procession performances also feature an "electric flower car" (*dian-huache*), which can be rented for the day. Here, attractive young women (who wear short dresses or bikinis) stand on the decorated stage of a flatbed truck singing karaoke to entertain the gods. As Avron Boretz notes, procession performances are yet another instance in which the manifestation of shamanism on Taiwan, although similar in many respects to Chinese shamanism, displays innovation and differences from Chinese popular religion: "[L]ocal innovation and adaptation, particularly since communication between Taiwan and the mainland were stifled after 1895, have had a profound influence on the form and practice of ritual performances" (Boretz 2003, 227).

Most performance troupes (*zhentou*) will include a wide range of individuals (listed here in no particular order). A male member of the temple community will carry a paper lantern bearing the name of the temple and its god, written in red ink. Another man will be charged with carrying a long pole from which hangs the black eight trigram flag. Processions also feature a man who dances along in the procession twirling a stick with a large brightly colored cylindrical parasol. Various temple members may also accompany the procession, wearing clothing—ranging from a baseball cap or tennis visor to shirt and pants—marked with the name of the temple.

Entranced male spirit youth (*jitong*) dance along in the procession, barefoot and dressed in red bibs and black or red pants. They wear the bibs so that they can strike their bare backs with ritual instruments. It is not uncommon to see female spirit youth (also barefoot and in trance) wearing special backless blouses, bibs, and pants in the procession. David Jordan remarks that the combination of sword dances, jumps, lunges, and martial arts moves used by these spirit youth as they move along in the procession resembles "an athletic ballet, magnificently rehearsed and enthusiastically performed, in the pugnacious tradition of Chinese shadow boxing" (Jordan 1972, 48). The spirit youth guard the gods of the temple, who ride in what is called the sedan chair (*jiaozi*), which is carried by two or four men depending on its size. The sedan chair is a wooden chair on which a smaller carved wooden image of the deity is placed for the duration of the procession. Five flags, representing the heavenly armies, hang from the back of the chair. Once the procession has arrived at the host temple, the smaller image of the deity and its inherent efficacy (*ling*) is passed into the inner altar (*tan*) and placed on one of the shelves (for a fee) near the inner altar, where it remains until the troupe returns to the originating temple (Pas 2003, 41).

Like the spirit youth, other performers in the procession are also believed to perform while they are in trance. These individuals are often boys from the temple community who have begun their training with a local temple master. They appear in the procession wearing traditional costumes and painted faces, becoming transformed into generals or martial deities (*jiang*). Avron Boretz notes: "The mask of face-paint of that particular deity, for instance, is said to inhere on the inner surface of the face of the actor for the rest of his life. The actors, then, are 'possessed' by the deities whom they represent as soon as they are costumed and ritually separated" (Boretz 2003, 228). The procession has a lighter side, featuring those wearing oversized, cartoonlike costumes of the legendary friends and temple guardians Fan and Xie, as well as the Monkey King (Sun Wukong), who tosses candy to the children in the crowd; also, the Vagabond Buddha (Jigong Pusa) stumbles along, sipping from a large gourd. Processions may also include a troupe of acrobatic dancers, composed of young girls, with older girls who perform to popular folk songs. There will be other troupes of dancers who perform to popular folk songs, with girls of various ages wearing aboriginal, traditional, or Western dress (such as pink taffeta princess costumes). Sometimes transvestites will play the role of the lead dancers in these dance troupes, flirting with the men in attendance.

Beliefs and Practices

Now that we have examined the more public forms of Taiwanese shamanism in procession performance, some time may be spent on a closer look at the particulars of shamanism on Taiwan—such as spirit writing and self-mortification—and examples of different types of mediums. Generally speaking, the specific beliefs and practices of shamanism on Taiwan can be divided into two categories. There are mediums who practice within the civil (*wen*) branch of mediumship, and mediums who practice within the martial (*wu*) branch. Spirit writing is a practice associated with the first branch, the civil; self-mortification is associated with the second, the martial. It must be borne in mind, however, that with commercial and economic changes to the Taiwanese religious landscape over the last fifty years have come innovations in religious tradition. Some less traditional mediums do not fall within either of the conventional branches of mediumship, instead performing both spirit writing and self-mortification.

Spirit Writing

Spirit writing (*fuji*) involves the use of a special Y-shaped instrument called a planchette or stylus to write Chinese characters in a container filled with sand. The planchette is usually held by two people who are partially possessed by the deity, but the characters produced when they hold the stylus above the sand are understood not to emanate from their conscious actions. Instead, these Chinese characters are perceived to be transmitted by the deity, who uses the bearers of the planchette as mediums through which to transmit messages from the spirit world. The traditional planchette is constructed from peach wood, and the underside holds a piece of willow wood. Both the peach wood and the willow (which makes contact with the sand) are believed to guard against malevolent forces (*bixie*) (Clart 2003; Jordan and Overmyer 1986).

An abbreviated method of spirit writing, taking less time and requiring fewer ritual instruments, also exists. In this form an entranced medium uses a pen (often red) to write characters on sheets of yellow paper. Like the individuals who hold the planchette during more traditional spirit writing sessions, these mediums are also partially possessed. What are produced during these spirit writing sessions are spirit-written morality texts (*shanshu*) offering advice. Once a spirit writing session has concluded, the texts transmitted from the deity are published by the host temple and made available to the temple community.

Self-Mortification

Self-mortification is performed by spirit youth of the martial branch. Donald Sutton summarizes the occasions that have traditionally been seen to warrant the use of self-mortification on Taiwan:

> For Tainan temples that have self-mortifiers, there are three kinds of occasions at which it is considered obligatory. The most important is in procession or pilgrimage to mark the encounter with another god's temple or his possessed medium. A second kind of occasion is a temple's events of transition at which chiefly temple members are present, for example at the dotting of the eyes (dianyan) of new images of gods, at the raising of the ridgepole in new construction, or at the initiation of a new medium. . . . Thirdly, self-mortification is occasionally utilized [on] behalf of families of the temple community, to exorcise a dwelling at night, to expel evil airs

(xieqi), or to exorcise objects such as unsanctified gods' statuettes that have brought bad luck (Sutton 1990, 101–102).

On these special occasions, martial mediums strike themselves with ritual instruments to demonstrate to all who watch the power of a possessing deity and to exorcise demons. Traditional ritual instruments consist of the five treasures (*wubao*): the prick ball, ax, barbed stick, dagger, and double-bladed barbed stick. Less traditional instruments include skewers, saws, and burning incense.

A medium will use any number of these instruments (but usually only one at a time) to strike his or her arms, back, face, and chest; sometimes the medium will also strike himself with lit incense. Spirit youth can show the strength of their possessing deity by the force with which they are able to strike their skin. Each strike of the body produces dramatic streams of blood that are wiped off by assistants who accompany the spirit youth. To wipe up the blood they use sheets of yellow paper colored with red ink, and they follow this action with the spraying or spitting of rice wine on the affected area.

Many Taiwanese observers have been quick to note that self-mortification is not what it appears to be. As mediums strike the skin on their foreheads, backs, and arms, for instance, they may merely open old wounds made when they were first initiated as spirit youth. Others explain that the five treasures are not sharp and cannot cut the skin. It is the paper, when applied to the skin, that transfers the red ink, which appears to "bleed" when it comes into contact with the rice wine. In spite of such skeptical remarks, however, the majority of the Taiwanese who attend self-mortification rites are in awe of the power of the spirit youth and the deity and regard self-mortification as an important part of the martial medium's role in Taiwanese society.

Types of Mediums

Spirit Youth

Normally, the spirit youth (*jitong; tâng-ki*) is an adult over the age of eighteen. There are both male and female spirit youth, but some roles of the spirit youth, such as self-mortification, are more commonly performed by men; others, such as fertility counseling, are more commonly performed by women. Spirit youth may speak Mandarin Chinese, classical Chinese, Taiwanese, or Japanese while in trance (see the case studies, below, for a discussion of two different spirit youth).

Most spirit youth still subscribe to the belief that spirit youth, if female, must have entered menopause, and that menstruating (or pregnant) women cannot enter the inner sanctuary of an altar or be present when a spirit youth performs self-mortification, or when a spirit youth becomes possessed by a major deity at a ritual (Ahern 1975). Here one sees the influence of Chinese popular beliefs on Taiwanese mediumship. Women as the yin and weaker aspect of the yin/yang dyad are believed to be ritually impure and polluting, owing to their role in childbirth and their menstrual cycles (Furth 1999, 74). However, these prohibitions and beliefs may be changing. New mediums such as the "true talents" (*zhencai*) and spirit diviners (*lingji*) can become possessed while menstruating, and being female is seen as a blessing rather than otherwise.

It has sometimes been said that spirit youth are uneducated and come from predominantly lower socioeconomic classes. That may have been the case many years ago, but today it is common to encounter spirit youth from a range of backgrounds. Spirit youth are factory workers, university graduates, former businessmen, temple owners, managers, housewives, real estate agents, and entrepreneurs.

Spirit youth perform many religious functions for the temple. They can be summoned to perform rituals in which they change fate (*gaiyun*) when the temple community has been experiencing bad luck, such as when a local business is failing. In that instance, it is common for the spirit youth to hand out talismans (*fu*) drawn on sheets of yellow paper. They are also called upon to heal people who have been feeling unwell. They perform during birthday celebrations for the god. Others perform rites of self-mortification, divination, or exorcism, and provide fertility and other types of counseling.

Daoist Ritual Masters

The Daoist ritual master (*fashi*) provides a link between the formal aspects of Daoist religion and the local traditions, often taking on the role of the shaman (Davis 2001, 11). Daoist ritual masters, in contrast to Daoist priests (*daoshi*)—who wear black hats and use classical Chinese—do not belong to the literati and do not inherit their positions. Rather, many Daoist ritual masters apprentice with an older ritual master until they have learned the spells, songs, dance steps, and other traditions they will use to perform their role as exorcists, relied upon to change fate. They wear red hats or bandanas (and sometimes sunglasses) and use vernacular Chinese during rituals for the local communities they serve. Many of these ritual masters work regular hours at the larger and more popular temples in Taiwan, providing a service to clients who visit them on their coffee and lunch breaks or after work.

True Talents

The true talent (*zhencai*) is a little different from the spirit youth and is commonly associated with the Unity Sect (*Yiguandao*), where the true talent is a young woman who is still menstruating. However, true talents may also be male, as in the case of those who work with spirit diviners, discussed below. Usually, a true talent is unmarried, vegetarian, well educated, and serves for between ten and twenty years, retiring once his or her mission has been completed. But true talents may serve for less time if they have been fated to do so, as, for instance, in the case of one true talent encountered by the author who became a medium of the god in order to undo the spiritual pollution he had acquired over the course of many years as a successful businessman. Like the spirit youth and other types of contemporary mediums on Taiwan, true talents come from a variety of social backgrounds. They also may speak Mandarin Chinese, classical Chinese, Taiwanese, Japanese, and even, at times, English.

There are three types of true talent. The first type is the medium who transmits the language and words of the deity. The second is the one who translates what the medium says, and the third is the one who does spirit writing.

Spirit Diviners

A more recent manifestation of Chinese shamanism on Taiwan, with influences from Buddhism, Daoism, and the Western New Age movement, as well as Christianity and Confucianism, is the spirit diviner (*lingji*). Spirit diviners are known by other names beginning with "spirit" (*ling*). They may call themselves spirit cultivators (*lingxiu*) or spirit mediums (*lingmei*). Spirit diviners have been in existence on Taiwan for at least fifty years but have become much more common in recent years, and especially since the lifting of martial law. Although it has been written that spirit diviners' beliefs and practices have an organizational structure (Paper 1996), none of the spirit diviners encountered by the author claimed a connection to any association or institution. Being a spirit diviner was not something one did as part of a temple organization or group. It was motivated by an individual need to find an end to suffering and to restore world harmony and peace.

Today spirit diviners are known for their ability to move the spirit (*lingdong*), and individuals are endowed with this ability to varying degrees. Usually one becomes more adept at moving the spirit the longer one does it and the more self-cultivated one's original soul becomes. Here spirit diviners' tenets draw on traditional Chinese Confucian self-cultivation practices to make one more virtuous through education, as well as more Western ideas of the soul, including New Age beliefs that doing good deeds creates world peace and harmony. With proficiency come variations in the practice. For instance, those who have just started to be able to move the spirit within them might be able to move only their arms in a meditative position or to burp (a common phenomenon in Taiwanese religion). In contrast, those who have been practicing for ten years can move their hands, burp, sing, dance, and even perform songs and dance with others. Who is it that "moves" these people? Although the same deity—for example, Guanyin, the Buddhist bodhisattva of compassion—may return to move a particular spirit diviner, that does not mean that the spirit diviners may not be moved at other times by the goddess Mazu, or even Chairman Mao Zedong, the Christian god, or the Virgin Mary.

Although there may be just as many male spirit diviners as female, the majority who perform songs and dances are female. These women do not need to have entered menopause before they become mediums, and they can be menstruating when they are moved by the spirit (a sort of semipossession experience). When they are moved they perform dances, none of which are rehearsed in advance. They are dances in which the spirit—for instance, Mazu—inspires the spirit diviner to perform. In this manner, the improvisational quality of the performance is unlike that of other forms of more traditional Chinese-influenced mediumistic performance—such as the spirit youth who serve martial gods (Sutton 2003). As one watches the spirit diviners move the spirit, one can see that their dances incorporate many influences, such as Chinese *qigong* (ch'i-kung) and *taiji* (t'ai-chi), as well as Western ballet, tap dancing, and pantomime, and Middle Eastern spinning, in the manner of whirling dervishes.

There are few restrictions on spirit diviners' performances—deities as well as famous dead people are known to move them from time to time. Unlike spirit youth, spirit diviners do not serve one temple or deity, and they do not perform self-mortification. Most are adamant that a spirit diviner with a pure and virtuous soul will not take money in exchange for these services. Those who do take money in exchange for relieving the suffering of others are perceived to be at a lower level of cultivation.

When asked why they became spirit diviners, most responded that they were looking for a way to end their own suffering. Some were counseled by true talents to become spirit diviners in order to get rid of a chronic condition, such as migraine headaches. Others were businesspeople who felt that their lives lacked meaning. Still others were responding to the suffering they saw around them and wanted to make a positive contribution to the world (Marshall 2003b).

Conclusion

All the Taiwanese mediums we have examined in this article seek to restore peace and harmony to the communities they serve (whether that community is a local village or the world), a practice that extends back into Chinese antiquity. But the beliefs and practices of the mediums discussed in this article also evoke an understanding of the changing cultural and social milieu of Taiwan. This change is reflected in the increasing variation seen among Taiwanese beliefs and practices, such as the expanding role of women in Taiwanese mediumship. There have been cultural changes, too, noticeable in the new languages that mediums speak while in trance, which now include Japanese and sometimes English. Although the Chinese legacy of shamanism can be seen in many aspects of mediumship—such as in the need to restore harmony, the importance of exorcism, and the use of talismans, to name just a few—other aspects are clearly non-Chinese in origin.

Case Studies

Mr. Tai

Mr. Tai is a fifty-one-year-old factory worker who serves as the spirit youth for three city prefect temples in Taiwan. He has been a spirit youth since his late teens and did not complete high school. He never married. He may be classed within the civil (*wen*) branch of mediumship, and he does not perform self-mortification.

On this occasion, Mr. Tai has been called because the temple community is experiencing a spate of bad luck. Although he was invited to arrive at the temple at a set time, it was understood that it would likely take a few hours for the deity to descend into him (very occasionally the deity might not descend at all). Before possession (or semipossession) takes place, the temple entrance and interior are exorcised and purified of any malevolent forces by burning spirit money and incense. The purification ritual is conducted by the "head of the table" (*zhuotou*)—the man who has functioned for many years as the spirit youth's assistant and interpreter while he is in trance. When the temple entrance and interior have been purified of evil influences, the spirit youth enters the temple and sits off to one side of the altar, where he waits for the deity to possess him.

After a period of more than an hour, the deity descends into the spirit youth, causing changes in his demeanor. He yells loudly and his body stiffens. (Other spirit youth may hop or dance, their voices may deepen, or an expression of sternness or of calmness may be seen on their faces). Then Mr. Tai moves to sit on a bench that has been positioned before the altar. The "head of the table" stands beside him and translates the words uttered by the spirit youth, which are often not Taiwanese or Mandarin but a combination of classical Chinese, Japanese, and gibberish. Then he poses the question to the deity: "Why has the community been experiencing bad luck?" The deity responds that he is displeased with the community because there are too few spirit youth serving him in the three temples. Whereas in the past there have been three, today there is only one. Two spirit youth have died in recent years and have not been replaced. A ritual must be held immediately so that the deity can choose a new spirit youth to serve the community. The deity gives instructions to the "head of the table" and other community leaders about how to prepare the temple for the ritual: where offerings are to be placed; where the musicians are to play; and how long the ritual should last.

It was deemed that the ritual was to last forty days, during which time one of the young men in the temple community who participated in the ritual would be called by the deity to serve as a medium. The forty-day ritual was performed at great expense to the temple community, and many men of appropriate age participated. However, the ritual failed to reveal a new spirit youth, and the community continues to experience bad luck, with businesses failing and members of the community experiencing poor health.

Mrs. Zhang

In a small southern Taiwanese village, Mrs. Zhang is a sixty-eight-year-old female spirit youth who serves two spirits, the male Xunhai and the Japanese Mazu (Shengmu), who is a protectress of orphaned children looking to be adopted. As a medium, she represents the complexity of Taiwanese shamanism, straddling the boundaries between the civil (*wen*) and martial (*wu*) branches of mediumship.

The first time that Mrs. Zhang heard the calling to be a spirit youth was at the age of forty-one. She did not believe in the powers of the spirit youth at the time, and it took a lot to convince her. The spirit returned over a four-year period to try to make her a willing medium, and eventually she became one at the age of forty-five. Shengmu had made the first contact with her and spoke first. Later Xunhai spoke through her. Both revealed their histories to her, and all of this was translated by another spirit youth, who helped her through the process.

When she finally became a spirit youth, she entered menopause. That happened because she had become possessed, and a spirit youth who was helping her during the initiation process said that she did not have enough power because she was contaminated by menstrual blood. The spirit youth made a talisman (*fu*) for her, writing a large symbol on a piece of yellow and golden paper. She was told to put the symbol in water and wash with it. After she used the talisman, she never had her period again. Her initiation lasted forty-nine days, during which time she had to live in the temple and endure several prohibitions, such as eating only fruit, drinking only water for three days, and praying only to the gods who had chosen her as a medium. The temple that she now owns and serves was built twenty-two years ago, a few years after she became a spirit youth, and it continues to be a strong force within the community. Initially it was managed by her husband, who was a fish farmer. When he died twenty years ago, her eldest son took over as manager of the temple. She has five children: one girl and four boys.

Normally, Mrs. Zhang becomes a medium of Xunhai once a week to solve common problems of members of the community. Xunhai is a young deity who speaks Taiwanese in a muffled voice and is good with children. When possessed by him, Mrs. Zhang does not wear shoes; she wears a red apron and holds six pieces of lit incense. Xunhai solves minor problems, such as when a child is being disobedient, someone is feeling unwell, a student needs to do better in school, or a family is experiencing repeated bad luck because of a *fengshui* problem (for example, with the orientation of their home). Most of these problems are solved by talismans that Xunhai produces. After listening to the patient and asking a few questions, Xunhai writes a sacred symbol with a calligraphy brush in black ink on a piece of yellow, red, and gold paper. The name of the patient is written on the back of the talisman. There are three talismans used by the medium, each with a different purpose. The first is to be mixed with water and drunk. The second is to be mixed with water and used to wash oneself. The third is to be kept with one at all times, to keep evil spirits away. Some patients are also given herbs with which to wash at home.

The second deity for whom Mrs. Zhang is a medium, the Japanese Mazu, is summoned only when people have more serious problems. As the Japanese Mazu, she speaks Japanese (although she has no formal education and cannot normally speak Japanese). She wears all white, with a yellow satin cape and hood. She also performs self-mortification with the five treasures, striking her forehead or back. There are never any scabs from the cuts. Sometimes she performs alone, and at other times she performs with other spirit youth who are male. As the Japanese Mazu, she will also dance and jump very high. During these performances she feels no fatigue and is refreshed when the celebration is over.

References

Ahern, Emily. 1975. "The Power and Pollution of Chinese Women." Pp. 269–290 in *Women in Chinese Society.* Edited by Margery Wolfe and Roxanne Witke. Stanford: Stanford University Press.

Berthier, Brigitte. 1987. "Enfant de divination, voyageur du destin" [Child of divination, traveler of destiny]. *L'Homme* 101.1: 86–100.

Boretz, Avron A. 2003. "Righteous Brothers and Demon Slayers: Subjectivities and Collective Identities in Taiwanese Temple Processions." Pp. 219–251 in *Religion and the Formation of Taiwanese Identities.* Edited by Paul R. Katz and Murray A. Rubenstein. New York: Palgrave.

Chang Kwang-chih. 1983. *Art, Myth, and Ritual: The Path to Political Authority in Ancient China.* Cambridge: Harvard University Press.

Chang, Mau-keui. 2003. "On the Origins and Transformation of Taiwanese National Identity." Pp. 23–58 in *Religion and the Formation of Taiwanese*

Identities. Edited by Paul R. Katz and Murray A. Rubenstein. New York: Palgrave.

Chen Mengjia. 1936. "Shangdai de shenhua yu wushu" [Mythology and shaman arts of the Shang dynasty]. *Yanjing xuebao* 19: 91–155.

Ching, Julia. 1997. *Mysticism and Kingship in China: The Heart of Chinese Wisdom.* Cambridge: Cambridge University Press.

Clart, Philip. 2003. "Moral Mediums: Spirit Writing and the Cultural Construction of Chinese Spirit-Mediumship." In *Negotiating Transcendence: Expressions of Ecstatic Performance in Religion and Theatre.* Edited by Alison Marshall. *Ethnologies* 25.1: 153–189.

Davis, Edward L. 2001. *Society and the Supernatural in Song China.* Honolulu: University of Hawai'i Press.

Furth, Charlotte. 1999. *A Flourishing Yin: Gender in China's Medical History, 960–1665.* Berkeley: University of California Press.

Guo Qitao. 2003. *Exorcism and Money: The Symbolic World of the Five-Fury Spirits in Late Imperial China.* Berkeley: Institute of East Asian Studies, University of California, Berkeley Center for Chinese Studies.

Hamayon, Roberte. 1998. "'Ecstasy' or the West-dreamt Shaman." Pp. 175–187 in *Tribal Epistemologies.* Edited by Helmut Wautischer. Aldershot, UK: Ashgate.

Høst, Annette. 2001. "What's in a Name? Neo-Shamanism, Core Shamanism, Urban Shamanism, Modern Shamanism, or What?" *Spirit Talk* 14: 3–6.

Jones, Charles B. 2003. "Religion in Taiwan at the End of the Japanese Colonial Period." Pp. 10–35 in *Religion and Modern Taiwan: Tradition and Innovation in a Changing Society.* Edited by Philip Clart and Charles B. Jones. Honolulu: University of Hawai'i Press.

Jordan, David K. 1972. *Gods, Ghosts and Ancestors: Folk Religion in a Taiwanese Village.* Berkeley: University of California Press.

Jordan, David K., and Daniel L. Overmyer. 1986. *The Flying Phoenix: Aspects of Chinese Sectarianism in Taiwan.* Princeton: Princeton University Press.

Katz, Paul R. 2003. "The Cult of the Royal Lords in Postwar Taiwan." Pp. 98–124 in *Religion and Modern Taiwan: Tradition and Innovation in a Changing Society.* Edited by Philip Clart and Charles B. Jones. Honolulu: University of Hawai'i Press.

Keightley, David N. 1983. "Royal Shamanism in the Shang: Archaic Vestige or Central Reality?" Paper presented at the Workshop on Chinese Divination and Portent Interpretation. Berkeley, June 20–July 1.

Marshall, Alison R. 2003a. "Engendering Mediumship: When Youths Performed the Rain Dances in Han Dynasty China." *Studies in Religion* 32.3: 83–100.

———. 2003b. "Moving the Spirit on Taiwan: New Age *Lingji* Performance." *Journal of Chinese Religions* 31: 81–99.

Overmyer, Daniel L. 2003. "Religion in China Today: Introduction." *China Quarterly* 174: 307–316.

Paper, Jordan. 1996. "Mediums and Modernity: The Institutionalization of Ecstatic Religious Functionaries in Taiwan." *Journal of Chinese Religions* 24: 105–129.

Pas, Julian. 2003. "Stability and Change in Taiwan's Religious Culture." Pp. 36–47 in *Religion and Modern Taiwan: Tradition and Innovation in a Changing Society*. Edited by Philip Clart and Charles B. Jones. Honolulu: University of Hawai'i Press.

Sangren, P. Steven. 1983. "Female Gender in Chinese Religious Symbols: Kuan Yin, Ma Tsu, and the 'Eternal Mother.'" *Signs* 9.1: 4–25.

———. 1988. "History and the Rhetoric of Legitimacy: The Ma Tsu Cult of Taiwan." *Comparative Studies in Society and History* 30: 674–697.

———. 1991. "Dialectics of Alienation: Individuals and Collectivities in Chinese Religion." *Man* 26: 67–86.

Sutton, Donald S. 1990. "Rituals of Self-Mortification: Taiwanese Spirit Mediums in Comparative Perspective." *Journal of Ritual Studies* 4.1: 99–125.

———. 2003. *Steps to Perfection: Exorcistic Performers and Chinese Religion in Twentieth-Century Taiwan*. Cambridge: Harvard University Press.

von Stuckrad, Kocku. 2002. "Reenchanting Modern Western Shamanism and Nineteenth Century Thought." *Journal of the American Academy of Religion* 70.4: 771–799.

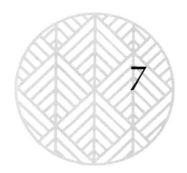

7

Body Cultivation in Contemporary China

DAVID A. PALMER

ODY CULTIVATION PRACTICES known as *qigong* (ch'i-kung; pronounced CHEE GUNG) were the most widespread form of popular religiosity in post-Mao urban China between 1979 and 1999. It is estimated that at the height of "qigong fever," in the middle of that period, more than 100 million people—above 20 percent of the urban population—practiced the gymnastic, breathing, and meditative exercises of qigong in some form or another. Hundreds of charismatic qigong healers and masters rose to fame and built organizations which, in the two cases known as Zhong gong and Falun gong, could claim as many adherents as the 40 million–strong Chinese Communist Party (CCP), if not more. This made them the largest mass organizations independent of government control in China. The movement known as Falun gong has become well known in the West since April 25, 1999, when it staged a 10,000-person protest around the CCP headquarters in Beijing. This protest was followed by a harsh state repression campaign against Falun gong, which has also led to the dismantling of most other qigong groups.

Media images of Falun gong repression and resistance should not, however, blind us to the complex reality of the qigong movement in the People's Republic of China. For much of the post-Mao period, government support played an instrumental role in the spread of the qigong craze. Qigong was touted as a cheap and powerful healing technology, as a "somatic science" that could lead to revolutionary discoveries for harnessing the powers of the human mind, and as a secularized training system that contained the key to the mysteries of traditional Chinese wisdom without the dross of religion or superstition. And yet, while this talk of modernization lent legitimacy to qigong, practitioners plunged into the legends and symbols of Buddhist magicians and Daoist immortals, dabbled in talismans and divination, and often experienced, through trance states, visions of popular demons and deities.

The fact that qigong is a type of body practice that blurs the boundaries between physical fitness exercises, mystic visualizations, and even apocalyptic militancy, opened a space for the massive spread of a body-centered religiosity. This religious phenomenon took place under the cover of health, sports, and science, outside the supervision of the official Religious Affairs Bureau. And yet the enthusiasm of Communist Party leaders for qigong in the 1980s, followed by their fear of Falun gong and other qigong groups today, suggests that body cultivation can come dangerously close to the religious roots of Chinese political power and authority.

This chapter begins with a brief overview of body cultivation in traditional China, followed by an account of the changing configurations of body cultivation in mainland Chinese society after 1949. It shows that while body cultivation was a fundamental aspect of traditional Chinese religion, it was also ideally suited for adaptation to the organization of modern life centered on the individual body. As such, qigong became a remarkable example of the modern reappropriation and transformation of Chinese religious tradition (for a detailed treatment of this theme, see Palmer 2005 or Palmer 2006).

Body Cultivation in Traditional China

Chinese notions of the body make no sharp distinctions between the mind and the flesh, and the term "body cultivation" refers to the varied Chinese traditions of training the body and the mind to conform with the pattern and power flows of the cosmos. The greater the body's correspondence with the cosmos, the more it taps into cosmic powers that can flow through the body, toward other bodies, and into the world. Body cultivation involves sets of movements and forms which aim for the attainment of specific goals and are transmitted through a training process which forms the basis of a tradition. It is an individual practice that usually involves the self-disciplined control of diet, posture, breathing, and thoughts. It is also a social practice, in which techniques and interpretive frameworks are transmitted from a master to disciples, and in which the powers gained from practice are used for a variety of ends within specific social and historical contexts.

Throughout history, Chinese body cultivation has involved a diversity of techniques. The dances and ecstatic healing practices of ancient Chinese shamanism were probably the source of later traditions of body cultivation. Invisible forces represented as demons and winds were later reconceptualized as cosmic breath (*qi;* see Unschuld 1985, 29–50). During the Warring States period (475–221 B.C.E.), gymnastics and breath training were practiced as forms of health cultivation, being described in philosophical works, notably the *Laozi* and *Zhuangzi,* as means of attaining unity with the Dao. Other texts mentioned body cultivation among the techniques for attaining immortality. In classical China, the proper training of the body through fasting and meditation was a prerequisite to self-cultivation and participation in rituals, which, to Confucius, aimed to foster social cohesion through the harmonious movement of bodies.

The emperor's body was seen as the center of the ordering of the cosmos: the appropriate movements of his body, through the space of the realm and following the cycles of the seasons, were essential to preserving the cosmic order. The empire was seen as an extension of the emperor's body: disorderly conduct by the emperor would cause chaos in the realm; natural disasters and calamities were seen as signs of the moral degeneracy of the emperor's body. The correspondence between the body of the emperor and the body politic was formalized in the medical theories of the Han dynasty, which applied the principles of government to the flows of *qi* in the body. The word for healing and government is the same in Chinese: *zhi.*

From the first century of the Common Era onward, Daoism developed a rich repertoire of body cultivation practices, ranging from the meditations on oneness of the Heavenly Masters movement to the Shangqing and Lingbao sects' visualizations of the divine landscape of the inner body. The inner alchemy tradition sought to refine the elixir of immortality through the manipulation and combination of cosmic energies in the body (see Robinet 1997). Body cultivation was also practiced by Daoist priests as a key to the mastery and efficacy of rituals conducted for local families and communities (see Schipper 1993). Buddhism introduced yogic meditation from India, practiced as a means of nurturing awareness of ultimate reality and, in the case of tantrism, of nurturing and controlling divine powers. The Shaolin

Practitioners of Falun gong meditate freely in Beijing in the period before the government crackdown, 1999. (China Features/Corbis Sygma)

and Wudang traditions of martial arts developed the use of body cultivation as the foundation of techniques of combat.

By the time of the Song dynasties (960–1279 C.E.), body cultivation had become widespread in many segments of society. Meditation by "sitting in tranquillity" became a popular practice of the Confucian literati, while sectarian groups disseminated body cultivation techniques among the common people. Those groups, which often espoused apocalyptic beliefs and delivered a message of salvation, commonly used the transmission of body techniques—including mantra recitation, breath control, sitting meditation, healing techniques, and martial arts—as a method of recruitment and expansion. Practice of the techniques could reinforce sectarian identity; the body became a vehicle for the nurturing and transmission of eschatological beliefs. Martial arts became more important in the sectarian repertoire in the nineteenth century, as increasing social chaos and banditry led to the multiplication of community self-defense groups. In the Boxer Movement of 1897–1901, certain forms of martial arts were believed to confer invincibility against Western military technology (Esherick 1987, 50–53; Cohen 1997, 16–30, 99–118).

By the early twentieth century, body cultivation was practiced among common people and among the elites, and became diffused in a wide variety of social contexts—it was even a fundamental part of training for the Chinese opera and acrobatic performance, which are closely related to the martial arts. The techniques varied greatly, but in most cases they involved breath training as a basic foundation. They were usually steeped in religious symbolism and transmitted secretly from master to disciple: mastering the arts of body cultivation was part of being initiated into an esoteric tradition. The process of initiation could last many years, as in the case of the Daoist priesthood, or it could take only moments, as in some sectarian movements that taught a secret mantra as a sign of membership. But in all cases, body cultivation was never an end in itself. It was always but one element of other social practices and conceptual systems, such as religion, government, medicine, mysticism, ritual, monasticism, defense, sectarian salvation, and the like. There was no single category to encompass the various forms of body cultivation, much less a self-conscious community or network of practitioners who could recognize each other in their common practice of these techniques.

The status of body cultivation began to change in the first half of the twentieth century with the introduction of Western values. In a society that privileged a mechanical, technological, rational worldview, traditional views of body cultivation were seemingly irrelevant to the bureaucracies, armies, and schools that mediated knowledge and power in the modern state. And yet, body cultivation was able to find a niche within these new social structures. It could do so by being reinvented, either as a modern technology for the mass development of healthy bodies or as a vehicle for a nationalist or mystical resistance to the alienation that people experience in modernity. As would happen in the qigong boom of the 1980s, both might occur at the same time.

Such a process began during the Republican era (1911–1949), when some authors popularized sitting meditation and other practices through widely circulated books that sought to eliminate the obscure esoteric language in which the techniques had traditionally been couched, and to present them in the idioms of psychology, physiology, and physics (see Kohn 2002). But it was under the communist regime that body cultivation became distinctive as part of a larger project of state expansion.

The Birth of Qigong

During the Chinese civil and anti-Japanese wars (1927–1949), Red Army and Communist Party units, entrenched in remote "liberated areas" and lacking access to modern medical facilities, encouraged the use of traditional local remedies for the care of the injured and ill. It was under such conditions that cadre Liu Guizhen, who had been suffering from ulcers and insomnia, obtained leave in 1947 to return to his native village in present-day Hebei province. While he was recuperating there, his uncle taught him a form of breathing exercise that, after 102 days of practice, cured him of his ailments. Upon returning to his post, he enthusiastically reported on the method's efficiency to his superiors, who ordered him to experiment with clinical applications of the method. Together with some colleagues, he researched classical medical texts on body cultivation, taught the techniques to other patients, and finally standardized two forms of exercise. The research group chose the term "qigong therapy" to designate the exercises.

The term "qigong," though it had appeared as early as the Tang dynasty (618–907), had rarely been used in the past, and it did not have the meaning of "breath training" intended by Liu Guizhen (on the etymology of the term, see Despeux 1997, 267). Qigong was promoted as a new category to encompass all body cultivation techniques that involved the training, control, and circulation of *qi* (ch'i; vital breath) in combination with bodily and mental discipline. Provincial party leaders supported his work and called upon him to found a qigong clinic in the city of Tangshan in 1953, followed two years later by the foundation of a qigong sanatorium in the exclusive seaside resort of Beidaihe, a favorite retreat for party elite. Liu Guizhen was honored by Vice President Liu Shaoqi, and he treated several of the country's top leaders. Qigong became recognized as a discipline of Chinese medicine, alongside herbalism, acupuncture, and massage, and national qigong workshops were held to train clinicians from hospitals and medical units around China.

Benefiting from such high-level political support, qigong quickly spread within medical institutions. Seventy qigong units were founded by the end of the 1950s. A national conference on qigong was held in 1959, and a national qigong training course was organized a year later. Books were published on the subject, and several research units began clinical and laboratory trials on the physiological effects of qigong. More than three hundred scientific articles on qigong had been published in Chinese journals by the early 1960s.

Thus institutionalized and modernized, qigong, together with the other disciplines of Chinese medicine, could be marshaled to serve the health policy needs of the new state. Indeed, after decades of civil war, the country's medical system was in ruins by the end of the 1940s. The answer was to enlist the hundreds of thousands of traditional doctors—whose practices had been suppressed by the previous Nationalist regime—to the cause of improving the health of the Chinese masses. They were assigned to state medical work units and educated in scientific methodologies (see Croizier 1968).

At the same time, practitioners of Western medicine, trained abroad or in missionary colleges, were considered tainted by their association with imperialist bourgeois culture and were accused of trying to place their scientific practice above political supervision. The institutions of Chinese medicine, on the other hand, as creations of the communist state, were more docile and grateful to party authorities. With the growing rift between Maoist China and the Soviet Union, Chinese medicine further benefited from an increasing nationalism and appreciation for native civilization.

Modern qigong was designed to serve the needs of the new medical institutions of the People's Republic: with qigong, body cultivation became an instrument of state power. Useful therapeutic techniques were secularized and extracted from their traditional social and symbolic settings, and master-disciple lineages were replaced by cohorts of "medical workers" operating in institutional settings. Secret transmission was replaced by formal training courses and the publication of therapeutic methods in medical journals. Instead of becoming the source of esoteric knowledge, practitioners' bodies were used as subjects for clinical research based on modern scientific biomedical categories. The effects of practice were described in physical and chemical terms, and the concepts of yin-yang and *qi* were standardized and materialized as expressions of "primitive dialectics" compatible with Marxist philosophy.

For reasons both practical and ideological, then, body cultivation thus flourished as a branch of institutionalized Chinese medicine in the 1950s. Entirely an instrument of state modernization and political campaigns, qigong during this period did not develop the alternative social networks and ideologies that would emerge in the 1980s. It did, however, acquire legitimacy and a niche within the state system, from which it could expand as a mass movement in the 1980s.

Mass Qigong

Together with almost everything else associated with traditional culture, qigong was attacked as a "feudal superstition" during the Cultural Revolution, and its medical institutions were closed: there were no officially sanctioned qigong activities in China from 1965 until its rehabilitation in 1978. However, one woman, Guo Lin, an artist and cancer victim from Guangdong province who had cured herself by practicing qigong during the 1960s, was brave enough to teach qigong to other cancer victims in the parks of Beijing as early as 1970. Although she was often harassed by the police, the number of people who came to practice qigong with her grew until she was able to train coaches to lead practice groups in other parks. An informal organization of practitioners was created to study and publicize her method. In 1977 she submitted a report to the health ministry which, summarizing seven years of experience teaching qigong, claimed that qigong was a cure for cancer. Her method, which advocated training the mind and body for the "ideological struggle against cancer," was published as the "new qigong therapy"; at the end of the Cultural Revolution, Guo Lin was invited to lecture in dozens of universities, factories, and official units. Thousands began to learn her qigong method in parks and public spaces around the country.

Guo Lin inaugurated a new form of qigong, heavily marked by the mass culture of the Cultural Revolution. Qigong was no longer confined to the medical institutions of the party elite; rather, it became a grassroots popular movement. Instead of professional medical workers providing one-on-one clinical instruction, amateur enthusiasts led free collective practice sessions in public spaces. The standardized set of exercises in Guo Lin's book could be learned by anyone and was replicable anywhere. Guo Lin became something of a celebrity. Her "new qigong therapy" quickly spread to most cities in China and even to several Western countries. Other qigong methods were also popularized and spread to all parts of China within less than a year. By the end of the 1970s, it was not rare to see more than a dozen different qigong methods being practiced in the same park on a given morning.

Ecstatic and Charismatic Qigong

Among the qigong methods that appeared in 1980, one of the most popular was "great crane qigong," which signaled the appearance of religious and charismatic motifs in qigong practice. This method was propagated by Yang Meijun, a seventy-seven-year-old woman who had been trained by her grandfather in a Daoist tradition in which one imitates the movements of the great crane, a symbol of immortality. Yang had participated in the anti-Japanese guerrilla war and had lived in the Communist Party base of Yan'an before the establishment of the People's Republic, then had concealed her knowledge of body cultivation until the end of the Cultural Revolution. Her "great crane qigong" was the first method to claim an explicitly Daoist heritage rather than an affiliation with modernized Chinese medicine. After Liu Guizhen (the cadre and communist clinician) and Guo Lin (the intrepid self-taught anticancer combatant) Yang Meijun emerged as the venerable inheritor of a secret lineage and as the possessor of concealed magical powers. Besides teaching her gymnastic exercises, she also used her powers to treat the ill by projecting her *qi* onto patients. Qigong was no longer exclusively a self-training exercise: by receiving the mysterious *qi* emitted by the master, patients entered into a new type of relationship with her and with the powerful traditions she was perceived to embody.

Two other immensely successful qigong methods launched around that time—the "flying crane qigong" and the "qigong of the spontaneous movements of the five animals"—triggered states of "spontaneous movements qigong." In these methods, after entering a state of deep relaxation through body and breathing exercises, the practitioner falls into a trance that lasts between thirty minutes and two hours, during which time he hits or massages himself, spontaneously carries out kung fu, *taiji quan,* or dance movements, or even falls and rolls on the ground. In this type of qigong, visions of gods or aliens were frequent. Large numbers of people in such trance states became a common sight in parks.

Another widespread phenomenon during the qigong wave was glossolalia, or "cosmic language," a condition analogous to what is commonly known as speaking in tongues. The most notorious promoter of this practice was Zhang Xiangyu, an actress who claimed to have been pushed by a puff of *qi* to run without stopping for days and nights on end, and who then played host in her kitchen to the Jade Emperor, the Queen Mother of the West, Guanyin, Sakyamuni, the Venerable Lord Lao, and other popular divinities. She heard a voice in "cosmic language" tell her to save humanity by teaching the "qigong of the center of nature" to the people, a method that attracted tens of thousands of devotees.

• • •

The spread of ecstatic qigong in the 1980s occurred in a context in which paramount leader Deng Xiaoping's policy of reforms and opening up had created the conditions for a religious revival. In the countryside, this revival manifested itself through the rebuilding of temples destroyed during the Cultural Revolution and through the reconstitution of ritual networks. In the cities, however, the renewed interest in religion was more diffuse: books on religious subjects found a large readership, and television serials on religious themes, such as *Journey to the West,* were smash hits. "Martial arts fever" added to the spiritual ferment. Kung fu novels and films from Hong Kong and Taiwan flooded mainland theaters and bookstalls, fueling the growth of a martial arts subculture. Itinerant martial arts troupes resurfaced and entertained crowds with their exploits. Blockbuster movies such as *Shaolin Temple* triggered a cult following among youth, who flocked to the temples of Shaolin, Wudang, and Emei in search of the secret teachings of a master.

These films and novels depict Buddhist monks and Daoist masters who can fly, disappear and reappear, and read people's minds—abilities they are said to have acquired through the mastery of "inner cultivation" (*neigong*) involving the body, breath, and mind control exercises associated with qigong. For thousands of kung fu fans, the magical feats of the past and the stunts of pulp films were not fiction: they could be mastered through initiation by a master.

A legend grew around the most famous qigong masters, many of whom were said to have demonstrated miraculous powers from their early childhood in a poor countryside surrounded by mountains, grottoes, and temples. Typically, they received initiation from as early as four years of age from a succession of mysterious sages, monks, and masters representing the esoteric traditions of Daoism, Buddhism, Confucianism, Chinese medicine, and the martial arts. Such an initiation is said to be the result of karmic predisposition (*yuanfen*)—the qigong master is one of the elect of the initiates, who possesses extraordinary power over the forces of the universe. After a period of incubation, during which the young master conceals his abilities, his initiators command him to "go out of the mountains" (*chushan*), to manifest his powers and his knowledge to the public in order to deliver the world from its agony.

Ecstatic qigong has been interpreted as a popular cathartic vehicle for the release of pent-up emotions after the torment of the Cultural Revolution

(Ots 1994). Qigong also offered the possibility for the private appropriation of public spaces in the socialist republic (Chen 1995). Indeed, ecstatic and charismatic qigong went beyond the earlier categorization of qigong as a therapeutic technique. After having been engulfed in a collective fusion with Mao Zedong during the Cultural Revolution, people could, by practicing qigong, rediscover their own bodies and subjectivities. Through exploring the inner universe of the body and directing the circulation of its energies, entering mystical realms through trances and visions, and connecting oneself (through a master) to ancient esoteric traditions, practitioners could enter an alternate world from the monotonous, regimented life of the socialist work unit (*danwei*) with its totalitarian, industrial-bureaucratic organization of bodies.

The work unit was a walled compound in which work, leisure, housing, and family life were contained and managed by a cadre of leaders (*lingdao*) who were in perpetual internecine struggle for control of state resources and prestige. Work was rarely challenging or rewarding, and unit members— enjoying the lifetime job security of the "iron rice bowl"—were often idle, subtly resisting arbitrary authority by putting out as little effort as possible. Information was mediated by a propaganda apparatus that impressed itself on the mind several times each day through the blaring of the People's Radio on loudspeakers. For those who were not politically ambitious, the work unit offered no hope for personal development or advancement, little contact with the outside world, and little space for personal subjectivity. In the cracked concrete yards of housing compounds and between the scraggly bushes of urban parks, however, the practice of qigong could open endless new horizons of experience and knowledge. Here, the body became a receptacle of and a conduit for traditional wisdom and mystical symbols. Hitherto unknown forms of energy inside and outside the body could be experienced, monitored, directed, and emitted, leading to a sense of better health and, often literally, heightened power. Qigong offered a way of personally appropriating and embodying this new world of knowledge, power, and experience—an alternative to the alienating world of the work unit, and one that could be legitimately and openly pursued under the guise of physical fitness (for other interpretations of the qigong boom, see Penny 1993, 179; Ots 1994, 126; Micollier 1999; Chen 1995, 361; Zhu and Penny 1994, 7; Zhu 1994/1989; Hsu 1999, 24; Heise 1999, 110; Xu 1999; Chen 2003).

Qigong Science

The experimentation with inner states through body techniques could also be conceived of as scientific research. The inner body became an instrument for observing the cosmos. Contrary to institutionalized science, in which a small number of specialists produce knowledge for passive consumption by everyone else, this was a type of scientific activity that anyone could engage in. Thousands of amateur scholars devoted themselves to studying classical texts on body cultivation and trying out different methods, exchanging observations and commentary in popular qigong journals. This was a conscious project of engaging in the prestigious activity of scientific research, with the body as the laboratory. A scientific attitude was seen as necessary to save body cultivation from centuries of superstitious dross and to enable qigong to create a new type of science. As one popular slogan put it: "Science will save qigong and qigong will save science." Here, scientism was not an abstract ideology but an embodied practice.

As a source of knowledge, qigong also fascinated the Chinese scientific community itself. By the end of the 1970s a handful of scientists had begun to conduct experiments on "external *qi*," the energy that is said to be sent by qigong masters toward their patients. Dr. Feng Lida began research at the National Navy Hospital, and Gu Hansen of the China Academy of Sciences Nuclear Research Centre announced that he had discovered the material basis of the "external *qi*" said to be emitted by qigong masters.

Meanwhile, the strange phenomenon of children reading with their ears made a sensation in the mass media. After the first case of such a child, in Dazu county, Sichuan, was covered by an official newspaper, similar phenomena were reported all over the country. Researchers from Beijing University published an article in *Ziran,* a popular science magazine, claiming that they had trained 60 percent of a sample of children to read without their eyes. The magazine subsequently published a series of articles on similar paranormal phenomena, stimulating widespread debate and speculation on what were called "extraordinary functions of the human body." On May 5, 1979, however, the *People's Daily* denounced "extraordinary functions" as quackery, antiscience, and idealism, momentarily leading the press to cease publishing such reports.

In spite of the controversy, interest in "extraordinary functions" of the human body did not diminish. Researchers from several universities gathered in

Shanghai in January 1981 to share their findings and discuss how to counter charges of idealism and pseudoscience. Extraordinary functions research groups were formed in several scientific institutions. A few months later, a second academic conference led to the foundation of the China Human Body Science Research Society, dedicated to research on extraordinary functions. Some persons with alleged extraordinary functions, such as Zhang Baosheng, became media celebrities. In 1982, scientists from several key universities conducted tests on some of these individuals and announced that their powers were "proven." Debate raged in the press, and the state propaganda bureau moved to put an end to speculation. But China's most influential scientist, Qian Xuesen, a graduate of MIT who was the principal architect of China's nuclear weapons program, successfully intervened before the central leadership on behalf of extraordinary functions research, which was now officially permitted and legitimized.

Meanwhile, researchers were continuing their experiments on qigong. In 1980, the Shanghai Chinese Medicine Research Institute announced that it had successfully tested "qigong anesthesia" by the emission of external *qi* onto patients undergoing surgery. Qinghua, China's most prestigious university for the physical sciences, also began experiments in 1980. Scientists began to theorize on the nature of *qi* and the effects of qigong. The emission of external *qi* appeared to be an extraordinary function which could be learned and nurtured through practice. Some qigong masters were also reported to have paranormal abilities such as ESP and telekinesis. Qigong increasingly came to be conceived of as a technique for attaining extraordinary functions.

Qigong, extraordinary functions, and martial arts began to merge in the popular imagination. Through assiduous qigong practice, anyone could hope to develop the extraordinary functions latent in the body. The supernatural feats of ancient Chinese popular legend, literature, and culture had been proven through real life experience and scientific observation. Qigong became the scientifically tested key to breaking the laws of classical physics. The old legends were true, qigong would turn them into science, and China would be at the forefront of a new global scientific revolution.

Qigong Fever

In early 1986, the China Qigong Scientific Research Association was founded on a triumphant note, as Professor Qian Xuesen proclaimed the new scientific

A man teaches qigong at a traditional-medicine hospital in Chengdu, Sichuan province.
(Keren Su/Corbis)

revolution. The creation of this academic body was heralded as a turning point in the history of science, as qigong advocates cried: "Qigong has left religion and folklore to enter the temple of science!"

Official recognition of qigong grew. Upon the instigation of Zhang Zhenhuan—revolutionary hero, retired Red Army general, and president of the new association—a large gathering of national leaders witnessed master Zhang Baosheng demonstrate his extraordinary functions at a meeting in Guangzhou in September 1986. Leaders of the Commission of Science and Technology for National Defense, which managed the country's huge military-industrial complex, promoted the military applications of qigong, and it was speculated that qigong masters could use their *qi* to deflect incoming ballistic missiles. One master was employed by the space agency to detect faults telepathically in a satellite before launching. Other masters were invited by the geological prospecting agency to detect underground mineral deposits.

The National Sports Commission organized qigong training to increase the abilities of Chinese athletes in international competitions, and the National Education Commission experimented with qigong training in primary schools to increase the intelligence of children.

Meanwhile, qigong fever was raised to a frenzy by a young and previously unknown qigong master, Yan Xin, who claimed to have been initiated since his early childhood by more than thirty traditional masters of medicine, martial arts, Buddhism, Daoism, and Confucianism. In early 1987 researchers at Qinghua University publicized the results of experiments showing that his external *qi* had changed the molecular structure of water at a distance of 2,000 kilometers. Yan Xin became an instant celebrity. He began a series of public lectures in large auditoriums and sports stadiums across the country. Entitled "Force-Conducting Experimental Lectures," they drew audiences of up to 20,000, lasted as long as ten hours without intermission, and were the scene of trance reactions and miraculous healings. Yan Xin gave more than two hundred mass healing lectures between 1987 and 1989. Before long, other qigong masters began giving "force-conducting lectures," and an industry was spawned selling the "force-conducting" audio-and videotapes of Yan Xin's lectures. The qigong grandmaster became a popular idol, combining in one body the powers of ancient wizard and of pioneering scientist.

"Qigong fever" expressed and combined many strands of utopianism in post-Mao China. At the level of the individual body, the practice of qigong can produce profound sensations and experiences that often lead to a heightened sense of health, empowerment, and understanding. These changes can produce a radical transformation in one's relationship with one's body and with the world, and a sense of connection with the ultimate power of the cosmos that is absent in the alienating routines of modern industrial culture. As a mass movement, qigong multiplied such experiences in millions of bodies, whose numbers grew rapidly, presaging the day when eventually all of China, and even the whole world, would experience and participate in the transformation—a transformation that would lead to universal health, the spread of superhuman and paranormal abilities on a wide scale, and the end of disease and suffering.

Such fantasies evoked visions of Daoist immortal realms, the Pure Land of Buddhism, and the millenarian eschatology of the sectarian tradition. They also revived the tradition of utopian consciousness that had been fostered through forty years of communism and Maoism—but one that, after the failure and pain of the Cultural Revolution, was turning inward into the body, into tending its sufferings, and into the dream that all would change once each body had been transformed. As such, because the effects of qigong could be felt viscerally by the practitioner, soothing and curing illness and pain as well as providing experiences of power and knowledge, qigong could stimulate the enthusiasm of the masses of all social and educational backgrounds. At the same time, for intellectuals and scientists, qigong reconciled the scientism of mainstream modern Chinese thought with pride in the achievements of Chinese culture. Qigong thus legitimized the study of Chinese traditions and held forth the promise of a revolutionary Chinese science, one that would restore Chinese civilization and wisdom to its true dignity and propel it to the vanguard of world scientific discovery. For party leaders and state officials, many of whom personally experienced the transformation of their bodies through practicing qigong or through being treated by qigong masters, the science of qigong offered the promise of national empowerment vis-à-vis the West: not only through creating a healthier, stronger, paranormal race of men and women but also through developing a new system of knowledge, both more advanced than that of the West and unfathomable to uninitiated foreigners.

(Note that qigong masters often refused to initiate foreigners into its higher levels, fearing that they would discover the secrets of qigong power, allowing them eventually to surpass the Chinese. Some leaders were also concerned that, through paranormal research, Western countries were already becoming more advanced in an area in which China had a natural advantage. China risked seeing the West make better use of qigong than China, just as it had done with the "four great inventions" of paper, gunpowder, the printing press, and the compass.)

Qian Xuesen and others saw in qigong the key to a renewed and reinvigorated Marxism based on the mind-body dialectic. Even after the Tian'anmen student protests of 1989, which led the party to become more suspicious of popular movements, some of its leaders saw in qigong a form of substitute faith: its exercises and mystical flights could distract people from political preoccupations.

End of Utopia

Throughout the 1990s a worn regime, devoted primarily to preserving its power and achieving international normality (notably through membership in the World Trade Organization) became increasingly distant from its utopian origins. The focus was now on integration into world capitalism. Money, competition, and corruption ruled. The new generation of party leaders, led by Jiang Zemin, were technocrats rather than revolutionaries, more interested in economics and hard technology than in the power of consciousness to accomplish transformation, be it of society or of the body.

China's scientific institutions, through increasing international exchanges, embarked on a process of integration with the worldwide scientific community. The "Chinese science" of qigong became less of a fascination, especially when scientists applied international standards to evaluate its claims. In 1988, members of the China Academy of Sciences invited the American Committee for the Scientific Investigation of Claims of the Paranormal (CSICOP) to visit China and investigate extraordinary functions. The committee's delegation witnessed fifteen demonstrations of alleged extraordinary function by subjects selected by qigong organizations. None of the demonstrations passed CSICOP's criteria. Articles critical of Yan Xin began to appear in the press, and Hong Kong newspapers became the forum for a heated anti-qigong polemic.

The news media reported an increasing number of cases of qigong quackery and of qigong practitioners unable to come out of trance, starving themselves to death while fasting, or displaying psychotic behavior. Psychiatric wards opened special sections for qigong-related disorders (on qigong deviation, see Chen 2003, 77–106). Some alleged qigong techniques, such as "electric qigong" and "lightweight qigong," were exposed as simple tricks bearing no relation to qigong. A growing number of researchers, including some within the qigong community, claimed that so-called external qi was merely psychological suggestion and self-hypnosis.

In response to these controversies, the government issued a new policy on qigong in October 1989, which included licensing qigong masters and taxing qigong organizations. Within a few months, more than half of all qigong masters, unable to obtain licenses, lost their jobs, and several qigong organizations and clinics, unable to pay taxes, closed their doors. Yan Xin's popularity began to wane. A "force-filled lecture" he gave at the Shanghai Municipal Stadium in March 1990, though attended by 23,000 persons, was surrounded by controversy (one audience member died during the lecture) and widely regarded as a failure. Anticipating political criticism, General Zhang Zhenhuan, the highest official in the qigong community, advised Yan Xin to leave China for the United States and to promote qigong in the West.

Through a policy of "no criticism, no promotion, no debate," the government enforced a precarious truce between advocates and opponents of qigong. But with the death in March 1994 of General Zhang Zhenhuan, who had been an influential promoter of qigong among the country's leaders, the adversaries of qigong seized the chance to lead a vigorous anti-qigong campaign. Throughout 1995, former qigong master Sima Nan waged a heated polemic against "pseudo-qigong" in a series of television and radio interviews, newspaper articles, and a controversial book entitled *The Inside Story on Miraculous Qigong* (Sima 1995). Anti-qigong articles appeared in the press all through 1995. The chairman of the China Academy of Sciences and several other influential Chinese scientists spoke or wrote against qigong, calling it pseudoscience, superstition, quackery, and a dangerous cult similar to the Aum Shinrikyo sect of Japan.

Qigong itself became increasingly commercialized, as masters and semiofficial sponsoring organizations saw the mass profits that could be made from turning qigong into a product. Qigong groups became better organized, as masters competed for the allegiance of the millions of practitioners willing to pay to attend force-conducting lectures, training workshops, and healing clinics, and to buy qigong books, tapes, videos, and paraphernalia. The young master Zhang Hongbao, for example, attempted to regroup qigong adepts under the umbrella of a vast commercial organization owning qigong universities, qigong hospitals, qigong cadre training institutes, and qigong business enterprises. His Zhong gong method condensed qigong techniques into eight ascending levels. As early as the second level, adepts were integrated into the organization's nationwide qigong training sales system. In 1994, Zhong gong claimed 30 million adepts and had become the largest mass organization in China outside the Communist Party. By the mid-1990s, the government began to discreetly limit the activities of the movement. Zhang Hongbao disappeared around that time and reappeared in the summer of 2000, seeking political asylum on the U.S. Pacific island of Guam.

Many qigong groups revealed, in their structure, ideology, and practices, an affinity with the heterodox sects of the precommunist era (Ownby 2003; Palmer 2003b). The term "sect" is used here in a sociological sense in the Chinese context, in reference to voluntary popular groups with charismatic leaders, distinct from state-recognized institutional religions and from traditional cults based on lineage, clan, village, social status, or profession. Increasingly, qigong was being propagated by structured organizations that used the teaching and practice of body cultivation to recruit adepts and disseminate a specific ideology. This ideology, which varied from one group to another, typically included an ideal of universal salvation that integrated elements of magical thought, millenarian eschatology, scientism, and romantic national-ism around the charismatic figure of the qigong grandmaster (Palmer 2003a, 90–96). It was inevitable that qigong transmission would lead to organized groups, as the circulation of body cultivation techniques, *qi,* healing, and money formed bonds between masters and practitioners that needed to be managed and formalized.

The attempt, which had been encouraged by the government, to enlist Chi-nese body cultivation into the service of socialist construction and then of a new Chinese-led scientific revolution, had ended up as a failure. Qigong had led to the emergence of a sectarian milieu, of organizations independent from the state whose structure, ideology, and practices weaved an alternative culture in the interstices of official structures. Thus in 1996 the government launched a campaign to "rectify" qigong associations, removing official recognition from groups that had strayed too far from official Marxism. A large number of qigong masters settled in other countries, opening new mar-kets for qigong's development abroad. In China, qigong circles were divided and disoriented by the criticism and increased control. But one group, Falun gong, though a target of this purge, continued to expand even as its master, Li Hongzhi, fled in 1996 to the United States.

Apocalyptic Qigong

While public opinion turned against the greed and quackery of many mas-ters, Li Hongzhi condemned the commercialization of qigong. Falun gong, the "qigong of the dharma wheel," linked the body cultivation of qigong to a moralistic, messianic, and apocalyptic doctrine. This strategy allowed the method to spread rapidly, attracting millions of qigong adepts, retired people, and marginalized intellectuals. Indeed, by the mid-1990s, the work unit system of lifelong security that had structured the lives of urban Chinese for almost fifty years was beginning to unravel under market-oriented re-forms and an ever-deeper corruption. This was not a time for flights of free-dom in an overstructured environment, like the qigong of the 1980s, but for finding certainty in a disintegrating social world. Exploiting nostalgia for the altruism of the Maoist days, Falun gong organized a movement of resistance against the growing social, moral, and spiritual decadence (Madsen 2000). Around 1994, Li Hongzhi began to teach that the purpose of body cultivation is not good health but spiritual salvation, a goal obtained by passing through the physical and social suffering that can result from practicing the fundamental virtues of truth, compassion, and forbearance. Falling ill, or suffering from the abuse of colleagues, bosses, or the police, became salutary trials through which the practitioner could reimburse his karmic debts. Falun gong no longer presented itself as a qigong method but as the great law or dharma (*fa*) of the universe, a doctrine with its own sacred scripture, *Zhuan Falun* (*Turning the Dharma Wheel;* see their website at www.faludafa.org). This dharma is said to transcend all forms of material organization, to be superior to all philosophies, laws, teachings, religions, and body cultivation methods in the history of humanity, and to offer the only path of salvation from the apocalyptic end of the *kalpa,* or universal cycle, in which the universe is destroyed (Palmer 2001).

There is no training of the breath in Falun gong gymnastics and meditation. Li Hongzhi acknowledges the existence of *qi,* but he claims that it is a lower and impure form of energy that the Falun gong disciple should not pursue. Whereas qigong involved opening the body to the cosmos, "collecting" *qi* from trees, the sun, and the moon, sending and receiving *qi* between practitioners, dabbling in all types of techniques, symbols, and concepts, the Falun gong practitioner must close his body to the lower influences of the world. He should not practice other techniques, nor read other qigong or religious books, nor engage in healing by emission of external *qi*—practices that all lead to possession by demons lurking in other methods, books, and bodies. According to Li Hongzhi, the body contains two types of matter, the demonic "black matter," which is an accumulation of bad karma for sins committed in past and present lives, and the "white matter" of virtue, which increases with good deeds and through the practice of Falun gong. When someone is rude, dishonest, or violent to another, he unwittingly gives his white matter to the victim and absorbs his black matter. All the more so if a Falun gong practitioner is verbally or physically abused while defending the dharma. In order to eliminate the karmic black matter and attain salvation, the disciple should attach himself exclusively to the "great law" or dharma— a connection that is embodied by the swirling Buddhist swastika that Li Hongzhi telepathically implants into the bellies of his followers, and by the countless invisible dharma-bodies with which he protects the sincere

Falun gong followers practice qigong in Hong Kong, April 2001. About twenty members of the Falun gong spiritual movement, outlawed in mainland China, demonstrated in central Hong Kong to press Beijing to stop its campaign of what they say is "unreasonable persecution." The demonstration in Hong Kong, where the group is legal, came on the second anniversary of a mass Falun gong protest in Beijing two years ago, which brought the group to the attention of authorities and led to its banning. (Reuters/Corbis)

practitioner. In Falun gong, then, the body is closed and protected from a demonic outside world; it becomes the site of a moral struggle between right and wrong; and it is viscerally attached to the master and his dharma through the implanted swastika and dharma-bodies. The disciple becomes a "dharma-particle" in the great body of the dharma. Falun gong became a new social body, in which the practitioners' bodies were the theaters of both personal struggle and of the apocalyptic battle between the demonic old world and the righteous dharma (Penny 2002).

The moral rigor, the active missionizing, and the strict discipline of Falun gong's organization allowed it to recruit successfully in all sectors of society, attracting tens of millions of adepts, particularly among retired people. In spite of its illegal status and its occultist philosophy, clearly at odds with the official ideology, Falun gong propagated itself openly and with impunity. Only a handful of journalists and scientists dared to criticize the group in the press, stressing its "superstitious" character and reporting on cases of adepts who had become seriously ill or had even allegedly died as a result of Li Hongzhi's teaching to refuse medical treatment.

At the time he moved his base to the United States, Li Hongzhi explained that salvation could be attained only through the public defense of Falun gong, without fear of the consequences of such action. The network of practice site supervisors was activated to mobilize the practitioners to react against any criticism through letter-writing campaigns, sit-ins, and peaceful protests directed at news media and government offices. The resistance, anchored in public displays of bodies in movement, was spectacular. Thousands of disciplined adepts appeared at strategic times and places, managing to obtain apologies, rectifications, and even—in the case of the Beijing television station—the firing of a critical journalist. Such actions had never before been seen in Communist China: an organized group with tens of millions of potential militants from all social strata and regions that did not hesitate to display its power in the public square and to intimidate the news media—which are, after all, mouthpieces for the party. In the beginning, the authorities were hesitant to intervene. A large number of CCP members were Falun gong adepts or sympathizers. Some leaders considered Falun gong's daily gymnastics a harmless and economical way to keep the masses of Chinese seniors occupied. Others feared the true influence of Falun gong and the risk of alienating Li Hongzhi's tens of millions of disciples.

Following the arrest of a dozen leaders of a Falun gong protest against a Tianjin magazine, however, more than ten thousand adepts silently surrounded the Zhongnanhai compound in Beijing, the nerve center of the party's power, on April 25, 1999. Perceived as a dangerous provocation by President Jiang Zemin, this demonstration triggered the deployment of the party's classic repressive apparatus, through a systematic campaign launched on July 22, 1999, which continues to this day: propaganda, mobilization of official organizations, work camps, psychiatric internment, torture, and so forth. Most Falun gong practitioners immediately gave up the practice, but a minority of adepts remained loyal to Falun gong and, in a spirit of martyrdom, continued to protest the repression, ready to sacrifice their bodies to display the power of Li Hongzhi's great dharma. Most of the other large qigong organizations were discreetly dismantled by the government. Only Falun gong has sur-

APOCALYPTIC QIGONG | 169

vived as an underground resistance movement that continues to flout government repression, under the eye of the international media (Penny 2001).

With the master's exile and the international media coverage of the crackdown, Falun gong became a U.S.-based world movement that presented itself as the innocent victim of a totalitarian genocide. Through the systematic use of protests, the news media, cyberspace, the hijacking of Chinese television signals, and the legal systems of Western countries, Falun gong systematically strove to embarrass party leaders on the world stage and to attract international condemnation of the repression. Today the Communist Party and Falun gong continue to wage a propaganda war before world public opinion, a war that draws heavily on gory images of mutilated bodies (see Powers and Lee 2002). Official Chinese sources show images of alleged Falun gong practitioners who, for instance, set themselves on fire or cut open their bellies to pull out the rotating swastika planted by the master (Eastday.com 2001). Falun gong literature and websites provide photographic documentation of the scarred and burned body parts of tortured practitioners (see www.faluninfo.net).

The CCP is now committed to the complete eradication of Falun gong. Although nonviolence characterizes Falun gong militancy, its symbolic power is all the more disruptive: the Zhongnanhai demonstration, in which thousands of adepts quietly surrounded the heart of the party for a full day, evokes images of a siege or of a strangling. Through this act Falun gong projected the image of a powerful organization, capable of mobilizing the masses, and one that is not afraid of the party. Political power today in China is only partially exercised through a machinery of control; more effective is the subjective perception of its power and the fear of falling into trouble. The reinforcement of such impressions through propaganda and the visible manifestation of power is thus crucially important. The Zhongnanhai demonstration threatened to shatter the fear of the people and to transfer symbolic power to Falun gong. Thus a Chinese practitioner who converted to Falun gong after the demonstration told me, in a menacing tone: "If the Party dares to act against Falun gong, Li Hongzhi will show his power." Indeed, between 1998 and 1999, each Falun gong demonstration seemed to bring about an increase in the number of practitioners.

The history of Chinese sectarianism shows that, if the majority of such groups have not become involved in politics, some, at certain points in their development, have turned into rebel organizations. In like manner Falun gong evolved from a qigong method geared to health and healing to become, in 1994, a doctrine of salvation based on a sacred book; then, beginning in 1996, the path to salvation included the "defense of the dharma" through an activism that would necessarily be interpreted in China as political behavior aimed at confronting and weakening the political order. In the repression campaign, and in Falun gong's response, the historical scenario of the sect rebelling against the state plays itself out once more, each side entrenching itself in its predetermined role and provoking the enemy's retaliation (see the special issue of *Nova Religio* 6.2 [2003] on Falun gong; see also Leung 2002).

Conclusion

The Falun gong conflict can be understood in terms of classical Chinese notions of the body and the state. The Chinese state perceives itself as a single body englobing and organizing the entire society. The center of the social body is the body of the emperor, whose power comes from its virtue derived from heaven, and which flows to the people, uniting their hearts through the ritual ordering of their bodies. This is the enduring inner source of political power, to which the external, military force of the state is but an auxiliary, used to suppress foreign bodies. Falun gong challenged the state's authority and legitimacy on four counts: (1) it attacked the moral corruption and lack of virtue of the party's leaders and presents an alternative source of moral authority in the body of Li Hongzhi and his dharma, thus touching at the very core of political legitimacy; (2) around the master's moral authority, and against the corruption of society, Falun gong formed a new social body, a foreign organism that challenged the unitary nature of the state; (3) the public protests and displays of Falun gong—notably the Zhongnanhai incident and other demonstrations before and after it, disrupted the state's ritual ordering of space and bodies and undermined its symbolic power; and (4) the deployment of a massive material apparatus of state propaganda and repression, and its inability to crush the bodies of practitioners, revealed the inner weakness of a political formation that, unable to base itself on a higher moral ground, could only resort to the tried and tested methods of Leninist political campaigns.

This chapter began with an overview of traditional Chinese notions of body cultivation and then showed how body cultivation evolved in the People's Republic of China through the modern qigong movement. In the 1950s and early 1960s, body cultivation was reformulated and institutionalized as part of the communist state's project of developing the health of the masses and of extracting and transforming all useful elements of traditional culture in the service of building the New China. During the Cultural Revolution body cultivation was banned, but the mass qigong model, pioneered by Guo Lin, was born. In the 1980s qigong underwent a shift from social utopia to the individual body and became a pathway to inner freedom and alternative worlds, often expressed in a religious idiom and symbolism, within the interstices of the state. Although still promoted and monitored by the state, qigong in that period increasingly escaped state control and became the locus for alternative networks of masters and practitioners. In the 1990s those networks gave birth to autonomous social bodies in the form of organized commercial or sectarian groups, one of which, Falun gong, became the focal point of resistance to the state and to the destabilization and corruption of a rapidly changing society. Each phase of Chinese socialist modernity—from its period of utopian state-construction to its postrevolutionary and market-driven phases—witnessed the appearance of new mutations of the Chinese tradition of body cultivation and, through them, different uses of religious symbols and forms of social organization, and a different relationship between the individual body and the body politic.

References

Chen, Nancy. 1995. "Urban Spaces and Experiences of *Qigong*." Pp. 347–361 in *Urban Spaces in Contemporary China.* Edited by Deborah Davis, Richard Kraus, Barry Naughton, and Elizabeth Perry. Washington, DC and Cambridge: Woodrow Wilson Center Press and Cambridge University Press.

———. 2003. *Breathing Spaces: Qigong, Psychiatry, and Healing in China.* New York: Columbia University Press.

Cohen, Paul. 1997. *History in Three Keys: The Boxers as Event, Experience, and Myth.* New York: Columbia University Press.

Croizier, Ralph. 1968. *Traditional Medicine in Modern China: Science, Nationalism, and the Tensions of Cultural Change.* Cambridge: Harvard University Press.

Despeux, Catherine. 1997. "Le *qigong,* une expression de la modernité chinoise." Pp. 267–281 in *En suivant la voie royale: mélanges en hommage à Léon Vandermeersch.* Edited by Jacques Gernet and Marc Kalinowski. Paris: École française d'Extrême-Orient.

Eastday.com. 2001. "Another Falun Gong Follower Set Himself Ablaze." http://english.eastday.com/epublish/gb/paper9/18/class000900002/hwz21198.htm (accessed on February 18, 2004).

Esherick, Joseph. 1987. *The Origins of the Boxer Uprising.* Berkeley: University of California Press.

Heise, Thomas. 1999. *Qigong in der VR China: Entwicklung, Theorie und Praxis.* Berlin: Verlag für Wissenschaft und Bildung.

Hsu, Elizabeth. 1999. *The Transmission of Chinese Medicine.* Cambridge: Cambridge University Press.

Kohn, Livia. 2002. "Quiet Sitting with Master Yinshi: The Beginnings of *Qigong* in Modern China." Pp. 90–99 in *Living with the Dao: Conceptual Issues in Taoist Practice* by Livia Kohn. Cambridge, MA: Three Pines Press. Originally published as "Quiet Sitting with Master Yinshi: Medicine and Religion in Modern China." *Zen Buddhism Today* 10: 79–95.

Leung, Beatrice. 2002. "China and Falun Gong: Party and Society Relations in the Modern Era." *Journal of Contemporary China* 11.33: 761–784.

Madsen, Richard. 2000. "Understanding Falun Gong." *Current History* 99. 638: 243–247.

Micollier, Evelyne. 1999. "Contrôle ou libération des émotions dans le contexte des pratiques de santé *qigong*." *Perspectives Chinoises* 53: 22–30.

Ots, Thomas. 1994. "The Silenced Body—The Expressive *Leib*: On the Dialectic of Mind and Life in Chinese Cathartic Healing." Pp. 116–136 in *Embodiment and Experience: The Existential Ground of Culture and Self.* Edited by Thomas Csordas. Cambridge: Cambridge University Press.

Ownby, David. 2003. "A History for Falun Gong: Popular Religion and the Chinese State since the Ming Dynasty." *Nova Religio* 6.2: 223–243.

Palmer, David A. 2001. "The Doctrine of Li Hongzhi. Falun Gong: Between Sectarianism and Universal Salvation." *China Perspectives* 35: 14–23.

———. 2003a. "Modernity and Millennialism in China: *Qigong* and the Birth of Falun Gong." *Asian Anthropology* 2: 79–110.

———. 2003b. "Le *qigong* et la tradition sectaire chinoise." *Social Compass* 50.4: 471–480.

———. 2005. *La "fièvre du* qigong." *Guérison, religion et politique en Chine, 1949–1999.* Paris: Éditions de l'École des hautes études en sciences sociales.

———. 2006. *Qigong Fever: Body, Science, and the Politics of Religion in China, 1949–1999.* London: Hurst.

Penny, Benjamin. 1993. "*Qigong*, Daoism, and Science: Some Contexts for the *Qigong* Boom." Pp. 166–179 in *Modernization of the Chinese Past.* Edited by Mabel Lee and A. D. Syrokomla-Stefanowska. Sydney: Wild Peony.

———. 2001. "Challenging the Mandate of Heaven—Popular Protest in Modern China." *Critical Asian Studies* 33.2: 163–180.

———. 2002. "The Body of Master Li." Unpublished paper, Australian Religious Studies Association. Available online at http://users.senet.com.au/~nhabel/Lectures/penny.pdf (accessed November 2003).

Powers, John, and Meg Y. M. Lee. 2002. "Dueling Media: Symbolic Conflict in China's Falun Gong Suppression Campaign." Pp. 259–274 in *Chinese Conflict Management and Resolution.* Edited by Guo-Ming Chen and Ringo Ma. Westport, CN, and London: Ablex.

Robinet, Isabelle. 1997. *Taoism: Growth of a Religion.* Stanford: Stanford University Press.

Schipper, Kristofer. 1993. *The Taoist Body.* Berkeley: University of California Press.

Sima Nan. 1995. *Shengong neimu* [The inside story on miraculous qigong]. Beijing: Zhongguo shehui chubanshe.

Unschuld, Paul. 1985. *Medicine in China: A History of Ideas.* Berkeley: University of California Press.

Xu Jian. 1999. "Body, Discourse, and the Cultural Politics of Contemporary Chinese *Qigong.*" *Journal of Asian Studies* 58.4: 961–991.

Zhu Xiaoyang. (1994/1989). "Spirit and Flesh, Sturm und Drang." Translated from *Shidai Chinese Sociology and Anthropology* 27.1: 35–47.

Zhu Xiaoyang and Benjamin Penny. 1994. "Introduction." In *The Qigong Boom.* Edited by Zhu Xiaoyang and Benjamin Penny. *Chinese Sociology and Anthropology* 27.1.

8

Protestant Christianity in Contemporary China

FRANCIS CHING-WAH YIP

OBSERVERS OF THE contemporary religious scene in China can hardly fail to notice the phenomenal growth of Protestant Christianity. "Today, on any given Sunday there are almost certainly more Protestants in church in China than in all of Europe" (Bays 2003, 488). According to a recent estimate, from 1949 to the turn of the century the number of Catholics in China increased from 3 million to more than 12 million, "surpassing the number of Catholics in Ireland." During the same period, the Protestant population has grown even faster, "multiplying from 1 million to at least 30 million adherents" (Kindopp 2004a, 1–2). The growth of the Protestant population has been much faster than that of the overall population in post-1949 China (Hunter and Chan 1993, 71). Such growth is especially remarkable considering the tremendous difficulties faced by Christians in China, especially during the first three decades of the People's Republic.

This chapter introduces Protestant Christianity in contemporary China in its historical, political, and religious-cultural contexts. It begins with an outline of the history of Christianity in China, with a special emphasis on the twentieth century, and briefly introduces the political and institutional framework related to Protestant Christianity. This is followed by an overview of the statistics and characteristics of the Protestant population in China today, and then a description and analysis of the various forms of Protestant Christianity in contemporary China. Instead of the usual dichotomy between the official "Three-Self" churches and the "house churches," it suggests several means of analyzing Protestant communities in China and depicts them using a fourfold typology. The emergence of new sects and cults, as well as so-called cultural Christians, will also be briefly mentioned. Finally a special instance is related of inter-religious encounter—Chinese Protestantism and Chinese popular religion.

Historical and Political Background

Early Encounters

Christianity came to China in several waves (see LeMond 1997). The first Christian missionary to China was not Roman Catholic or Eastern Orthodox or even Protestant, but rather a Nestorian monk named Alopen. Nestorian Christianity took its name from its founder, Nestorius, a Syrian monk from Antioch who became the patriarch of Constantinople. Emphasizing the distinction between Christ's divine and human natures, he opposed the use of the title "Mother of God" (*Theotokos* in Greek) for the Virgin Mary. He was excommunicated in 431 by the Council of Ephesus, which was dominated by his rival, Cyril, the patriarch of Alexandria. He died in exile in the Egyptian desert in 451 (Moffett 1998, 169–184). His influence continued in what was called "the East Syrian church," "the Persian church," or "the Assyrian Church of the East." Alopen, a Nestorian monk, traveled from Persia along the ancient Silk Road and in 635 came to Chang'an, the capital of the Tang dynasty in China. The Tang emperor Taizong tolerated the new religion and even ordered the building of a Nestorian church in the capital. As a famous memorial tablet erected in 781 shows, Jinjiao (as the religion was called in Chinese) adopted Buddhist terminology to express its theology. Nestorian Christianity in China flourished until 845, when the Tang emperor Wuzong, who favored Daoism, suppressed Buddhism and other foreign religions (ibid., 287–314; Whyte 1988, 31–40).

While Nestorian Christianity disappeared in China, it still continued among some Central Asian tribes. People from these Christian tribes, notably the Keraits, later became members of the royal family of the Mongolian empire through intermarriage. This included Sorkaktani, the daughter-in-law of Genghis Khan and the mother of Kublai Khan, a great ruler of the Yuan dynasty (1279–1368) in China. During Kublai Khan's reign Nestorian Christianity flourished once again, with the capital Khanbaliq (present-day

Illustration from a seventeenth-century Chinese manuscript of the Jesuit missionary to China, Matteo Ricci, and his first convert. (Hulton Archive/Getty Images)

Beijing) being a metropolitan see. The Yuan dynasty also saw the first arrival of European Christians in China, including Marco Polo, his father, and his uncle. The first Roman Catholic missionary to reach China was John of Montecorvino, a Franciscan who became the first archbishop in China. Both Roman Catholic and Nestorian Christianity disappeared when the Chinese drove out the Mongols and established the Ming dynasty (1368–1644) (Moffett 1998, 442–475; Whyte 1988, 40–48).

Christian missionaries were unable to establish a long-term presence in the Chinese empire until 1582, when the Jesuit Matteo Ricci arrived in southern China. Erudite in both European science and Chinese thought, he successfully won converts in the imperial court, including Xu Guangqi. For Ricci and other Jesuits, Christianity was in harmony with and fulfilled Confucianism. Rituals that honored Confucius and venerated one's ancestors were considered traditional Chinese customs. That view was later challenged, however, by the Dominicans and Franciscans, who regarded such rituals as idolatrous religious practices. The dispute, known as the Rites Controversy, intensified in the early decades of the Qing dynasty (1644–1911). The pope eventually prohibited the participation of Chinese Catholics in such rituals. The Chinese emperor Kangxi felt offended by such foreign intervention as a sign of contempt for traditional Chinese customs. His successor, Yongzheng, issued an edict in 1724 banning Christianity in China. The ban continued until the last decades of the Qing dynasty, when the Western powers militarily forced the opening of China (Whyte 1988, 49–80).

Protestantism in Pre-1949 China

The modern encounter of China with Christianity was, unfortunately, made possible by imperialism, a fact especially important to our understanding of Protestant Christianity in post-1949 China (see Lutz 2001). The first Protestant missionary to enter China, Robert Morrison of the London Missionary Society, arrived in 1807 in Guangzhou, the only port open to foreign trade. He was allowed to stay only because he was an interpreter with the East India Company, which brought opium to China. He and those who came later faced serious difficulties. The turning point was 1842, when China was forced to sign a treaty that ceded the island of Hong Kong to Britain and opened five treaty ports for foreign trade and residence after its defeat in the First Opium War, by which Britain retaliated against China for attempting to eradicate the illegal importation of opium. Subsequent defeats forced China to sign similar treaties with other foreign powers, including the United States, France, Germany, and Russia. In addition to seizing territorial rights, extraterritoriality, and economic privileges, these unequal treaties also gave freedom and protection to Christian missionaries. Numerous European and U.S. mission groups took the opportunity to enter China, including both denominational missions and nondenominational mission organizations, such as the China Inland Mission, founded by Hudson Taylor. Besides engaging in direct evangelism and social services, they also set up schools and universities, published newspapers, and translated books that introduced Western thought to China. Christianity, especially Protestantism, thus contributed much to the societal and cultural modernization of China. It is also worth noting that several leaders of the series of revolutions that eventually overthrew the monarchy in 1911 and established the Republic of China were Protestant Christians. Yet Christianity's close ties with Western powers often invited the charge of its being a collaborator with imperialism. The title of a 1922 survey report, *The Christian Occupation of China,* added more credibility to the charge. An anti-Christian movement arose with a growing nationalism that demanded an end to persistent foreign domination (Whyte 1988, 95–159; Leung 1988, 34–153).

It was within such an atmosphere that Protestantism in China moved toward greater indigenization. Many Protestant denominations added the term *Zhonghua* ("Chinese") to their official names. The National Christian Council was established, with Chinese Protestants taking up leadership roles. Some denominations, particularly those with a Presbyterian or Congregational background, united to form the Church of Christ in China, the largest denomination in China before 1949. There were also attempts at the indigenization of theology and liturgy. Yet the mainline Protestant denominations remained dependent in various ways—financially, organizationally, and the like—on Western missionary societies. Meanwhile, a sector of Chinese Protestantism that was "independent of foreign missions, autonomous in operations, and indigenous in ideas and leadership" (Bays 1996, 309) developed on Chinese soil. It included federations of independent congregations, such as the China Christian Independent Church (Zhongguo Yesujiao zhilihui); independent churches, such as the True Jesus Church (characterized by its Pentecostalism and antiforeignism); the Jesus Family (strongly millenarian, communitarian, and Pentecostal); and the Local Assemblies or Little Flock (founded by Ni Tuosheng, better known in English as Watchman Nee; the Local Assemblies were influenced by the Brethrens and Holiness traditions). There were also influential evangelists and revivalists, such as Wang Mingdao and Song Shangjie (John Sung) (ibid., 310–316; see also Hunter and Chan 1993, 119–123; Leung 1988, 156–171). "In the 1940s, the various independent Chinese Protestants may have accounted for 20–25 percent of all Protestants" (Bays 1996, 310).

Protestantism in China after 1949: The Formation of the Three-Self Patriotic Movement

The victory of the Chinese Communist Party (CCP) and the establishment of the People's Republic of China (PRC) in 1949 brought seismic changes to the religious situation that surpassed even the disruption caused by Japan's invasion of China (1937–1945) and the civil war (1945–1949). To attain the revolutionary goals of liberating China from feudalism, imperialism, and capitalism, the CCP sought to bring all aspects of society and culture—including religion—under its effective control. The official Marxist ideology regarded religion as a symptom of the presocialist society, and even as the "opium of the people." Christianity was even more problematic because, according to the CCP, which was zealously nationalistic, the Western religion had been a collaborator and a tool of imperialism. However, under the CCP's strategy of the united front, which emphasized "seeking the common ground, while reserving differences" (Wickeri 1988, xxi), Christianity could be tolerated by the atheistic party and would not be considered an enemy of the Chinese people if it were "patriotic"—that is, if it cut off all ties with the West and actively followed the political leadership of the CCP. This was part of the background to the formation of the Three-Self Patriotic Movement.

The idea that a church should be self-governing, self-supporting, and self-propagating (thus Three-Self) originated from two nineteenth-century missionary administrators. Some Chinese Protestants advocated similar ideas in the late nineteenth century (ibid., 36–41). After 1949 the idea was taken up by Protestant leaders who turned it into a "patriotic movement." Under the encouragement of the CCP, a group of Protestant leaders led by Wu Yaozong (Y. T. Wu) launched a nationwide signature campaign asking leaders of the Protestant community to endorse a document commonly known as the "Christian Manifesto" (Jones 1963, 19–20), which emphasized that the Chinese Protestant church had to purge itself of all imperialist influences and to fulfill the goal of self-government, self-support, and self-propagation within the shortest possible time (Jones 1962, 54–55; Ying and Leung 1996, 36–38).

Anti-imperialism intensified as the Korean War broke out in June 1950. The whole nation, including Christians, rallied against the United States. In April 1951 the government called a meeting of Protestant leaders in which the Chinese churches were required to sever immediately and completely all links with missionary boards, including personnel and financial support. The meeting established a Preparatory Committee of the Chinese Protestant Resist America Aid Korea Three-Self Reform Movement, a new structure to lead the Protestant churches, replacing existing ecumenical institutions. This was the prototype of the National Committee of the Three-Self Patriotic Movement (TSPM) established at the national Protestant conference in 1954 (Xu 2004, 115–116; Whyte 1988, 230–233; Ying and Leung 1996, 51–62). Similar Three-Self organizations were set up at provincial and municipal levels. They became the official interface between the party-state and the Protestant churches.

Protestantism under Leftist Politics

The April 1951 meeting launched a "denunciation movement" that soon spread nationwide. U.S. missionaries and Chinese Protestant leaders were singled out and publicly criticized in denunciation meetings by their former colleagues and associates for being "running dogs" of U.S. imperialism and enemies of the nation. Study classes for thought reform and re-education began to be held in many places (Ying and Leung 1996, 67–79; Wickeri 1988, 134–146; Whyte 1988, 221–226, 229; Jones 1962, 63–76). Within such a hostile atmosphere, most missionaries had left the country by 1952 (Hunter and Chan 1993, 24). Indigenous and independent Protestant churches such as the Jesus Family, the True Jesus Church, and the Little Flock—which did not rely on foreign personnel or financial support—were also under attack, and their chief leaders were arrested. A few years later, Wang Mingdao and a few other influential preachers who refused to cooperate with the TSPM were charged with "counter-revolutionary" crimes and were imprisoned (Wickeri 1988, 157–168; Whyte 1988, 240–244; Jones 1962, 102–111; Ying and Leung 1996, 92–97). In the late 1950s, many more church leaders, including those within the TSPM structure, were denounced for being "rightists" or "reactionaries."

The 1950s saw a shrinking of institutional Protestantism in China. Schools, hospitals, and social services, which had relied heavily on overseas funding, were either disbanded or taken over by the government. Others, such as theological seminaries and publishing houses, were turned over to the TSPM. Many were eliminated because of mergers. The number of churches was greatly reduced after the Great Leap Forward in 1958 as pastors were required to engage in "material production," churches were closed, and church buildings were confiscated or given to other work units. Denominations, seen as a vestige of imperialism, were eliminated as churches were consolidated and worship rituals unified (Xu 2004, 116–117; Kindopp 2004b, 124–126; Hunter and Chan 1993, 24–25; Deng 1997, 96–102).

During the Cultural Revolution (1966–1976), especially during the early chaotic years, all institutional religious activities disappeared. Church buildings were confiscated, converted for other uses, damaged, or even destroyed. Protestant ministers, including TSPM leaders, were physically abused, publicly ridiculed, sent to the countryside for labor reform, removed from their homes, or confined in ad hoc prisons. Many Christians were tortured, their homes ransacked, and their religious books burned. Yet many of the faithful continued to gather at home to worship. The growth of such home gatherings laid a foundation for the phenomenal church growth after the Cultural Revolution (Wickeri 1988, 179–187; Whyte 1988, 288–304, 316–340; Kindopp 2004b, 126).

Protestantism after the Cultural Revolution

The death of Mao Zedong and the arrest of the Gang of Four in 1976 put an end to the Cultural Revolution. The political victory of Deng Xiaoping at the Third Plenum of the Eleventh Central Committee of the CCP in December 1978 brought a decisive reversal to the leftist policies. Economic development and modernization, rather than continuous revolution and class struggle, became the paramount goal of the party-state. Economic reform and the "open door" became a long-term policy. The market economy and other measures that encouraged individual initiative were gradually introduced and expanded. The control of the party-state in many aspects of society was relaxed. Administrative structures related to the implementation of religious policies, such as the United Front Work Department (UFWD) and the Religious Affairs Bureau (RAB), were re-established, and churches began to reopen. The Third

National Christian Conference, held in 1980, revitalized the TSPM organization and created the China Christian Council (CCC), which takes care of pastoral and ecclesiastical matters, while the TSPM continues its political roles. Bishop Ding Guangxun (K. H. Ting) was both the chairperson of TSPM and the president of the CCC. On the initiative of Ding and others, the Amity Foundation, an organization committed to channeling the resources of overseas churches in support of education, health, social welfare, and Bible printing in China, was founded in 1985. In 1991, the CCC became a member of the World Council of Churches (Lambert 1994, 26–50, 266; Wickeri 1988, 185–190; Whyte 1988, 322–354, 420–422; Hunter and Chan 1993, 79–80). In 1996 the Chinese Christian Church Order, which provides a unified and binding framework of church governance and ministry, was adopted by the Sixth National Christian Conference (ANS 1996a; 1997; see also Chao and Chong [1997] for a history of Protestantism in China after 1949 from a perspective sympathetic to, and hence with more information on, the house churches).

Political and Institutional Framework

In addition to Catholicism, Daoism, Buddhism, and Islam, Protestantism is one of the five legitimate religions recognized by the PRC. While it is tolerated, it is subject to various forms of control by the party-state. In China, it is the CCP that holds the real power and formulates policies to be implemented by the state. The most important policy document on religion is what is known as Document 19 (MacInnis 1989, 8–26), issued by the Central Committee of the CCP in 1982. It states that patriotic believers can and must form a united front in the common effort for socialist modernization. Freedom of religious belief is protected—which is also stated in Article 36 of the constitution of the PRC—but it is relegated to private life. The same article in the constitution also asserts that the state protects "normal religious activities," a phrase often used in Document 19. Since what is "normal" is not explicitly defined, it is left to the decision of the political authorities, subject to the prevailing political climate. While religious activities on a family basis are tolerated, Protestant gatherings in homes for worship should not be allowed in principle, though they should not be rigidly prohibited. Criminal and anti-revolutionary activities done under the guise of religion are to be suppressed. All patriotic religious associations (including the TSPM) should follow the leadership of the party and the government and should assist them in the implementation of religious policies (Hunter and Chan 1993, 48–51; Spiegel 2004, 41–44; Lambert 1994, 51–57).

After 1989, the CCP was more concerned about foreign and domestic hostile forces that might undermine its rule. The subversive potential of religion was demonstrated in the events in Eastern Europe. In such an atmosphere, Document 6, promulgated in 1991, prescribed more legal restrictions on religions, while the basic tenets of Document 19 were upheld. The central government issued several regulations in the mid-1990s governing the religious activities of foreign nationals and the registration, management, and inspection of religious venues. Nonregistered religious venues were proclaimed illegal and could be shut down. In 2000 a Ministry of Public Security document made use of a new definition of "heretical cults," originally formulated to eradicate the Falun gong, to characterize as "cults" fourteen Protestant groups and their offshoots. Besides these policy documents and national regulations, provincial and municipal authorities also issue various regulations and implementation rules governing religious activities (see Lambert 1994, 69–70 for some common stipulations in local regulations). The TSPM also gives guidance on matters such as what is a proper sermon; in addition, it attacks unorthodox beliefs and reminds local churches not to baptize minors (Spiegel 2004, 44–48).

The CCP's policy on religion, as part of the strategy of a united front, is carried out by the party's UFWD, which has branches at various administrative levels, and by the government's RAB (now renamed as State Administration for Religious Affairs), which has branches in provinces and major cities. The RAB is responsible, for example, for the administrative control of religious venues. Also involved in the implementation of religious policy is the Public Security Bureau (PSB) at all administrative levels, which is responsible for cracking down on "illegal" religious activities, often by arrests and fines. Church affairs are managed by the TSPM and CCC, known collectively in Chinese as the "two committees" (lianghui). From the 1980s onward, the TSPM/CCC have done a lot for the development of the church, such as the opening of churches, the printing of Bibles, the provision of theological education, and the launching of social services. The UFWD and the RAB are involved in the appointment of the leaders and members of the two committees. Some of them are believed to be party members or appointees. However, the TSPM/CCC are not totally subservient to the control of the party-state; they have some capacity to represent the Protestant churches, such as in negotiating for the return of church property (Hunter and Chan 1993, 53–64).

The Protestant Population in Today's China

How many Protestant Christians are there in China? There is no reliable answer to that question. According to 1999 official statistics, there were more than 13 million Protestants, not including those not yet registered, and each year 500,000 to 600,000 people are newly baptized. There were 1,300 pastors (300 of them were women) serving 13,000 churches and 27,000 meeting points (congregations without a regular pastor) (CTR 2000, 155). In 2004 the official estimate of the number of Protestants went up to over 16 million, with more than 70 percent living in the countryside. There were altogether 50,000 churches and meeting points (Overview 2004). However, the actual number of believers must be higher, as many of them go to what are called house churches—that is, churches and meeting points not registered or affiliated with the TSPM/CCC. The PSB in 1995 noted that Protestants numbered 25 million (Yamamori and Chan 2000, xiv), which seems to have included Protestants outside the official TSPM/CCC umbrella. People associated with or sympathetic to house churches gave even higher estimates, with claims of the number of Protestants in house churches alone ranging from 60 to 80 million. But, as the analyst who mentions such claims concludes, it is "virtually impossible to make an accurate estimate of the total number of house church believers in China" based on the available evidence: "[T]here are tens of thousands of smaller groupings and individual isolated meeting points," and no one can visit them all (Lambert 2003, 8–10). A further complication is that even if we have accurate figures for Protestants in house churches, as well as those under the TSPM/CCC umbrella, we still cannot get an accurate figure for the total number of Protestants, because there are people attending both TSPM/CCC churches and the house churches. A former house church member says: "In my experience as a house church participant for years, there is a huge overlap of those who go to both open churches and house churches" (Wang 1997, 180). Thus we have to take any estimate of the total number of Protestants in China with great caution. In any case, Protestants clearly outnumber Catholics, estimated today to be about 10 million. That is in contrast to the situation before 1949, when there were about 3 million Catholics but only 700,000 to 1 million Protestants (Bays 2003, 491). This might be partly explained by the relative "flexibility" of Protestantism, which can depend heavily, if not totally, on laypeople and can function anywhere, with or without a roof (see Leung 1999, 225).

What we know with a greater certainty is the uneven geographical distribution of Protestant Christians in China. They concentrate mainly in three regions. The central Chinese provinces of Henan and Anhui have the largest Protestant populations. TSPM estimates from the late 1990s for the two provinces are 5 million and 3 million, respectively. The second region is the coastal provinces of Zhejiang (1,500,000), Jiangsu (1 million), Shandong (800,000), and Fujian (700,000). The third region is the ethnic minority areas in southwest China, such as Yunnan (800,000) and Guizhou (360,000). (The provincial figures are from the table, compiled from various official sources, in Lambert 2003, 8. See also Lambert 1994, 155, for a map.)

The Protestant population is only a tiny minority of the total population in China. Even if we take an estimate of, say, 30 million Protestants, it is still just 2.3 percent of the total population (nearly 1.3 billion). In some areas, however, the Protestant population is higher. For example, 2.8 percent of the population of Zhejiang province is Protestant Christian. Within the province, the Protestant population in Wenzhou city is 9 percent and in Dongtou county, 12 percent (CTR 2000, 154).

The majority of the Protestant population consists of four overlapping groups: rural people, illiterate and semi-illiterate people, elderly people, and women (Ying 2001, 286). More than 70 percent of the total Protestant population are rural (Overview 2004, 154). In Henan, Zhejiang, and Jiangsu, the three provinces with the largest number of Protestant Christians, rural people constitute 80 to 90 percent of the Protestant population (Ying 2001, 289). A 1995 survey revealed that in Henan, people with a low level of education (including the illiterate and those with only primary education) constituted 51 percent of the total population, while Protestants with a low level of education formed 88 percent of the total Protestant population. In Zhejiang, 23 percent of the population was illiterate or semi-illiterate in 1990. But in the case of Protestants, illiteracy was more than 70 percent in 1991 and 55 percent in 1995. Big cities were not much better. However, the situation seems to be improving (Ying 2001, 294–295). The aging trend of the overall Chinese population also occurs among Protes-

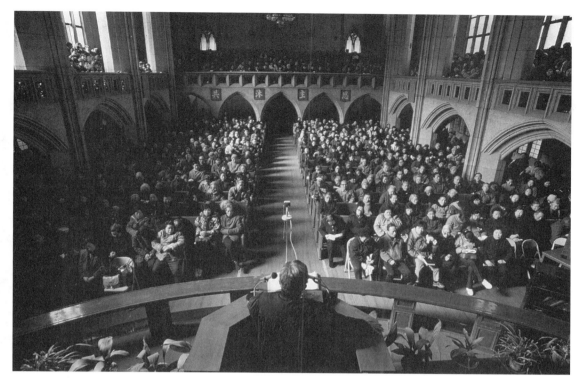

A service at the Protestant church on Xizang Zonglu Road, Shanghai. The church, known as the International Church, is very popular. (Bojan Brecelj/Corbis)

tants. Take Shanghai city as an example: a study of 12,000 Protestants baptized there between 1980 and 1990 in five churches showed that 63 percent were over sixty, while only 17 percent were below forty. But the proportion of the younger generation seems to be on the increase. A 1997 survey showed that the youth population (between eighteen and thirty-nine) was 30 percent, while those over sixty was 34 percent. According to a recent survey in Hubei province, 26 percent were over sixty-five, while young people (between eighteen and thirty) constituted 13 percent; 2 percent were children (ibid., 296), despite the official prohibition against the proselytization of minors. Another scholar predicts that the expansion of the market economy and the social mobility it entails might increase the numbers of young people, people with more education, and professionals joining the urban churches (Dunch 2001, 203).

Varieties of Protestantism in China

China is a large country with a geographic area similar to that of the United States. A Chinese province may have the size and population of a country in Europe, and thus it is easy for outsiders to overlook the great economic, social, ethnographic, linguistic, and cultural diversity in China. The Chinese population is composed of the Han Chinese and minority ethnic groups. Even among the Han Chinese, who share a common written language, there is an enormous diversity of spoken Chinese, sometimes even within a province. There is a rich regional and local diversity in culture. On the socioeconomic scene, traditional subsistence farming in central China goes hand in hand with modern industrial capitalism in the coastal cities. Rich entrepreneurs who consume expensive health supplements coexist with farmers who cannot afford the medical costs associated with a minor illness. Such social and cultural diversities correlate with varieties in religion.

Adding to the complexity are the variations in the implementation of official policies in different locations. The policies and decisions of the central government in Beijing might be variously interpreted and implemented by local officials in various provinces, cities, and counties. In areas where local officials take a leftist approach to religion, even Christian activities organized by a registered TSPM/CCC church may be suppressed. In some other areas officials have good relationships with Christians; even the unregistered house churches may be allowed to flourish. Thus, as the authors of a masterful study of Protestantism in contemporary China remind us, "to speak of 'Christianity in China' is only useful at a high level of abstraction, as when talking of 'Christianity in Europe'" (Hunter and Chan 1993, 9). The account of Protestantism in China being outlined in this chapter can be only a highly generalized account of a highly complex reality.

Aspects for Analysis

Inadequate Views

Two different views of Protestantism in China are frequently expressed. The first view, shared by some overseas evangelical groups, posits two separate and opposing systems of Protestantism: the Three-Self churches versus the house churches. On the one hand, there are the churches under the control of

TSPM/CCC organizations. They are considered more loyal to the communist party-state than to God. What they have done is seen at best as a strategy of survival and at worst as a betrayal of their Christian faith. On the other hand, there are the house churches, which are believed to be the majority of Protestant communities in China. They are regarded as the only embodiment of authentic Christianity in China. They suffer persecution because they refuse to compromise their faith.

The second view, advocated by TSPM leaders and their sympathizers, underscores the TSPM as a patriotic movement that has helped Protestantism cut its ties with imperialism and become truly Chinese. The existence of unregistered house churches is downplayed, and their alleged hostility toward the TSPM is dismissed. House churches are Christian home gatherings that emerged for the sake of convenience, inasmuch as churches are not sufficient in number and often too far away for many people, especially those in the countryside. Persecutions are explained as occasional aberrations of the established policy of religious freedom or as lawful actions against illegal activities in the guise of religion.

A Nuanced View

Both views oversimplify the reality. A more nuanced view should begin by differentiating the various aspects or dimensions of Protestantism in contemporary China. The following aspects, among others, can be considered when analyzing a Protestant community in China:

Historical origins: whether the community is the legacy of a Western mission or of indigenous Protestant movements in China;

Institutional affiliation: whether the community is affiliated with the TSPM/CCC establishment, and the extent to which it is subject to the latter's control;

Church-state relation: the community's relation to the party-state;

Geographical position: the community's position on the urban-rural spectrum;

Religious form: whether the community's beliefs and practices belong to an official or popular form of Protestantism;

Theological orientation: the characteristics of the community's theology.

The next two sections describe varieties of Protestantism in China today.

Types of Protestant Communities in China

Three-Self versus House Church?

We begin with the commonplace bifurcation between Three-Self churches and house churches. These are convenient labels with which to designate Protestant communities that are registered or affiliated with the TSPM/CCC establishment and those that are not. But the labels are not adequate. The term "Three-Self" was originally used to describe a church that was self-governing, self-supporting, and self-propagating. If we take this original sense, then the houses churches are as much Three-Self as those churches within the TSPM/CCC hierarchy. The term "official church," which is sometimes used (for example, Hunter and Chan 1993), can be a good alternative, if it is not confused with the term "state church." Similarly, we may consider using the term "established church," which refers to a church officially recognized by the state and supported by civil authority, if we make it clear that it does not refer to a church of the "official religion," which simply does not exist in China. The term "house churches" is even less adequate, as some of them are actually meetings of several hundred people in the open or in large self-constructed church buildings. Thus the term "autonomous Christian communities" was suggested as a more adequate alternative (ibid., 81).

The Three-Self churches and the house churches are often seen as rival camps. That may be true when leaders of a local TSPM organization collaborate with the local PSB to suppress autonomous Christian communities that might be seen as potential threats, socially or religiously. It may also be true in cases when leaders of an autonomous community refuse to join the TSPM/CCC because they regard it as a state apparatus to persecute true Christians. But between these two extremes there are instances of peaceful coexistence and even tacit cooperation.

> For example, many TSPM pastors have more sympathy for the autonomous leaders than for their own hierarchy, and take opportunities to protect them. On the other hand, many house church members have no particular objection to the official church, but either have practical difficulty in attending services there or seek something more or something different. At a local level the two groups co-exist and many people participate in both (ibid., 87).

A Fourfold Typology

It would be helpful, therefore, to differentiate the types of the Protestant communities, instead of forcing them into the dichotomy of Three-Self or house church. A Hong Kong scholar has distinguished four types (Leung 1999, 50–52):

1. Churches under the administration of TSPM/CCC. They usually have church buildings and are served by full-time ministers. Most are found in big cities, but some are in counties with a large Protestant population. They are directly under a TSPM/CCC organization and subject to its regulation.

2. Meeting points under the authority of TSPM/CCC. Some of these are in cities, but most are located in a suburb that is not remote. They have a fixed venue for meetings, but not necessarily a church building. They might be served by regular volunteers but rarely by full-time ministers with formal theological training. Many of them are under the supervision of a TSPM-administered church, whose clergy will regularly come to administer Holy Communion and to train volunteers. Most of these meeting points are registered, but some are refused registration by the local government.

3. Semi-independent rural meeting points. Most of these meeting-points were set up by lay people after the 1950s or by itinerant evangelists or laypersons after the 1980s. Most of them do not object to having some connection with the TSPM/CCC. They might have registered with the government, or they might want to register but have been refused. Since many of them are located in remote rural or mountainous areas, they do not get much support from the TSPM/CCC, even if they have joined it. For practical reasons, their members and natural leaders might not be willing to be controlled by the TSPM/CCC.

4. Urban and rural meeting points that are unregistered and refuse to join TSPM/CCC. Many of these meeting points were set up by pastors or lay people who suffered persecution in the 1950s and 1960s. They refuse to join the TSPM, as they regard it as a tool for the government to eradicate Christianity. The sectarian and exclusivist position of indigenous Protestant communities, such as the Little Flock and the True Jesus Church, from which some of these meeting points originate, also leads to their uncooperative stance toward the TSPM. Some of them were set up by itinerant evangelists after the 1980s. As

their evangelizing was deemed illegal, they have been marginalized, suppressed, or even arrested, thus accounting for their opposition to the authorities. Only this type constitute the house churches that are in principle opposed to the TSPM.

Besides the usual focus on the institutional affiliation with TSPM/CCC, this typology of Protestant communities in China also brings in the urban-rural dichotomy, which largely explains many differences among the communities (Lambert 1994, 133; Bays 2003, 497).

> Except for the urban-rural dichotomy in Protestantism in China—which accounts for different levels of affluence, education and openness to Western ideas—almost *all* forms of Protestant Christianity in China tend to be evangelical, lay centred, non-liturgical, decentralised, diffuse, and influenced by both Western theologies and Chinese cultural traditions (Wickeri 1994, 15).

Protestant Communities in China Today

Type 1 churches—and to some extent, type 2—have inherited the legacy of the Western missions. Compared with the other types, their services are more liturgical, their congregational participation more restrained. The services look similar to those of the European and U.S. traditions. Many hymns are well-known British or U.S. classics, sung, sometimes by choirs, in the original tunes and with translated Western lyrics, played on piano or organ. Sermons are evangelical, usually expositions of biblical texts, and characterized by an emphasis on personal piety, spiritual and ethical perfection, and salvation, making use of relational (instead of legal) terms and the paradigm of family relationships to interpret Christian beliefs. Rarely are there sermons on eschatology or spiritual healing, subjects that are strongly discouraged. Exorcism and other practices and teachings deemed by the government as superstitious are not permitted. The theology of the congregations is basically conservative and evangelical (Hunter and Chan 1993, 75–76; Bays 2003, 493–494; Dunch 2001, 198; Oblau 1996).

Although Protestantism in China has, according to TSPM/CCC officials, entered a "post-denominational era," the influences of different traditions can still be felt in type 1 and type 2 churches. Besides the Western denominational traditions, the indigenous Chinese Protestant traditions are also present. According to some recent observations, congregations of the Little Flock are integrated into the TSPM/CCC network in many parts of China. As they do not recognize an ordained ministry, they are eager to block the institutionalization of the CCC. They practice the breaking of bread usually on Sunday night, and some women may cover their heads, according to their traditional practice. In some regions True Jesus Church congregations are also integrated into the TSPM/CCC network. But in some other regions they remain separated, as local authorities do not allow them to register—on the grounds, for example, that their practice of baptizing people in the river even in winter endangers public health. Being Sabbath observant, the True Jesus Church Christians worship on Saturday. That is also the case for Christians from the tradition of Seventh Day Adventists (Oblau 2001, 35; Bays 2003, 495).

The fact that churches of types 1 and 2 are under the TSPM/CCC hierarchy does not mean that they are necessarily docile toward the authorities. Many church leaders negotiate with the government to expand their sphere of activities. Worship services, prayer meetings, and Bible study classes for youth, women, the elderly, and married couples have been developed, and there are instances in which churches may have children's Sunday school, previously disallowed, by first starting child care for worshiping parents. Some churches have also managed to offer charitable and welfare services. There are interventions from government authorities, but congregations have used various forms of resistance—such as voting out church officials who have strong support from the RAB, filing lawsuits against government authorities, and waging nationwide campaigns to defend their rights (Kindopp 2004b, 130–131). Leaders of the national TSPM/CCC also use their positions and resources to voice complaints against government authorities. For example, the nationally distributed Protestant magazine *Tian Feng* has revealed and criticized the widespread practice of government officials' appointing church workers, by publishing an article written by a RAB official in Henan province (ANS 1996b). Also, Bishop Ding Guangxun reportedly has written to the RAB protesting the appointment of party members (who of course are atheists) as church leaders (Deng 1997, 180).

Many churches of types 3 and 4 have inherited the legacy of the indigenous Protestant churches, such as the Little Flock and the True Jesus Church, or are influenced by those traditions. Their traditions are critical of the hierarchical

Hong Kong Chief Executive Tung Chee-hwa smiles as he receives a Bible from Reverend Cao Shengjie, president of the state-sanctioned China Christian Council. The honorary president of the council, Bishop K. H. Ting, looks on at this opening ceremony of a Chinese Bible exhibit in Hong Kong. (Anat Givon/AP Photo)

and institutional character of mission-founded churches and of the liberal theology found in some Western denominations. Local congregations enjoy a high degree of autonomy, and their services permit a high degree of participation. Inasmuch as many members are illiterate, especially those in the rural churches, congregations sing hymns that are adaptations of local popular folk tunes to Gospel texts or are composed of simple melodies in the local ethnic style, with lyrics in colloquial language. They stress direct spiritual experience, especially in conversion, healing, speaking in tongues, and prophecy. Such stress on the immediacy of personal spiritual experience, together with the tendency toward allegorical interpretation of the Bible, is regarded as an important characteristic of Chinese Protestantism in general (Bays 2003, 494–495; Dunch 2001, 199, 203–204; Kindopp 2004b, 133; Oblau 2001, 31). Besides these common characteristics, there is also considerable diversity among these Protestant communities:

Some are clearly Pentecostal, others are on the margin, while many are simply of the conservative evangelical type. Some are exclusivist to the extreme and reject the validity of any other group, while others are conciliatory and willing to work together, including working with Three-Self churches (Tang 2002, 28).

Some type 4 meeting points—that is, autonomous Protestant communities that refuse to be affiliated with the TSPM/CCC—have formed networks. It was reported that in August 1998 representatives from large networks in Henan and Anhui issued an open letter calling on government authorities to end their attack on the Chinese house churches, to release all house church Christians from labor reform camps, and to spell out a definition of "cult," the term sometimes used in suppressing groups that refuse to join the TSPM. In November 1998, representatives of four networks issued a Confession of Faith, spelling out their theology, including their position on eschatology and aspects of Pentecostalism (Aikman 2003, 89–95, 293–307). Large-scale arrests of the leaders of these networks were reported in 1999–2000. Arrests and repressive measures were reported in later 2002 and the first half of 2003. On the other hand, it was reported that government officials were in contact with leaders of large networks. It is increasingly the case that local officials allow house churches to register directly with the government without coming under TSPM control (Kindopp 2004b, 140).

Special Varieties of Protestantism in China

New Sects and Cults

The lack of formal theological training in the rural areas, and religious persecution of unregistered Protestant groups, have resulted in the flourishing of various sects and cults. These include more or less orthodox Protestant groups such as the one called the Born Again Sect, or Full Scope Church, which emphasizes a definitive conversion experience including weeping in the confession of sins. Such groups "are heavily experiential and revivalist in emphasis, stressing direct personal experience of God, centered on literal reading of the Bible, spread by itinerant preachers with little in the way of formal education (theological or otherwise), but a great deal of dedication and enthusiasm. Suspicion of the state, and of the TSPM/CCC for its ties to the state, are characteristic, as is an otherworldly and often eschatological orientation" (Dunch 2001, 201). Others are heterodox or pseudo-Christian groups that "denounce orthodox Christian congregations, perform alleged spectacular miracles, promise deliverance from an imminent apocalypse, and demand obedience and resources from their followers" (Bays 2003, 497). They include the Established King, whose founder claimed to have succeeded Jesus and preached an impending end of the world; the Lightning from the East, whose founder claimed that Jesus Christ has already returned as a female messiah, that only those who believe in her can be saved, and that a kingdom of judgment without grace for unbelievers had come; and many others (Lambert 1998, 6–7; Kindopp 2004b, 141).

Cultural Christians

Since the 1980s, an increasing number of Chinese intellectuals in universities and research institutes have become interested in Christianity as an integral part of Western culture. Many of them were in the fields of history and philosophy. They conducted research, wrote books, and translated works on the theology, history, art, and literature (including the Bible) of Christianity. Some of them have become Christians and received baptism. Others are not converted but agree with the beliefs and values of Christianity. In either case, such intellectuals do not participate in any Christian church in the usual sense of that term, and they are reluctant to reveal their personal beliefs. A few of them are both religiously committed to Christianity and have produced sophisticated theological writings. Yet they are seldom invited to participate in the meetings of Protestant leaders or seminary professors. On the other hand, academic conferences and publications on Christianity seldom include church leaders and seminary professors. This underscores the great separation in mainland China between intellectuals in the Protestant churches and intellectuals in secular academic institutions who specialize in Christianity. What is especially significant is that most "cultural Christians" were not introduced to Christianity by the churches but through their academic studies and translation experiences. As one of them described it, it was evangelization without missionaries. At the same time, they have become missionaries, spreading Christianity to other intellectuals in academic circles without the help of institutional churches (Bays 2003, 498–499; Zhuo 2001; Lam 2004).

Protestantism and Chinese Popular Religion

Official and Popular Protestantism

Is there a Chinese Protestantism? If yes, where is it, and how Chinese is it? The answer does not seem to be found in the official Protestantism promoted by Bishop Ding and other leading figures of the national TSPM/CCC. The dominant discourse of Chinese Protestant theology they have constructed consists of theological affirmations of the goodness of non-Christians (especially communists), and of the history of the Chinese communist revolution, the present socialist system, and the Three-Self movement, using ideas such as the cosmic Christ, the presence of the Holy Spirit in culture and society, the incarnation of the Logos in a Chinese context, the providence of God in China, and an optimistic, process-theological view of creation and eschatology (Yip 1997, 83–128). This is an attempt to adapt Protestantism to the Chinese context. But there is no sign of its wide acceptance, even among churches under the administration of the TSPM/CCC. What is widely accepted and practiced in various Protestant communities is substantially different from the official version.

> While the official version emphasizes a sober, theologically liberal and politically motivated Christianity, what we can see on the ground are communities whose faith is experience-based, affective-emotional and materially efficacious. The social dimension is absent. If the official version emphasizes some form of theological and political "orthodoxy," then the grassroots communities stress more "orthopraxis" (experience-based baptism of the Spirit, speaking in tongues, healing) and "orthopathy" (deep sense of conversion and repentance that externalises in yelling and weeping) (Tang 2002, 28).

The following section examines more closely this widely accepted, hence popular, version of Chinese Protestantism, with particular reference to its encounter with Chinese popular religion.

Affinities and Interactions between Chinese Protestantism and Chinese Popular Religion

Not a few scholars have suggested that Protestantism in China, especially in rural areas, has many affinities and interactions with Chinese popular religion. "Interaction with indigenous traditions is arguably the most important single formative factor of Chinese Christianity" (Hunter and Chan 1993, 141). A Chinese ethnologist uses the term "Chinese folk Protestantism" (*Zhongguo minjian jidujiao*) to describe the popular form of Protestantism in China (Sun 1994, 47–48).

There are several areas of similarity, affinity, and interaction between Protestant Christianity and popular religion in China: healing, exorcism, morality, and beliefs in retribution and reciprocity.

Healing

Healing is perhaps the most widely reported reason for conversion to Protestantism in contemporary China. "ccc representatives report that in rural areas generally at least half of all conversions are motivated by healing experiences that are either personal or witnessed in the family. In many local places, church people claim a ratio as high as 90 percent" (Oblau 2001, 27). Praying for the sick is a significant part of worship services and prayer meetings (Tang 2002, 27), and one that is not restricted to the countryside. Urban Christians, including those affiliated with the ccc, and even students at Nanjing Theological Seminary practice it (Oblau 2001, 28). But in contrast to Pentecostal communities elsewhere, praying for the sick is done in a "democratic" way: "[A]ny believer can do it, no special healing charismata or any particular ecclesial status is required" (Oblau 2001, 28; see also Tang 2002, 27).

In Chinese popular religion, people often pray to a god and offer sacrifices to ask for healing. Chinese people do not find it difficult to pray to Jesus Christ for healing. A study of several accounts of healing reveal a similar structure. Usually a nonbeliever had been suffering from an illness (physiological or psychological) for a period of time. Medical treatment or Chinese popular religion was tried but was not effective. Often as a last resort, the sick person tried Christianity (probably regarding it as a functional alternative to traditional Chinese folk religion) or was approached by Christians who earnestly prayed for her and asked her to believe in Jesus. Suddenly or gradually, the illness disappeared. She converted to Christianity either during the healing process or shortly after that. Her moving testimony led her family members and others to become Christians (Yip 1999, 135).

Exorcism

Driving out evil spirits through rituals, words, or other means (such as writing a charm or talisman) to defend against possible intrusion by ghosts is an important feature in Chinese popular religion. According to one report from a rural area in Jiangxi province, although 60 percent of the Protestant Christians were illiterate and 90 percent could not read the Bible, they were still eager to buy one. They wrapped the Bible with a red cloth and stored it as something precious. If someone were ill, they would place it beside the pillow, believing that it could suppress evil forces and exorcise evil spirits (Sun 1994, 49). Cases of exorcism have also been reported. In one case, a demon reportedly jumped from one villager to another, "until the whole village of 250 people had been exorcized and all believed in Christ" (Ming 1986, 12).

Morality

It is not difficult to notice the affinities between the moral emphasis of Chinese Protestantism and the morality of Chinese popular religion. Confucianism, which had dominated the Chinese educational system for many centuries, has a strong concern for morality, especially relationships within the family, such as filial piety. Confucian morality left an impact on Chinese culture in general and Chinese popular religion in particular, as expressed in ancestor worship. In a county in Anhui province, it was reported that filial piety was the most frequent theme in sermons and hymns. Moral exhortations were also a dominant theme in hymns sung by a group in Henan. Chinese Protestants believe that becoming Christian makes for good intrafamily relations, including the relations between mother-in-law and daughter-in-law, which is the site of many family disputes in Chinese households. The high moral standards and uplifting moral presence of Christians in China have been recognized by party officials and social researchers alike. Christians do not smoke, gamble, or fight, and there are few disputes involving them (Yip 1999, 140–142, 160–162). In southwest Yunnan province, local government officials even actively introduced and promoted Protestant Christianity to combat widespread opium addiction—with successful results. Not only did the people's health improve but also their economic situation, for Christians did not need to spend money on the costly sacrifices required by local folk religion (Yamamori and Chan 2000, 28–35).

Retribution and Reciprocity

Chinese popular religious beliefs include the notion of retributive causation (*yinguo baoying*): good deeds will reap good rewards, while bad deeds reap bad retribution. Retribution is also a belief of Chinese Protestants. A survey of some Protestant Christians in Jiangxi reveals that they understand God as having the power of immediate retribution. If one is devoted to God, one will get protection; if not, one will get punishment (Sun 1994, 49). Illness and suffering are often seen as God's retributive punishment (Yip 1999, 142–143).

Related to the notion of retribution is the idea of reciprocity, which is the key to understanding the relations between humans and spirits (gods, ancestors, and ghosts) in Chinese popular religion. People give favors (such as food offerings) to spirits in expectation that the spirits will grant favors in return (ibid., 123). Such a "remarkably pragmatic, even mercantile attitude toward the physical benefits of divine blessings" that characterizes Chinese popular religion has also permeated Chinese Protestantism (Oblau 2001, 29). A telling example of the Chinese Protestant belief in reciprocity can be found in a report that is worth quoting at length:

> Christians interviewed in Fujian stated that they offered money to the church just as they had previously offered incense to the Buddha, believing that it was a symbol of their piety, and that the more they offered the more help they would receive. The concept of reciprocity was strongly held, and on the walls of a church in Fuzhou there were numerous letters of praise and thanks to Jesus after success in examinations, obtaining a scholarship to a Canadian university, healing of ailments, happy betrothals and finding employment. A phrase commonly used to praise a Chinese god is *youqiu biying*: "infallibly granting requests for favours." Almost identical terms were used in the Christian environment of the church (Hunter and Chan 1993, 144).

Conclusion

What we have seen above supports the conclusion that Protestantism in China is a functional alternative to Chinese popular religion. The fact that many people seek help from Christians as a last resort for curing sickness serves as good evidence of that fact. There are also cases of "Gospel villages" in which Christianity has replaced the traditional role of Chinese popular religion in various aspects, such as having church workers officiating in funerals and giving blessing to familial and public businesses (Guang 1990). But Protestantism is not just an alternative; it is also regarded by Chinese Protestants as a more efficacious alternative to traditional popular religion. A sociologist told a story about a middle-aged Christian who, until the end of the 1950s, had called on the Buddhist bodhisattva Guanyin when troubled by ghosts or illness. However, as Guanyin seemed to be less and less effective, someone introduced her to Christianity and taught her to pray to Jesus. That brought good fortune. She and her friends now prayed to Jesus. The sociologist described this as "co-opting by Christianity of traditional belief patterns" (Hunter 1990, 18). Numerous cases cited in a fairly comprehensive study of Protestantism in rural China show that there were many similarities, affinities, and interactions between Chinese Protestantism and Chinese popular religion, and that many Protestant peasants understand and practice their religion in ways and forms that are very similar to the beliefs and practices of Chinese folk religion (Leung 1999, 223–227, 233–234, 408–424).

Based on the above discussion, it is evident that Chinese Protestantism has been shaped by and has interacted with Chinese popular religion in the following way:

> Attracted by the claimed superiority in terms of efficacy of Christianity, some Chinese people who had been practicing traditional popular religion turned to Protestant Christianity in distresses or crises such as illness. Their ready acceptance of Christianity was facilitated by the numerous similarities between these two traditions. They actualized their conversion in no compromising manner. Deities, rituals, and other manifestations of their former religion (Chinese popular religion) were consciously rejected, and they devoted themselves to the individual and communal practices of this new faith. We should note, however, that *their acceptance of Protestant Christianity was based on and informed by the ideas, categories, conceptual scheme, worldview, etc., of the very religious tradition they consciously rejected.* These ideas, categories, conceptual scheme, worldview, and so on, continue to be operative in helping them to understand and appropriate the new religious tradition (Yip 1999, 148–149; original emphasis).

With regard to healing and exorcism, praying to Jesus is seen as a more efficacious alternative to the traditional deities. With regard to morality, Chinese Protestants appropriate Christian moral teachings in a Chinese way, upholding filial piety and family harmony. With regard to the divine-human relationship, they relate with the Christian God in terms of the ideas of retribution and reciprocity, which are essential elements in Chinese popular religion.

In these various ways, Protestantism looks appealing to the rural people in China. In many other ways, Protestantism also looks attractive to urban Chinese. The following passage by an expert in Chinese Protestantism helps to explain the grounds for its popularity in China.

> Protestantism seems thoroughly rooted in Chinese society, with some aspects of it strongly reflecting affinity to traditional cultural patterns and others appealing to modernity. It offers varied appeals to its followers: its beliefs provide an explanation of suffering, an ethical code and a promise of salvation, all at a much cheaper cost than traditional rituals in local communities, because of less expense for ritual offerings, operas and feasts. Socially, it provides fellowship in a wide variety of organizational forms, from small home groups to large congregations. Yet it also offers personal affirmation and, especially for women and young people, an outlet for their energies and development of musical, organizational or preaching skills. For example, numbers of rural teenagers have found in networks of Protestant groups a vocation of travelling evangelism. Psychologically, different forms of Protestantism can offer for intellectuals or the urban middle class an identification with the West and modernization, or an eschatological prospect which may appeal to poor peasants left behind by the economic reform (Bays 2003, 502).

References

Aikman, David. 2003. *Jesus in Beijing: How Christianity is Transforming China and Changing the Global Balance of Power.* Washington, DC: Regnery.

Amity News Service, China Christian Council. 1996a. "Chinese Christian Church Order Adopted." *Amity News Service* 96.8.5. http://www.amitynewsservice.org/page.php?page=1065.

———. 1996b. "RAB Official: RABS Must Not Appoint Church Officers." *Amity News Service* 96.7.2. http://www.amitynewsservice.org/page.php?page=1075.

———. 1997. "Chinese Church Order." Amity News Service 97.11.7. http://www.amitynewsservice.org/page.php?page=978.

———. 2003. "Women in the Chinese Church: A Few Facts and Figures." *Amity News Service* 12.5/6.4. http://www.amitynewsservice.org/page.php?page=612

Bays, Daniel H. 1996. "The Growth of Independent Christianity in China." Pp. 307–366 in *Christianity in China: From the Eighteenth Century to the Present.* Edited by Daniel H. Bays. Stanford: Stanford University Press.

———. 2003. "Chinese Protestant Christianity." *China Quarterly* 174: 488–504.

Chao, Jonathan (Zhao Tian'en), and Rosanna Chong (Zhuang Wanfang). 1997. *Dangdai Zhongguo jidujiao fazhan shi, 1949–1997* [A history of Christianity in socialist China, 1949–1997]. Taipei: CMI.

CTR. 2000. "Statistics for the Protestant Church in China: 1999." *Chinese Theological Review* 14: 154–156.

Deng, Zhaoming. 1997. *Cangsan yu junjing: sishi duo nian lai de Sanzi Aiguo Yundong* [The vicissitudes of the Three-Self Patriotic Movement in the 1950s and its predicament today]. Hong Kong: Christian Study Centre on Chinese Religion and Culture.

Dunch, Ryan. 2001. "Protestant Christianity in China Today: Fragile, Fragmented, Flourishing." Pp. 195–216 in *China and Christianity: Burdened Past, Hopeful Future.* Edited by Stephen Uhalley, Jr., and Xiaoxin Wu. Armonk, NY: Sharpe.

Guang. 1990. "Gospel Villages." *Bridge* 40: 12–14.

Hunter, Alan. 1990. "A Sociological Perspective on Chinese Christianity." *Bridge* 44: 16–18.

Hunter, Alan, and Kim-kwong Chan. 1993. *Protestantism in Contemporary China.* Cambridge: Cambridge University Press.

Jones, Francis Price. 1962. *The Church in Communist China: A Protestant Appraisal.* New York: Friendship.

———, ed. 1963. *Documents of the Three-Self Movement.* New York: National Council of Churches of Christ in the U.S.A.

Kindopp, Jason. 2004a. "Policy Dilemmas in China's Church-State Relations: An Introduction." Pp. 1–22 in *God and Caesar in China: Policy Implications of Church-State Tensions.* Edited by Jason Kindopp and Carol Lee Hamrin. Washington DC: Brookings Institution.

———. 2004b. "Fragmented Yet Defiant: Protestant Resilience under Chinese Communist Party Rule." Pp. 122–145 in *God and Caesar in China: Policy Implications of Church-State Tensions.* Edited by Jason Kindopp and Carol Lee Hamrin. Washington DC: Brookings Institution.

Lam, Chun, ed. 2001. *Zhongguo jidujiao jiaohui fazhan: yuanyin yu luxiang* [Protestant church development in China: How did it happen and where is it leading?]. LWF China Study Series, vol. 5. Geneva: Lutheran World Federation.

Lam, Jason Tsz-shun. 2004. "The Emergence of Scholars Studying Christianity in Mainland China: Religion." *State and Society* 32.2: 177–186.

Lambert, Tony. 1994. *The Resurrection of the Chinese Church.* Wheaton, IL: Harold Shaw, OMF.

———. 1998. "Modern Sects and Cults in China." *China Study Journal* 13.3: 6–8.

———. 2003. "Counting Christians in China: A Cautionary Report." *International Bulletin of Missionary Research* 27: 6–10.

LeMond, John G. 1997. "A Brief History of the Church in China." *Word & World* 17: 144–153.

Leung, Ka-lun (Liang Jialin). 1988. *Fu lin Zhonghua: zhongguo jindai jiaohuishi shi jiang* [Blessing upon China: Ten talks on the contemporary church history of China]. Hong Kong: Tin Dao.

———. 1999. *Gaige kaifang yilai de Zhongguo nongcun jiaohui* [Rural churches of mainland China since 1978]. Hong Kong: Alliance Bible Seminary.

Lutz, Jessie G. 2001. "China and Protestantism: Historical Perspectives, 1807–1949." Pp. 179–193 in *China and Christianity: Burdened Past, Hopeful Future.* Edited by Stephen Uhalley, Jr., and Xiaoxin Wu. Armonk, NY: Sharpe.

MacInnis, Donald E., ed. 1989. *Religion in China Today: Policy and Practice.* Maryknoll, NY: Orbis.

Ming. 1986. "Demons and Ghosts in China's Countryside." *Bridge* 15: 11–12.

Moffett, Samuel Hugh. 1998. *A History of Christianity in Asia.* Volume 1: *Beginnings to 1500.* 2d rev. ed. Maryknoll, NY: Orbis.

Oblau, Gotthard. 1996. "Protestant Sermons in China: Harbingers of an Evolving Contextual Theology." *China Study Journal* 11.1: 16–28.

———. 2001. "Pentecostal by Default? Reflections on Contemporary Christianity in China." *China Study Journal* 16.3: 23–37.

Overview. 2004. *Zhongguo Jidujiao gaikuang* [Overview of Chinese Protestantism]. http://www.chineseprotestantchurch.org.cn/other/gaikuang.htm.

Spiegel, Mickey. 2004. "Control and Containment in the Reform Era." Pp. 40–57 in *God and Caesar in China: Policy Implications of Church-State Tensions.* Edited by Jason Kindopp and Carol Lee Hamrin. Washington DC: Brookings Institution.

Sun, Shanling. 1994. "Zhongguo minjian Jidujiao" [Chinese folk Protestantism]. *Nanjing Theological Review* 21: 45–51.

Tang, Edmond. 2002. "'Yellers' and Healers—Pentecostalism and the Study of Grassroots Christianity in China." *China Study Journal* 17.3: 19–29.

Wang, Jiali. 1997. "The House Church Movement: A Participant's Assessment." *Word & World* 17: 175–182.

Whyte, Bob. 1988. *Unfinished Encounter: China and Christianity.* London: Collins, Fount.

Wickeri, Philip L. 1988. *Seeking the Common Ground: Protestant Christianity, the Three-Self Movement, and China's United Front.* Maryknoll, NY: Orbis.

———. 1994. "Understanding the Church in China: A Review Article." *China Study Journal* 9.2: 11–16.

Xu, Yihua. 2004. "'Patriotic' Protestants: The Making of an Official Church." Pp. 107–121 in *God and Caesar in China: Policy Implications of Church-State Tensions.* Edited by Jason Kindopp and Carol Lee Hamrin. Washington DC: Brookings Institution.

Yamamori, Tetsunao, and Kim-kwong Chan. 2000. *Witnesses to Power: Stories of God's Quiet Work in a Changing China.* Waynesboro, GA: Paternoster.

Ying Fuk-tsang (Xing Fuzeng), and Leung Ka-lun (Liang Jialin). 1996. *Wushi niandai Sanzi Yundong de yanjiu* [The Three-Self Patriotic Movement in the

1950s]. Hong Kong: Christianity and Chinese Culture Research Centre, Alliance Bible Seminary.

———. 2001. "The Development of Christianity in Contemporary China as Revealed from Its Social Composition." *Jian Dao* 15: 285–318.

Yip, Francis Ching-wah (Ye Jinghua). 1997. *Xun zhen qiu quan: zhongguo shenxue yu zheng jiao chujing chutan* [Chinese theology in state-church context: A preliminary study]. Hong Kong: Christian Study Centre on Chinese Religion and Culture.

———. 1999. "Protestant Christianity and Popular Religion in China: A Case of Syncretism?" *Ching Feng* 42.3–4: 130–175.

Zhuo Xinping. 2001. "Discussion on 'Cultural Christians' in China." Pp. 283–300 in *China and Christianity: Burdened Past, Hopeful Future.* Edited by Stephen Uhalley, Jr., and Xiaoxin Wu. Armonk, NY: Sharpe.

9

Women in Contemporary Chinese Religions

TAK-LING TERRY WOO

Introduction

This chapter begins by examining the three central elements of this chapter: women, contemporary societies, and Chinese religions. Next the chapter focuses on the four main divisions within Chinese religions: folk religion, Confucianism, Daoism, and Buddhism, the last of which some may consider a foreign religion and not indigenously Chinese.

Women of various qualities and capacities form and determine the shape of Chinese religions: old and young; schooled and unschooled; clever and slow-witted; wise and foolish; cultivated and rash; religious and secular; spiritual and materialistic; active and torpid; moral and immoral; wealthy and destitute; famous and obscure; kind and cruel. These women may be grandmothers, mothers, aunts, daughters, nieces, nuns, priestesses, teachers, managers, politicians, business owners, laborers, and friends.

The contemporary societies in which these women live may be urban or rural; industrialized or developing; capitalist or socialist; democratic or oligarchic; Chinese or Western. Societies that include a substantial number of Chinese include city-states such as Singapore; the previous British Crown colony of Hong Kong; the People's Republic of China, situated on the mainland; the island of Taiwan, the "other" China; and, of course, the populous diaspora communities located primarily in Southeast Asia, Europe, and North America. The markedly different political, economic, and cultural histories of these areas further contribute to the enormous range of conditions under which women practice and understand their Chinese religions.

Mainland China has been communist since 1949, and its ideology has been generally hostile to its indigenous religious heritage; that was particularly true during the Cultural Revolution, from 1966 to 1976. Taiwan and Singapore, on the other hand, influenced by capitalism and democracy, have tended toward conserving some semblance of a society based on Confucian values, permitting traditional religiosity to continue. Hong Kong, a colony until 1997, has, like Taiwan, experienced a surge in the popularity of Buddhism over recent years; it is the most Westernized of the East Asian Chinese populations and has a strong Christian presence. We will see that these different histories have had tremendous influence on women in their understanding and practice of Chinese religions.

Chinese religions, when understood in terms of what is elite and popular, formal and informal, and in terms of the differences between the religious specialist and the ordinary devotee, typically display four main streams. The first is embodied in the various road shrines and temples for the various spirits, gods, and goddesses of folk belief and practice; the second is seen in ancestral shrines, and the cultural beliefs and practices rooted in Confucianism; the third, in the heterogeneous beliefs and practices categorized under the unwieldy mass called Daoism; and the fourth, in the numerous gray- or saffron-robed Buddhist monks and nuns and their many temples. The unruliness of the multitudinous shrines, temples, and institutions is compounded by two additional elements: the lack of a unitary source of authority in these religions, and the tendency toward syncretism. This means that a woman can simultaneously hold Confucian values, belong to a Daoist temple, and pray for help to Guanyin, a Buddhist bodhisattva of compassion—and all without exclusive allegiance to any particular monk, nun, priest, priestess, or organization.

The varieties of experience contained within the heading "Women in Contemporary Chinese Religions" thus mean that this chapter can hope to offer only a glimpse, an impressionistic montage—assembled with snapshots and portraits of particular women, in their familial and societal functions, and at a particular time and location in history. Women may embody these many differences and live out their beliefs and practices within the broader context of Chinese religions as curious bystanders, casual participants, inducted devotees, specialists, or leaders.

Folk Religion

The young and the old, the new and the traditional coexist with ease in crowded and ultramodern Hong Kong. On a sloping concrete pavement, just up the hill from the throbbing central financial district where fashionable women can be seen in stylish European and U.S. designer wear, stands an open, sooty street shrine not much larger than 4 by 6 by 10 feet, set off by a rudimentary metal railing. On the various shelves of the structure are images of gods and goddesses; several coils of mustard-yellow incense are lit and hang, scenting the air. An old woman of about sixty to seventy years of age can be seen dusting off the altar and sweeping the area inside and around the shrine. Men and women, young and old, stop and step into the shrine to offer sticks of incense.

Half an hour away by an efficient and internationally acclaimed subway system, north across the harbor on Kowloon peninsula in a vertically stacked light-industrial residential area, is further evidence of folk religion. An old woman can be seen taking care of another road shrine. Leaving untouched the apples and oranges placed in a tray, she takes out the burned incense sticks and puts new ones into a censer in front of a simple 8-by-11-inch sheet of red paper in an ordinary photograph frame that is leaning against a tree. On it is a dedication printed in yellow-gold ink for the spirits of the five directions and the god of fortune of the vicinity.

Shrines like these are often dedicated to one particular spirit, god, or goddess with little regard to sectarian affiliations. What is of crucial importance is their reputed efficacy. Confucian, Daoist, and Buddhist figures alike can also be found in restaurants and shops. In Hong Kong, offerings of incense and fruits are made routinely to the spirit of the earth; the historical Martial Duke Guan (Guan Gong; also known as Guandi, or Lord Guan), who lived during the latter part of the second century, is also a favorite; as is Tian Hou, the Empress of Heaven. But these spirit shrines are no longer found only in East Asia. They have migrated along with Chinese immigrants to North America.

For example, in Toronto's Spadina-Dundas Chinatown, there is a particularly intriguing shrine in a Chinese-Vietnamese bakery that holds two figures: Guan Gong and Guanyin. When the middle-aged owner was asked why there were two statues being offered fruits and incense side by side, and not the usual one, she answered without hesitation and enthusiastically in Cantonese:

Worshippers make offerings, Kowloon City, Hong Kong. (Mike McQueen/Corbis)

Guan Gong is a male spirit and was installed for her husband, whereas Guanyin, a female spirit, was brought in for her because she wanted a feminine presence in the shop. She said she felt that the coexistence of male and female brought a balance of energy. The pan-Chinese sense of and desire for harmony and balance, explicitly in male and female energy and expressed often in the notion of yin-yang (shady and bright side of the mountain), can be traced back to the divination text known as the *Book of Changes* (*Yijing*). The male (*qian*) is understood to be the creative, heavenly aspect; the female (*kun*) is its counterpart, the receptive, earthly aspect (Sommer 1995, 5). This rudimentary notion of two generative sources can be traced back some 2,500 years.

Young women in their twenties and thirties from mainland China, working in the retail stores and restaurants in the various Toronto Chinatowns, when asked about the absence of shrines in their shops answered that such displays are superstition; they offered that such practices reflect the behavior of an older generation. They noted that they are not involved in that sort of practice, and a few confessed to being Christians.

Confucianism

Many Chinese women have converted to Christianity; does this mean that they have abandoned Chinese religions? Many more have tacitly adopted the modern belief and practice of secularism; does this mean that they have forsaken Chinese religions? The answer is an ambiguous one. There is, on the one hand, the anticipated distancing from Chinese religions; yet, on the other, there is an interest, a will, and an effort made at religio-cultural recovery. One aspect of this may be gleaned through the life and work of a recently deceased (2001) scholar of international reputation, Professor Julia Ching, who taught at the University of Toronto. Born in Shanghai in 1934, Ching escaped from China during World War II and finished high school in Hong Kong. Not unlike other families that could afford to do so, and that had been exposed to Western influences, she studied abroad. She was unusual, however, because for two decades she served as an Ursuline Catholic nun.

While working as a nun in Taiwan, Ching discovered a new interest in Chinese philosophy. She completed a master's degree at the Catholic University of America in Washington, D.C., and continued on for a doctorate, writing about Wang Yangming, a Neo-Confucian, at the Australian National University in Canberra. She left her vocation as a nun, became a professor, and eventually married. Professor Ching's tricontinental reach, though unusual for her time, has now become commonplace for many Chinese immigrants.

Ching may not have situated herself unreservedly within the lineage of the New Confucians who are trying to resuscitate Confucianism; but she lauds the spirit of humaneness (*ren*) by describing the humane or exemplary person (*junzi*) as one who takes on the political responsibility to change and transform society. She quotes the eleventh century scholar-official, Fan Zhongyen, noting that the exemplary person is "the first to take on the worries of the world, and the last to enjoy its pleasures" (Kung and Ching 1989, 88). Ching goes on to comment on the relevance of Confucianism in the modern world, writing that if we understand Confucianism to be

> a dynamic discovery of the worth of the human person, of the possibilities
> of moral greatness and even sagehood, of one's fundamental relationship

to others in society based on ethical values, of an interpretation of reality and metaphysics of the self that remain open to the transcendent—all this, of course, the basis for a true sense of human dignity, freedom, and equality—then Confucianism is very relevant and can remain so, both for China and for the world (ibid., 90).

Nevertheless, Ching was critical of the way in which Confucianism theorized about and treated women, quoting the notorious lines from *Analects* 17:25: "Women and servants are to be treated severely. If you are familiar with them, they become impudent; if you ignore them, they are offended." She was critical of how the core teaching about humaneness (*ren;* also translated as "benevolence" or "compassion") was incompletely propagated, neglecting the welfare of women. She found even deeper trouble with Confucianism because of the remark about servants, so that

> with Confucius, it was not only the relation between man and woman that was governed by patriarchalism and authoritarianism, but the other basic human relationships as well. Even though all of these were conceived as being reciprocal, they could easily be used to justify the domination of the father over the wife and children and above all of the princes over their subjects (ibid., 121).

Ching is referring to the five relationships here: first, the emperor and minister; second, the father and son; third, older and younger siblings; fourth, husband and wife; and fifth, friends. The first of each of these pairs of relationships is construed as senior, the second as junior. These relationships are, as Ching notes, to be reciprocal. The senior is to be benevolent, always looking out for the junior and taking care never to treat the junior in a way that she herself would not want to be treated. The junior, on the other hand, is to be loyal; she is to be obedient and follow the senior. Here, the role of women becomes specific. Women have three "follows" in their lives: first, as a daughter, she is expected to follow her father; as a wife, she is expected to follow her husband; and in old age or after the death of her husband, she is to follow her son.

When dynastic rule ended in 1911, the emperor-minister relationship—along with the offices of the Empress Dowager, the Empress, numerous princesses, and various grades of concubine—disappeared with it. Many women yielded to the commanding calls to progress. The rhetoric of liberation from the New Culture Movement and the May Fourth Movement (1919) demanded that women be rescued from Confucianism, which was derided as "the teaching of rites that consume people" (*chiren de lijiao*). Ching, born fifteen years after the May Fourth Movement, was heir to this early-twentieth-century ferment.

This was a heady time for women: the call for democracy, personhood, and freedom was in the air. Foot-binding was declared illegal and female infanticide declared abhorrent. Public elementary and secondary schools were built for all girls in lieu of home education, not only for the rich ones, and a few, like Ching, eventually went on to university. In time, after World War II, polygamy became illegal in all communities where Chinese made up the majority population, including China, Taiwan, Singapore, and Hong Kong.

We see in Ching a prototypical, inconsistent, and dichotomous reaction to Confucianism. Even as she agreed with the disestablishment of state Confucianism, and even as she was one woman among many in the vociferous denunciations against China's foremost familial and political ideology, she nevertheless pointed to particular ideals and practices within it that she spoke of favorably. This tendency is reflected elsewhere, among the larger population.

There is, for example, the diffused but persistent continuation in the idea of filial piety (*xiao*)—that is, acting in deference, with respect and consideration for one's seniors—as a first step to moral development; it was spoken of approvingly by Ching, in Chinese children, even in diaspora. A concrete illustration of this is the popularity of the ancestral tablets housed in Buddhist and Daoist institutions alike—for example, respectively, in the Fo Guang Shan temple in Mississauga, just west of Toronto, and in the Darcy Street Fung Loy Kok temple in downtown Toronto.

For some traditional families, religious paraphernalia like paper gold nuggets, money printed as Hell Notes, paper clothes, cars, airplanes, stoves, houses, and paper versions of other such commodities may be burned as offerings to ancestors on special days of remembrance, such as Qing Ming (Clear and Bright), the third day of the third month in the lunar calendar, marked off for sweeping the tomb. When seen in this way, ancestor veneration, an observable ritual demonstrating filial piety, continues to be an integral part of some Chinese families.

This dissonance between successful institutional disestablishment and willful cultural preservation comes partly from the women themselves. It is they who, as grandmothers, mothers, and primary caregivers, propagate filial piety in the contemporarily small extended or nuclear family, but who continue to look after the often patrilocal and patriarchal ancestral shrines at home and in temples. In so doing, some women continue to transmit the hierarchical values of senior and junior implicit within the relationships between parent and child, and older and younger siblings. By this means the women themselves gain definition and status; they remain at the heart of the family, binding all of its members together through the notion and practice of filial piety.

The two defining elements here are the logistics of whose family name the children should take and which ancestors should be venerated, as well as the ethos of deference and respect. The first has traditionally been patriarchal and subject to much criticism; the second has also been censured by scholars like Ching for encouraging authoritarianism.

Born in the 1950s, a generation younger than Julia Ching, I have offered another view of why it may be helpful to resuscitate an ailing Confucianism. This perspective is secular and is not based upon the Christian presumption that all human beings are equal before God. Instead, I have suggested that it is important to accept and start from the demonstrably unequal qualities of human beings; the unequal assignment of intellectual, psychological, economic, and spiritual capacities can be understood to be basic, and such differences form the field of cultivation. This position seeks to recover and adapt the Confucian notions of senior and junior as a means to encourage the development of self-cultivation, or the cultivation of one's body (Woo 2003, 112).

Confucianism suggests that the external discipline of one's body through the curbing of one's appetites and the extension of one's consideration of others, when nurtured from birth by the practice of filial piety in both girls and boys, can influence or bring about an attitude of yielding, of mindfulness of one's own mistakes, and the effort to do one's best before reprimanding others. Such a discipline, when adopted widely, can act as a balance, on the one hand, to the secular West; on the other, it can be a complement to the prophetic West Asian traditions and a contemporary global politics that seems bent on and fueled by confrontation.

This ambivalence that Chinese women have about Confucianism and the tension between its potentially negative authoritarian grip and its efficacy in instilling self-discipline is captured well by a scholar who stands outside of the tradition. Theresa Kelleher writes that although Confucianism had "contributed to the victimization of women, it also gave them a sense of self-discipline, esteem for education, and respect for public service that has enabled them to enter into today's political and social realm in the number and with the effectiveness that they have" (Kelleher 1987, 157). The truth of this can, ironically, be seen in the success of women in Buddhism—the Chinese foreign religion.

Buddhism

Universal Aspects

The attacks on and disestablishment of Confucianism have been so successful that even as it is now being championed through attempts to resuscitate it, it has faded away and become so diffused that it functions more like a personal philosophy within Chinese culture. The would-be resuscitators are the overwhelmingly male New Confucians in Hong Kong, Taiwan, and Boston—where scholars at Harvard and Boston University have taken to calling themselves the Boston Confucians. Ironically, the willingly and skillfully domesticated foreign religion, Buddhism, has become the primary religion by which Chinese religion is identified; many or perhaps most ordinary women rally around it as a point of spiritual cultivation. Not only does it call Chinese women; it has also been a point of convergence for the ordination of Tibetan and Theravadin nuns from South and Southeast Asia.

The monastic rules (*lü*) for nuns (*biqiuni*) were first given to the Chinese by Sri Lankan Buddhist communities (*seng*) in the fourth century of the Common Era. During our own time, the Dalai Lama has encouraged female devotees of Tibetan Buddhism in the West who want to become nuns to take ordination from Chinese nuns, or Vietnamese and Korean ones, because the order of nuns had never been established in Tibet (see www.sakyadhita.org).

But it is not only Tibetan nuns who take their vows outside their own tradition. Two high-profile Theravadin nuns, Chatsumarn Kabilsingh and Ayya Khema, have also received ordination from Chinese nuns, because the Theravada lineage of nuns disappeared from Sri Lanka and India in the eleventh century. Kabilsingh is a professor who is a well-known activist in issues of social justice in her native Thailand. Ayya Khema (1923–1997) was born Ilse Ledermann of Jewish parents in Berlin; she escaped Germany in the 1930s, stayed in Shanghai for a short time and was interned by the Japanese during the war, immigrated to the United States in 1949 when the communists were taking over, and started practicing meditation during the 1960s while traveling around Asia with her husband. She began to teach meditation in the 1970s and became a Theravadin "nun" in 1979; she

A group of Tibetan Buddhist women, Tsethang, Tibet. (Alison Wright/Corbis)

participated in the nuns' ordination ceremony at Fo Guang Shan's Hsi Lai temple in Los Angeles in 1988. Ayya Khema wrote about her experience in this way:

> We received a rigorous, almost military-style training, almost all in Chinese. We were treated most generously and did not have to pay anything for lodging, food, and clothing. It would have been better if they had immediately established some Western nuns there, since only one of the Chinese nuns spoke English and the temple was intended for the spreading of the Teaching in the West.
>
> After we had received training daily for four weeks, many hours a day, the great day of the ordination arrived. This meant both the day and the night for the nuns, because we had to be ordained twice—once by ten monks, who had all been monks for at least thirty years; and again by ten *bhikkunis*, who had all been *bhikkunis* for at least twenty years. We all completed the process successfully, although the Western monks and nuns often had no idea what was going on, because the proceedings were not translated. But we understood the essential. I was glad when it was over, since every bone in my body ached (Lopez 2002, 184).

While the westerner Ayya Khema was traveling through Asia in the 1960s, Sun Shuyun, a film and television producer, was born on the mainland. In 1999, eleven years after the non-Chinese nuns were ordained through the Chinese monastic code in Los Angeles, Sun began her journey, tracing—by her travels through Central and South Asia—the journey taken by Xuanzang, a Chinese monk who made a pilgrimage to India in the seventh century. She had decided to do this as a personal commitment to understanding her maternal grandmother's world; her adventures are recorded in *Ten Thousand Miles without a Cloud* (2003).

China

Sun had lived through the Cultural Revolution as a child and adolescent, and experienced the repercussions of the calculated destruction of tradition. Her interest in Chinese religions is less theoretical than that of Ching and Woo; rather, she explores Buddhism, her grandmother's faith, as a gesture of filial commitment. Sun attended Beijing University, won a scholarship to Oxford, and lives now in England. Even as she confesses that she does not share her grandmother's beliefs, she also admits that what she has learned about Buddhism will stay with her for the rest of her life.

Sun's grandmother was born in 1898 in a small village in Shandong; she was a devotee of popular Pure Land Buddhism, a devotional sect of Chinese folk Buddhism. There were three temples in the village where she grew up, and, reflecting the words about balance from the Chinese-Vietnamese bakery owner in Toronto, one temple, for men, was dedicated to Guandi; the remaining two temples, where women went to pray, were dedicated to the God of Earth and Guanyin. Pure Land devotees believe that they can avoid being reborn into this world—that is, avoid the cycle of rebirth—by being reborn in the Western Paradise of Omitofo (the Buddha Amitabha). Their spiritual discipline consists of good works, prayer, offerings to Guanyin, and the chanting of the mantra *namo-Omitofo* ("homage to Amitabha Buddha").

Shuyun's grandmother would count beans to keep track of how many prayers she had said. She prayed for her seven dead children and husband, and to join them in Western Pure Land; she also prayed for Sun, so that she might not suffer too much as the unwanted daughter; for her grandson, Sun's brother, and the health of the entire family; for enough food; and for her son-in-law, Shuyun's father, that he not be a target in the many campaigns of the Cultural Revolution (Sun 2003, 28).

One of Sun's "earliest and most enduring memor[ies] was of her [grandmother's] bound feet" being in her face, because they shared a bed, sleeping head to toe, until Sun went off to university. In one of the most intimate descriptions of their grandmother and granddaughter relationship, Sun describes one way in which she cared for her grandmother:

> The first thing I learned to do for her, and continued doing right up to my teens, was to bring her a kettle of hot water every evening to soak her feet. The water was boiling and her feet were red like pigs' trotters, but she did not seem to feel it—she was letting the numbness take over from the pain, the pain that had never gone away since the age of seven when her mother bound her feet. It was done to make her more appealing to men (ibid., 23).

Shuyun had a very close relationship with her grandmother because she felt that her grandmother had protected and loved her by paying the most attention to her among all her grandchildren, so that she would not feel uncared for and unloved by her father. Sun's father was born in 1930, an older contemporary of Ching and a dedicated, secular, and idealistic communist from northern China who, nevertheless, after the birth of two daughters wished for a son; he was bitterly disappointed when Sun, the third daughter, was born. She describes how apologetic her mother was, for in the latter's northern village, there was a saying: "A hen lays eggs. A woman who cannot produce a son is not worth even a hen."

Sun notes plainly that in the past, her father could have taken a concubine to bear him a son; or, she, the unwanted girl, could simply have been drowned. But because neither of these alternatives was possible under the communists in the 1960s, she bore the brunt of her father's disappointment as the "unwanted daughter" (ibid., 22). So even as drastic measures to kill off traditional religions were executed at the external, broader political level, deep-seated cultural attitudes remained within individual personalities and families.

Sun relates how her grandmother stated reality as she understood it at the time of her birth. Perhaps out of a wish to protect her daughter, Sun's mother, she confessed to being responsible for the birth of a daughter, an inferior being. She reasoned that because Mao Zedong's reforms, which mandated the closing and destruction of temples and the conversion of incense factories into toilet paper manufacturers, she had been prevented from going to the temple to pray and offer incense to Guanyin; thus her prayers for a boy had gone unnoticed by heavenly beings (ibid.). When Sun's father, who had dedicated his life to fighting superstition, heard this he flew into a rage:

> To hell with all your superstitious crap. What is so good about your gods up there? If they're as good as you boast, how come they let people live in such misery before? How come they were so useless in protecting your children? You know what? They are not worth a dog's fart (ibid., 23).

At this, Sun's grandmother picked up her third granddaughter, the unwanted baby daughter, and walked out of the room. Sun then went on to describe another pivotal point in her family's life: the breech birth of her brother. She recounts how her mother almost bled to death; how her father, previously disdainful of his mother-in-law's superstitious beliefs, when frightened to death looked to her for help. Her grandmother, rattled and with teeth chattering like castanets, tried to calm him down. While her son-in-law, Sun's father, paced about "like a caged animal,"

> Grandmother knelt down and began to pray loudly to Guanyin, holding tight to Mother's hand. "I have been praying to you for more than fifty years," she pleaded urgently. "If you have too much to do and can only help me once, please do it now. I need you more than ever. I am begging you." She promised she would do anything if the boy was delivered safely: she would produce a thanksgiving banquet for Guanyin for seven days; she would go on a pilgrimage to her place of abode in southern China even if she had to pawn her bracelet, her only piece of jade; she would tell her grandchildren to remember the loving kindness of the Bodhisattva for ever (ibid., 33).

Sun's mother and brother both survived, and as the Cultural Revolution continued her father became a changed man. He lost his idealism and became less interested in his work; he had more time for his children and even bought his mother-in-law candles for rituals held on the Ghost Festival (*Guijie;* also known as Ullamabana), which falls on the fifteenth day of the seventh month of the lunar calendar. It is believed that for the entire month, the gates of hell are opened so that the dead will mingle with the living; although this was originally a Buddhist festival, it has become a part of popular tradition.

In her travels, Shuyun learned of Buddhisms that were different from her grandmother's. In Dunhuang in northwestern China, for example, she met

Shan Ren, a laywoman who was designated as her helper by the abbot at the Thunderbolt Monastery, where she stayed to experience monastic living. Shan was obviously well educated and very knowledgeable about Buddhism; that, to Sun, seemed incongruous with her being a Buddhist since none of the educated people she had previously encountered were religious. Shan's faith made her different from many of her contemporaries, who were often either atheists or devout communists and viewed Buddhism as superstition; Shan was the same age as Sun's parents. When Sun shared her doubts about an intervening deity, Amitabha, Shan Ren remarked that she sounded like someone with an affinity for the Chan (Meditation) School, which is "concerned with what one can do oneself: gaining insight into how things really are, achieving inner freedom and abandoning attachment to worldly pleasures. It does not rely on performing ritual or on books, but calls for self-discipline and constant meditation" (ibid., 397).

But even as Sun learned about different types of Buddhism, there was one trait or belief that she observed to be the same for all of the Buddhists she met: they had "the idea that you can change your life by changing the way you look at it. Your mind is what matters, and you can transform it" (ibid., 442). Shuyun saw in Shan Ren and her grandmother a selflessness that had helped them to transform and transcend the cruelties and vagaries of the times they lived in. They remained kind and compassionate, unlike her father and his communist comrades, who, with the fiasco of the Cultural Revolution, had became bitter and had died depressed (ibid., 38–39).

Sun thus captures, through her narrative, the radical changes and constancies in attitudes toward traditional culture and religion over the course of the tumultuous twentieth century by focusing on three generations of women: starting with her maternal grandmother, then her mother, and finally herself. She experiences and describes the transformation of the largest Chinese religio-cultural sphere, mainland China, from within, in contrast to Ching and I, who write from diasporic perspectives, as minority citizens who have lived much of our lives in Western countries.

Finally, in memory and appreciation, Shuyun ends her book with this testament to her grandmother, who had lived an unimaginably difficult life and yet remained to the end unbent by hardship:

> I placed on her grave bananas, oranges and grapes that I had bought her,
>   the simple things she never tasted in life.
> Softly, I said Amitabha for her (ibid., 446).

Buddhism is slowly being restored in China. During my visits to Guangzhou and Xi'an during December 2001 and 2003, respectively, there was evidence that many old Buddhist temples were being restored, but there was also a noticeable gap in the pace of development and renovation between Guangzhou and Xi'an; unlike Taiwan, which will be discussed later, most of the clergy I saw were monks. When I commented on and asked about these differences, Shi Changrui, the head nun of the small Wangji Temple in Xi'an, joked that the larger, famous temples across China have all been assigned monks by the government. On a more serious note, she pointed out that there are more nuns than monks nationally; in Shaanxi province, however, there are more monks than nuns. Moreover, she continued, the general rate of economic development is uneven across China; the temples along the southern coastal provinces are in better condition architecturally and financially, simply reflecting economic reality.

Dharma teacher Changrui observed further that the larger temples in Xi'an were in better shape than her small temple because the temples of historical significance can charge entrance fees, while a small temple like hers relies entirely on donations from occasional visitors and devotees who attend ceremonies performed on the first (the new moon) and the fifteenth (the full moon) of each month in the lunar calendar. She spoke at length about the difficult situation for nunneries in Xi'an, saying that while she had about forty-five nuns who work with her, more live at the temple during the summer because the winter in Xi'an is cold and the temple has limited heating.

Changrui and a group of nuns started work on Wangji Temple in 1997–1998, but after five or six years the temple was still in need of much repair; they simply do not have the funds to finish the renovations. Moreover, she noted that 200,000 RMB will be needed to run the temple annually if she is to achieve her vision of starting a school. Changrui herself went to college in Fujian to learn more about Buddhist doctrine; she hoped, however, that local women would not have to travel so far to get an education.

Wuzhenxi Temple, a small temple in the village of Lantian, southeast of Xi'an, is run by an elderly monk, dharma teacher Hongdao, with overseas connections. The restoration of the temple started in 2000, and the inauguration of the statue of the Buddha at the Opening the Light (*kaiguang*) ceremony was held three years later, in 2004, on the twenty-third day of the first month. The temple is cared for by lay people when the monk is away. The lay manager works outside the temple during the day; his wife, Chen Xiuxian, who is thirty, and another young woman, Li Li, who is eighteen, look after the temple.

When asked about the temple, Li Li explained enthusiastically that its history goes back to the Sui dynasty (589–618). She continued with stories about the paintings on the walls and the various statues in the temple: the reclining Buddha (*wo fo*); big belly Buddha (*dadu fo*); Compassionate Child (*shantong*) and Dragon Girl (*longnü*), a young boy and girl, respectively, both associated with Guanyin; and Guanyin. When asked if the flat-chested statue denoted a male Guanyin, Li Li was adamant that even though flat-chested and wearing a low-cut robe, Guanyin is undeniably a woman. When more questions were directed at Li Li, she went to the side compartments to fetch Chen Xiuxian.

Chen Xiuxian became a nun (*guiyi;* "took refuge") when she was twenty-seven; she married the temple manager at twenty-eight and hoped to become a mother. When asked why some women choose to become nuns, she answered that many do so for family reasons or because of an unstable personal life; she added that women who leave home (*chujia*) to become nuns for such reasons usually regret their decision later. Xiuxian went on to say that many women do not become nuns because of traditional values; women often stay home to look after their parents or marry and start a family of their own. She explained that she believed in Buddhism because it teaches people to become good (*shan*).

Taiwan

Across the Formosa Straits, Buddhism has fared much better. It gained many of the reformist Buddhist monks that the communists drove out, resulting in a bloom in Buddhism in a concentrated area on the island of Taiwan. Nuns have been at the forefront of this new flourishing. Dharma teacher Zhengyan is an illustration of that phenomenon.

Zhengyan was born in Taiwan in 1937, and her secular name is Wong Jun-yun; she is the third daughter of a button tailor and his wife. While she was still very young, she was given to her aunt and uncle, her father's younger brother and wife, who had no children at the time (Ching 1995, 155). She is a contemporary of Sun Shuyun's parents, Shan Ren, and Julia Ching, but all lived in very different milieus.

After Japan had taken the island in 1895, it encouraged an elementary education in Confucianism, science, and Japanese language; the colony was also suffused with Buddhism. When Zhengyan was six, Taiwan became a major naval base for Japan. At the end of World War II, the communists gained ascendancy over the Nationalist Party and won the civil war in 1949; the latter therefore retreated to Taiwan from the mainland, with many Buddhist clergy following.

Zhengyan is a famous nun who founded the Buddhist Association for the Merit of Overcoming Difficulties and Compassionate Relief (Fojiao kenan ciji gongde hu; also known as the Tzu Chi Compassion Relief Society) in 1966 in Hualian. She was exceptional from the start. Although not a disciple of the famous monk Yinshun, she was ordained by him in 1963. Yinshun was one of the monks who had gone to Taiwan after the communist revolution. He was a disciple of Taixu (1890–1947), a reformist monk who in 1915, during World War I and while absorbed in the same experiences as those who initiated the New Culture Movement and the May Fourth Movement, reacted by developing a plan for reorganizing the monastic community in China. He criticized the popular Buddhism that Sun's grandmother had adhered to, instead stressing the need for Buddhist social activism. Compassionate Relief (*ciji*) is one fruit from the seeds planted by Taixu in mainland China; it is active in the areas of charity, medicine, education, and culture. Zhengyan speaks simply, on audiotape, about the process she went through before settling on her choice of Buddhism. She notes how she had, as a young girl, reached out to Christianity because, at the time, there was a Christian doctor that she had heard about; it was rumored that "he had removed a part of his own skin and the skin of his wife, to transplant it onto the burned body of a child." Zhengyan went on that, even though he was a foreigner and a white man, she nevertheless admired him for his actions (ibid., 271).

But she found Christianity wanting and unsatisfactory, not because it was foreign, since Buddhism too is foreign, but because she found that "in Buddhism, there is logical explanation, scientific proof, and philosophical reasoning" (ibid.). But she did not find Buddhism entirely satisfactory, either; in the recording she goes on to say this:

> In the eyes of many, Buddhism is a passive religion and an escape from reality. Buddhism is also viewed as the superstitious belief of the ignorant poor, who lived in backward nations and belonged to the lower class of society.
>
> And that was when I decided to bring Buddhism back to its original form, as Buddha had wanted it to be twenty-five hundred years previously.

> I promised myself that my followers and I would prove to the world that Buddhism is a positive and active way of living and that we Buddhists would continue with our good deeds to help the suffering masses and bring joy to those living in sorrow (ibid.).

Zhengyan was especially spurred into action when Catholic nuns on a mission in Taiwan claimed that Buddhism was "concerned only with personal liberation and not with social ills." She strove to prove the Catholic nuns wrong. In 2002, Compassionate Relief was reported to have provided more than U.S.$20 million per year in charity for projects around the world, including famine relief in Africa and the building of hospitals, colleges, and research centers (ibid., 227). After the 1999 earthquake in Taiwan, Zhengyan made the following remarks in a public speech:

> If we look at society now, we notice that more and more people are creating bad karma. People used to be industrious, thrifty and conservative. They might not have created blessings, but they hardly created any bad karma. But people now use any means to gratify themselves. To reach that objective, they even fight and injure each other.
>
> When people create bad karma together, the land will fight back. Therefore, natural disasters happen. On the other hand, people can also make good karma together. That is why I hope to reduce the bad karma and increase the good (ibid., 233).

Zhengyan's strategy in creating good karma offers a handy illustration of the Buddhist notion of skillful means. Compassionate Relief devotees take what the existing culture offers and start their practice from that; consequently, Chinese Buddhism is suffused with Confucian ideas. When Ching Yu-ing asked Zhengyan for an interpretation of the Confucian notion that "We must take care of all old folks as if they were our parents and tend to all the youngsters as if they were our own children," Zhengyan agreed that all old and young should be taken care of as if they were one's own family. She notes especially the Mother-and-Sister Association within Compassionate Relief, wherein 130 women pay regular visits to students in various schools. Zhengyan adds that all children need attention and someone to talk to; children in Taiwan can now get that attention not only from their own mothers and sisters but from Compassionate members as well. She finishes her commentary to Ching Yu-ing by saying that Compassionate Relief members follow that particular Confucian teaching and put it into action; she further emphasizes that one of the songs composed by a devotee for the foundation tells the world that "under heaven everyone should be loved, trusted, and forgiven" (ibid., 108–110).

But even as Zhengyan has become one of the most successful representatives of Buddhism in Taiwan, is deeply loved and respected, enjoys fame and garners tremendous financial support, she is still subject to the eight special rules, or weighty regulations (*bajingfa*), imposed only on nuns. They are as follows:

1. A senior nun, even if with a hundred years' standing, must pay obeisance to a monk who is junior to her, even if he has just been ordained.

2. A nun must not take up residence in a district where there are no monks.

3. A nun must wait for the monks' congregation to come and appoint the day of fasting at the time of the full moon.

4. A nun must invite criticism from both the monks' and nuns' communities at the end of her residence.

5. If guilty of serious misconduct, a nun must undergo penance of half a month toward both communities.

6. A novice must seek ordination from both communities at the end of her two years of practice of the six rules.

7. A nun must not revile nor abuse a monk in any way.

8. A nun cannot rebuke a monk formally, whereas a monk is allowed to reprove a nun officially.

Lin Guoliang reports that during a ceremony for the welcoming of a relic of the Buddha (*fosheli*) in Taiwan, there was widespread incredulity and perhaps, he writes, even dissatisfaction when the polished and well-accomplished Zhengyan went on stage to pay homage to the monk-elders.

This discomfort with the first rule levied against a nun is not an isolated case: Lin cites another situation, this time at a summer camp in China. The incident was related to him by Professor Wang Leiquan of Fudan University in Shanghai. During a Buddhist summer camp, a nun bowed to all monks before giving a dharma-talk or sermon, after which a young woman stood up and said, "I had originally intended to *chujia* [become a monk or nun], but seeing this custom, I do not wish to *chujia* anymore" (Lin 2003, 248–249).

The two incidents illustrate the tension between the perceived traditional misogyny, or at least gender inequality and female subservience, in Buddhism and contemporary opinions about gender equality. Dharma master Xingyun (Hsing Yun), founder of Fo Guang Shan, another vastly successful Buddhist organization in Taiwan, has moved decisively to remove the historical differentiation between monks and nuns that is represented most clearly by the eight special rules and five obstructions (*wuzhang*). The latter are mentioned in the *Lotus Sutra* and state that a woman cannot achieve the rank of Brahma, Indra, chief guardian of the four quarters, world conqueror, or Buddha, suggesting therefore that women have to be reborn as men before they can achieve release from transmigration.

Xingyun gets to the heart of the Buddhist understanding of equality by appealing to the Mahayana notion of emptiness. He quotes chapter 5 of the *Diamond Sutra:* "Whatsoever that has characteristics, that is also delusion; if one perceives that the many characteristics are not-characteristics, then one perceives the *Rulai* (*Tathagata,* Thus Come One, Thus Gone One or the Buddha)" (Xingyun 2002, 240). He further cites the precedent of Baizhang Huaihai (720–814), a famous Chan master who, according to tradition, established the monastic rules for the Chan school (*Chanyuan qinggui*), which were more suitable to Tang culture, thereby circumventing rather than changing or destroying the Indian *vinaya* (ibid., 243).

In *The Development in the Community of Nuns* (*Biqiuni sengtuan de fazhan*), Xingyun writes at length about the historical importance of women within the Buddhist tradition, making much of slim historical data. He notes also that in 1998 at Bodh Gaya, the ordination of nuns was brought back from China to South Asia, where it had disappeared, when forty young women from Sri Lanka came forward to receive tonsure; he goes on to enumerate twenty famous contemporary Chinese nuns from different lineages, thirteen of whom are also mentioned in the Digital Museum of Buddhism in Taiwan (see References, below), which includes twenty-seven nuns in contrast to forty-six monks. Xingyun lists their many accomplishments: building temples; bringing Chinese Buddhism into the international arena by erecting temples and doing missionary work; establishing Buddhist schools; editing encyclopedias; setting up and teaching in universities; creating cultural foundations; and setting up charity foundations.

One such nun, Yifa, a member of Fo Guang Shan, is active in the United States; she received her doctorate from Yale University, spent 2001–2002 as a visiting scholar at Harvard University, and in 2002 published *The Origins of Buddhist Monastic Codes in China: An Annotated Translation and Study of the*

Ordination scroll of Empress Zhang *(detail), 1493. (San Diego Museum of Art/ Gift of Mr. and Mrs. John Jeffers) See page 229.*

Chanyuan qinggui. Yifa is active in missions within the field of universities; in the same year her book was published, she instituted and brought to life her conception of a one-month residency program for university students and organized the first annual summer Monastic Life Program, which seeks to bring interested North American and European students to Fo Guang Shan's home temple in Gaoxiong (Kaohsiung), Taiwan.

Xingyun's essay, which mentions Yifa as one of the twenty famous contemporary nuns, concludes with four points that nuns might attend to and focus on in the future: first, equalizing the status between monks and nuns; second, like monks, nuns should take up work outside of the temple by focusing on the development of culture, education, and mission and charity work; third, clerical communities must organize themselves and systematize various aspects within the institution, thereby minimizing and eliminating inconsistent administration; and fourth, there should be equal access to education, so that both monks and nuns will be equally well educated (ibid., 244–245).

The irony is clear: a prominent and successful monk is leading the call to gender equality and has created one of the most vibrant of Chinese Buddhist communities, staffed by many monks who are not only highly educated but also active in the world, living out the ideals initially put forward by Taixu the reformer. Xingyun is not, however, entirely positive in his estimation of women. In the penultimate paragraph of his essay, he gives a rather traditional account of female characteristics, writing that even as women tend to be attentive to details, are compassionate, and kind, thereby making practice easier for them, they can also be small-minded, limited in their intellectual reach, and lacking in wisdom when compared with men (ibid., 244).

It is also important to bear in mind, however, that in advocating for his female disciples, Xingyun was labeled Leader of the Women's Work Team. Once, when confronted by a monk who had just taken tonsure complaining about a senior nun at Fo Guang Shan not bowing to him, Xingyun noted that deference must come from the heart, with respect gained from experience, and cannot be regulated by a single rule (ibid., 234). Nevertheless, it remains a question whether the community at Fo Guang Shan will elect a nun as the head of its organization in the future.

At the beginning of the twenty-first century it is Buddhism, the *foreign* Chinese religion, that is most often identified in the popular imagination of the West as the primary formal religious affiliation of the Chinese community. There are many reasons for this, two of which rest in the characteristics of the Buddhist and Daoist organizations. First of all, there is the fact that the Buddhist community has had to be well organized in order for its monastic community to survive. This organization was responsive to the pressing demand for change at the end of the nineteenth and the beginning of the twentieth centuries, integrating some of the values from the secular New Culture and May Fourth movements. But perhaps more important, Buddhism had an international aspect, so that the local and global elements were able to work together, reinforcing each other, and so that the successful Chinese reform movements might be understood as having succeeded within a larger global sphere.

Secondly, there is the historical weakness of Daoism, which is in part engendered by fuzzy boundaries regarding what passes as Daoism, and the lack of a central authority to adjudicate legitimacy. That in turn results in identification with some nonlineage affiliated, self-identifying popular religious practices, such as divination and spirit possession, as Daoist, which in turn results in charges of superstition. Early European and U.S. missionaries were particularly antagonistic toward this element of superstition in the indigenous religions, and that aversion was later taken up by the Chinese themselves. Because religious Daoism is primarily local to East Asia, there were few resources to draw upon from outside the area when Daoism suffered a setback from 150 years of attack from secular reformists, from the New Culture Movement to the Cultural Revolution. There is currently, nevertheless, a revival of Daoism in China.

Daoism

With Daoism, we move into a religion that is amorphous when compared with Confucianism and Buddhism, for not only are the connections between individuals, groups, and communities difficult to trace but, in addition, personal information about novices, nuns (*nüguan*), and masters (*daoshi*) is neither readily available nor easy to gather. As a Daoist master on Hua Shan noted, protocol discourages the asking and answering of personal questions about and by the clergy.

Buddhist and Daoist ritual specialists are very easy to tell apart: first and foremost, Buddhists shave off their hair; Daoists do not. Instead, they wear their hair in a topknot. In terms of clothing, the standard garb for Daoist women is the same as men: loose black pants and a plain white tunic. During more formal religious ceremonies, however, Daoists wear ritual clothing that is typically yellow with a black trim, easily distinguishable from the plain brown or gray robes worn by Buddhist nuns. Daoist nuns may also wear a black cap over their hair-knot. Nuns who carry out key ritual functions may also wear more elaborate vestments such as a gold wrap shaped like a flame, a symbol of spiritual realization. The fabric of vestments worn at important festivals is still more elaborate, frequently embroidered with symbols that give an air of brilliance and majesty. When Daoists performed vital roles at the imperial court, no expense was spared in the production of stunning vestments befitting the splendor and dignity of the occasion. One of the most well-known depictions of the richness of Daoist material culture is the ordination scroll of Empress Zhang, dated 1493. The scroll depicts the investiture of the Empress Zhang as a Daoist master. Of particular interest is her yellow robe, a splendid example of the intricate and sumptuous ritual garments used during Daoist services at the imperial court (see illustration on page 227).

The material cultures of Daoist nuns and masters are, and have traditionally been, very different from those of Buddhist nuns. And there is another difference: whereas all buddhas and early disciples of Siddhartha Gautama, the historical Buddha, are portrayed as men, Daoism has many female deities, such as the Queen Mother of the West (Xiwangmu), the Mother of the Pole Star (Doumu), the Old Mother of the Primordial Lord of the Morning and Evening Clouds (Xiayuanjun laomu), and Lady Mysterious Lass of the Nine Heavens (Jiutian xuannü). Guanyin is often the only female figure in the overwhelmingly male Buddhist pantheon, and even though she is frequently but not always portrayed as female, she is at least most often understood to be female. This polymorphous Indian Guanyin, most often presented in her feminized form in China, has been readily absorbed into the host of Daoist and other indigenous feminine deities. For Buddhism, most of the common buddhas and bodhisattvas other than Guanyin are again male: for example, there are Samantabhadra, who symbolizes virtue; Manjusri, who symbolizes wisdom; and Maitreya, who symbolizes the hope for a future teacher and enlightenment. In stark relief, there are many efficacious female spirits in Daoism, such as Tian Hou in Hong Kong, or the Old Mother of Mount Li (Li shan laomu) in a village just outside of Xi'an.

The Old Mother of Mount Li is a Daoist goddess conflated with Nüwa, the female creator god in Chinese mythology, and the Old Mother of the Ultimate Nothingness (Wuji laomu). The placard outside the hall dedicated to her explains that she "gave birth and transformed ten thousand things, is an early ancestral deity and creator deity of the people of Hua-Xia." It goes on to say that she created people out of the yellow earth, refined colored rocks to complete the gray green sky, instituted marriage, and created the eight moral treasures: filial piety, fraternity, loyalty, trustworthiness, decorum, righteousness, incorruptibility, and honor. This is radically different from the masculine world of Buddhism. Moreover, that these Confucian virtues should be attributed to a female deity is of special interest because it reinforces and makes visible the bedrock of an indigenous impulse: syncretism. The Old Mother's birthday is given as the fifteenth day of the sixth lunar month, and her antiquity is attested to by the date in which the hall dedicated to her was built: circa 200 B.C.E., during the Qin-Han period.

Although personal details about Daoist religious specialists are not easy to come by, both a novice at the Hall for the Old Mother of Mt. Li (Lishan laomu gong) and a Daoist master at a temple at the foot of Mt. Hua, northeast of Xi'an offered general remarks about the religion. The novice at Mt. Li sat at the front of the temple as the receptionist, greeting visitors. She seemed to be in her early twenties and, unlike most female Daoists, did not have long hair. Rather, her hair was cut short and unevenly, which she explained was standard practice for a novice. She explained further that one simply starts the process toward ordination by paying respects to a person one wishes to have as a teacher (*bai shifu*). When asked about the structure of advancement through the spiritual ranks, her explanations were vague, saying simply that the teacher would know when the novice is ready for the next step. When questioned further about practices, she answered that chanting scriptures (*nianjing*), sitting in meditation (*dazuo*), and studying by herself were all parts of her practice. She also commented that if a novice should wish to attend school formally, she is free to pursue her ambitions. The young novice continued, saying that there were about seven women at the temple. Three were in their twenties and thirties, the rest in their fifties.

At the temple at the foot of Mt. Hua there are six words chiseled into a rock: "benefit others" (*li ta*) and "all humanity is equal" (*renlei pingdeng*). This notion of equality cuts to the heart of Daoist internal practices, since both men and women are believed to have the capacity to become immortals (*xian*). The practices, however, are necessarily different for women and men because of their physiological differences: a woman's practice is to stop the flow of her menstrual blood, which is her essence (*jing*), whereas a man's is to prevent the loss of his semen, which is his essence, by avoiding ejaculation (Despeux and Kohn 2003).

The Daoist master at the Mt. Hua temple, like the novice at Mt. Li, did not discuss this aspect of the practice. Dressed in the common blue Daoist casual wear, she had her hair put up in the Daoist style and was sewing in the courtyard of a side compartment at the back of the temple. It was difficult to tell her age; she might have been fifty-five or sixty-five. Her description of religious practices confirmed the information provided by the novice. The structure of morning and evening worship, meditation, and study is reminiscent of and similar to Buddhist practices. When asked why there seemed to be more men in both Daoist and Buddhist temples, she answered that the surrounding villages are poor, and many young men are unemployed; thus they join the temples for work. She then echoed what dharma teacher Changrui of the Buddhist Wangji Temple had said, that the southeast coastal area is better developed; hence, more Daoist schools for women (*kundao yuan*) can be found there, particularly in Shanghai. The Daoist master went on to suggest, as did Chen Xiuxian at the Buddhist Wuzhenxi Temple in the village of Lantian, that tradition plays a part in limiting the number of women who leave home to pursue a religious vocation. She intimated that the women have to stay home to look after the young and the elderly; she intoned confidentially that women under fifty could cause a lot of trouble at temples, but she did not elaborate. She did note, however, that the temple on Mt. Hua likes to take women who are over fifty. She volunteered with enthusiasm that there was a senior female practitioner (*dashangfang*) in her seventies who lived on the mountain and asked if I would be interested in seeking her out. She went on to say that this woman resumed her practice only after the Cultural Revolution because she had to hide in society during the unfriendly times.

As Daoism is being restored in China, it is receiving support from Taiwan and Hong Kong, where Daoism had experienced an earlier revival in recent years. Daoist nuns in Hong Kong can be observed wearing their familiar yellow robes while performing funeral rituals. In Taiwan, Daoist women, like Buddhist nuns, are also becoming more prominent. For example, Weng Taiming, the celibate head of the Institute of the Way and the Power (Daode yuan), has gained a strong reputation. Her charitable work has been compared favorably with that of the Buddhist Zhengyan and her Compassionate Relief organization. Ho Wanli notes that Weng Taiming is celibate and unusual because she had succeeded in "slaying the dragon"—that is, stopping her menstrual flow—in her forties. Although relatively slow to start and comparatively unknown when compared with Taiwan's Buddhist nuns, Daoist women are starting to adapt themselves to the challenge of modernity; they have become more prominent, and aspects of their social work have been made more visible while the traditional Daoist focus on health and longevity is simultaneously maintained (Ho 2003).

Conclusion

The concern for the quality of lives for women, rooted in Western feminism, has clearly made an impact on the lives of religious women in Chinese religions, but the effects have been varied. Particular schools of Buddhism such as Fo Guang Shan, interested in reform and the spread of Buddhist ideals, have made strong public statements regarding policies about the place of women in their beliefs and organizational practices. Confucianism and Daoism, on the other hand, have been less coherent, forceful, and visible in their presentation of the place of women in their teachings.

Despite these differences, there seems to be a common thread running through the formal traditions: the concern for the quality of women's lives and work in the larger context of the community and society. In short, the concern is directed at strengthening the community within the Confucian context of self-discipline and personal cultivation. This is reminiscent of the teaching in the Confucian *Great Learning,* where it is written: "From the Son of Heaven to the common people, everyone must consider developing the self to be the fundamental root of things" (Sommer 1995, 39).

Perhaps that is why the formal aggregate of Chinese religion has remained distinctively Chinese: it is less about enlightenment and salvation in the world to come, and more about cultivating one's character and maintaining harmony in the natural and human worlds. Women are not exempt from this responsibility. The different practices and methods come from, or perhaps aim toward, one primary inclination: harmony. Perhaps Confucianism has not gone so far away.

References

Ching Yu-ing. 1995. *Master of Love and Mercy.* Nevada City, NV: Blue Dolphin.

Despeux, Catherine, and Livia Kohn. 2003. *Women in Daoism.* Cambridge: Three Pines.

Digital Museum of Buddhism in Taiwan. National Taiwan University, Chinese Centre of Buddhist Studies, and National Taipei Fine Arts University. http://ccbs.ntu.edu.tw/formosa/index-people.html.

Ho, Wanli. 2003. "Daoist Nuns in Contemporary Taiwan." Paper Presented at the international conference on "Daoism and the Contemporary World," Boston University, June 5–7, 2003.

Kelleher, Theresa. 1987. "Confucianism." Pp. 135–159 in *Women in World Religions.* Edited by Arvind Sharma. Albany: State University of New York Press.

Kung, Hans, and Julia Ching. 1989. *Christianity and Chinese Religions.* New York: Doubleday.

Lin Guoliang. 2003. "Fojiao nei de nan-nü pingdeng wenti" [The question of equality between men and women in Buddhism] *Pumen xuebao: Du hou gan* [Universal Gate Buddhist Journal: Readers' Reflections] 2003: 247–253. Kaohsiung: Fo Guang Shan Foundation.

Lopez, Donald, Jr., ed. 2002. *Modern Buddhism: Readings for the Unenlightened.* London: Penguin.

Sommer, Deborah. 1995. *Chinese Religion: An Anthology of Sources.* New York: Oxford University Press.

Sun, Shuyun. 2003. *Ten Thousand Miles without a Cloud.* London: HarperCollins.

Woo, Terry. 2003. "Confucianism." Pp. 99–118 in *Her Voice, Her Faith: Women Speak on World Religions.* Edited by Arvind Sharma and Katherine K. Young. Boulder, CO: Westview.

Xingyun. 2002. "Biqiuni sengtuan de fazhan" [The development in the community of nuns]. *Pumen xuebao* [Universal Gate Buddhist Journal] 9: 233–245. Kaohsiung: Fo Guang Shan Foundation.

10

Contemporary Chinese American Religious Life

JONATHAN H. X. LEE

CHINESE RELIGIOUS LIFE comes in multiple expressions: it is ritualistically lively, adaptable, inventive and, overall, syncretistic. Scholars have traditionally defined and investigated Chinese religion in terms of the combined interaction among Confucianism, Daoism, Buddhism, and popular religious myths and rituals. Their work, however, has tended to locate Chinese religions within the sphere of Chinese culture and history. It has tended to ignore the religious experience of Chinese diaspora communities, those culturally distinct populations outside the People's Republic of China, the Republic of China on Taiwan, and other states and territories where ethnic Chinese are either a majority population or a significant cultural force (for example, Singapore). Within the United States, Chinese Americans have created specific enclaves of culturally significant communities referred to as Chinatowns both in the past and today. The inhabitants of those communities point to the historical, social, political, linguistic, and economic diversity that complicates the Chinese American religious landscape.

In order to understand the religious life of Chinese American diaspora communities, it is important first of all to understand the distinctive features of these communities in a larger historical context. This broad historical context can be divided into three phases: first, the early political doctrine that specifically excluded Chinese immigration; second, the ideal of the United States as a melting pot; and third, the meaningful pluralism that is the heart of the new American religious landscape. This chapter seeks to explain how Chinese religious institutions and communities functioned in each of these historical contexts. Secondly, this chapter offers two case studies, one from the early period and one from contemporary times, that reflect the changing boundaries of Chinese religious life on U.S. soil. Thirdly, the chapter surveys two emerging transnational Chinese religious organizations whose global structure is creating a new kind of religious community. Although these examples are primarily based on Chinese American religious temples and communities in California and secondarily in other parts of the United States, they all reflect wider phenomena in contemporary Chinese American religious life. The chapter concludes by giving consideration to the changing dynamics of Chinese religious life in contemporary diaspora communities.

Historical Context

The Early Period

Between 1848 and 1882, waves of Chinese immigrants came to California in search of gold. They came predominantly from the southern province of Guangdong. The Chinese pioneers began by establishing Chinatowns, re-building and re-creating a sense of traditional community. The majority of these immigrants were young men in their working prime, chosen by their families to journey to "Gold Mountain" (*Jinshan;* Cantonese: *Gam San*) in the hope of striking it rich and returning home after several years abroad. The discovery of gold at Sutter's Mill in 1848 had evoked a deep gaze toward the West Coast. Caucasian tradesmen recited embellished stories of gold and prosperity in the United States in order to convince young Chinese men to travel across the Pacific Ocean, but their real motive was to trade in "China-men." The possibility of finding gold was more legendary than real for the Chinese miners: even though there was a lot of gold to mine, they faced stiff racial prejudice from Caucasian miners as well as from local and state governments. The best example of this was the establishment of the 1850 Foreign Miner's Tax, which was enforced mainly against Chinese, who often had to pay more than once.

San Francisco was a major port of entry for Chinese immigrants during the early period of the Gold Rush. In the later 1840s there were some 325 Chinese forty-niners; by 1851, 2,716; and by 1852, 20,026 (Takaki 1989, 80). In 1876, the Pacific Mail Steamship Company began regularly scheduled runs between Hong Kong and San Francisco. Between 1870 and 1883, an average of 12,000 Chinese immigrants were arriving through the port of San Francisco each year. And by 1870 there were 63,000 Chinese living on U.S. soil—between 75 and 80 percent of them in California. Hence, in the Golden State there were many Chinese communities of varying sizes along the coast, from as far south as Baja and San Diego to as far north as Mendocino.

Life in the United States was arduous. Discriminatory immigration laws beginning with the Page Act of 1875 had affected the number of Chinese women who were eligible to immigrate, and as a result the early Chinese communities were composed mainly of bachelors. They were hit again with discriminatory laws that hindered their ability to establish a family when the state's antimiscegenation law extended in 1906 to include Chinese men. The pinnacle of discriminatory legislation, however, occurred in 1882, with the passage of the Chinese Exclusion Act (extended in 1892 and again in 1904) prohibiting Chinese laborers from entering the United States and resulting in a large decrease in the Chinese immigrant population in the early twentieth century. This demographic decline resulted in the gradual disappearance of Chinatowns throughout the West Coast. For example, the Chinese communities in California towns such as Cambria, Riverside, Mendocino, and San Luis Obispo slowly disappeared as the remaining Chinese moved northward to San Francisco or southward toward Los Angeles—two cities with major Chinese centers and more possibilities for employment. Those years, however, witnessed an increasing number of Chinese American families, which resulted in a new generation of acculturated English-speaking Chinese Americans who grew up between the 1930s and 1940s.

Chinese exclusion was finally repealed with the passage of the 1943 and 1965 Immigration and Nationality Reform Acts, which lifted the anti-Chinese feature of U.S. immigration policy. The repeal of Chinese exclusion affected the Chinese American landscape substantially: the population increased from 106,334 in 1940 to more than 2.4 million in 2000, most of that number being recent immigrants. The last three decades have therefore witnessed a rich transformation in the underlying terrain of Chinese American religious communities.

From "Melting Pot" to "Religious Pluralism"

The liberalization of immigration policy after 1965 paralleled the changing mainstream attitude and belief in U.S. culture. The initial American perception of Chinese people was ambiguously positive: they were seen as diligent, clean, industrious, and endowed with the potential to become good citizens. But once economic competition in agriculture and gold mining increased, that attitude quickly shifted to one of exclusion. The first decade of the twentieth century had ushered in the great image of the melting pot, a process of assimilation by which diverse peoples from around the world gathered on U.S. soil and, over a period of time, acculturated themselves into mainstream American life. Chinese immigrants, however, did not melt into U.S. mainstream society smoothly. In terms of their religious practices, the first generation of Chinese Americans were creative in their attempts to "fit in." That is well illustrated with the use of the term "church" instead of "temple" for their religious institutions. The historic Taoist Temple in Hanford, California, was officially the "Taoist Church" up until the late 1970s. Despite such attempts, however, Chinese immigrants found it difficult to assimilate. Because of their physical, cultural, and linguistic differences, mainstream U.S. society concluded that the Chinese were resisting assimilation. As a result, they were perceived as potentially dangerous and subversive to the American way of life.

The end of World War II ushered in the countercultural movements that began to question the normative vision of U.S. social life, and with it the expectation that immigrants would assimilate into mainstream society. The civil rights movements of the 1960s and 1970s not only expressed dissatisfaction with racist beliefs and public policies but also revealed a fundamental problem with the concept of assimilation. To the extent that the American way of life was normatively white and middle class, it was impossible for whole segments of the population ever to become fully "American." The imagined consensus promoted by those who favored assimilation could be sustained only by excluding people with dark skin, non-European ancestries, and limited incomes—in particular, Asian immigrants. The civil rights movements not only demanded practical changes in public policy; they also demanded a transformation of U.S. national self-identity. They insisted that Americans recognize themselves to be a pluralistic people, that there were diverse and legitimate alternative ways of being American. This produced a pluralistic attitude toward American life, one that resembles a "salad bar"—indicating that Americans and American life come in a variety of styles, cultures, religions, languages, and so on.

Between 1882 and 1965, exclusionist attitudes gave way to the melting pot idea, which then gave way to the cultural pluralism of the 1980s. Since 1965

A family's prayers are sent to heaven with the scent of burning incense. Many sticks of incense are placed together in a burner at the Kong Chow Buddhist Temple in San Francisco's Chinatown. (Phil Schermeister/Corbis)

there has been a rejuvenation of Chinatown communities across the United States, especially in San Francisco, Los Angeles, New York, Chicago, and Houston. These regions have also experienced the formation of new China-towns in rural areas. In all of these areas, the formation of the new China-towns has occurred and continues to occur as a result of the continuous flow of Chinese emigrants from Taiwan, Hong Kong, mainland China, and the Indo-Chinese from Southeast Asia. In these recent communities, temples and religious businesses have rapidly appeared on the new pluralistic religious landscape.

Contemporary Chinatown communities are now multigenerational, multinational, and heterogeneous. Chinese immigrants are creating and liv-ing in "culturally Chinese" communities outside of China, Taiwan, and Hong Kong. It is possible for them to live without speaking English, to have conti-nuity between the way they live their lives in the United States and the way they lived their lives back home. The religious lives of the new Chinese American communities are therefore as diverse and complex as the communities in which they are located. This stands in direct contrast to the early homogenous bachelor society, which did not reflect the intrinsic diversity in Chinese religious life. The following two case studies illustrate this extraordinary change in Chinese American religious life.

Early Period Case Study: The Temple of Kwan Tai

History of the Temple

In 1854, seven Chinese junks set sail for "Gold Mountain," but only two made it to the California coast. One landed at Monterey Bay, the other on the Mendocino coast at Caspar Beach. Many of the Chinese immigrants who made their home along California's coast introduced seaweed farming and abalone drying as commercial export industries. They gathered, dried, and exported seafood resources, including seaweed, kelp, and abalone, back to China. The historic Chinese community in Mendocino was one such community. As these coastal communities developed, the Chinese created a community by establishing homes, building restaurants and shops, and constructing religious institutions. Shortly after their arrival in Mendocino, the Chinese immigrants built a small cabin temple dedicated to Guandi (Kwan Tai), a deified general from the Three Kingdoms period (third century C.E.), regarded as a god of military affairs, literature, wealth, and business. By the 1860s, some 500 to 700 Chinese made Mendocino their home.

The Temple of Kwan Tai sits on a parcel of land at 45160 Albion Street in the historic district of Mendocino, facing the Pacific Ocean. It is perched on a south-facing hillside above Albion Street. This placement of the temple is consistent with the Chinese practice of geomancy (*fengshui*), according to which temples and large palatial buildings should always face south. The Temple of Kwan Tai is colloquially known as the Joss House. The word "joss" is believed to be an adaptation of the Portuguese word for god, *deos*. Hence, a temple where the Chinese venerate their gods became known as a "joss house."

The exact date of the temple's founding is unclear. The earliest written document of the temple's history is a Sanborn Insurance Company map that dates it back to July 1883. However, based on the oral history of George Hee,

Loretta Hee McCoard, left, and her sister Lorraine Hee Chorley, right, look out the windows of Kwan Tai Temple in Mendocino, California. The temple, once used by the Chinese who built the railroads and chopped timber on California's north coast, is a monument to one family's devotion to tradition and the story of a vanished population. (Eric Risberg/AP Photo)

born in Mendocino in 1897, the temple dates back to 1854. Hee recounts that his grandfather, in combination with the other Chinese residents, constructed the temple when they purchased the property and built it with twelve dollars worth of virgin redwood. Successive members of the Hee family have held and preserved the temple since 1871, when the deed of the property was signed over to Lee Sing John. In 1979, the temple was registered as California Historical Landmark No. 927. A report written by the California state architect dates the construction to the early 1850s based on the materials used to build the temple, which supports the Hee family's estimate.

In 1995, members of the Hee family deeded the temple property to a newly established Temple of Kwan Tai, Inc., a nonprofit organization whose mission is to preserve and restore the historical landmark as a celebration of

Mendocino's community diversity. In addition, it will serve as a place in which to educate local schoolchildren and surrounding community members about the history and contributions of the Chinese in the United States. The nonprofit organization was established so that they would be able to solicit funds to support the restoration project. Before the establishment of the nonprofit organization, ownership of the temple's property was shared among six members of the Hee family.

In 1998–1999 the Temple of Kwan Tai received a thorough historic building assessment by architect Laura Culberson, who works for the architectural firm of Carey and Company of San Francisco. The assessment was partially funded by the Cynthia Woods Mitchell Fund of the National Trust for Historic Preservation. Culberson's report provided the documentation and prospective plans for restoration that enabled the temple to secure restoration funds through the California Resources Agency. Culberson concluded her report with a statement on the significance of the Temple of Kwan Tai:

> The Mendocino Joss House is an invaluable resource to the State of California. It is the only surviving physical document (made more significant by its continued use from the early 1850s), which retains its original integrity and marks the now mostly lost history of the Chinese in Mendocino. Mendocino was one of the few communities along the Pacific North coast that housed a substantial Chinese community. Although Mendocino's Chinatown burned in 1910, the knowledge of its existence and the cultural and historical relationship between the Joss House and the Chinese community are significant aspects of local and state history (Temple of Kwan Tai n.d.).

The architect's report, however, revealed that although the temple had remarkably survived for nearly 150 years, it was in serious need of stabilization and renovation. The foundations had to be supported, which involved raising the building, leveling it on steel support beams, digging new footings, and bringing the structure up to code. The exterior walls were removed temporarily to put in additional support and to place insulation between the interior and exterior walls. The exterior wall on the east side was replaced because the lumber was not salvageable. Additionally, the interior floor had to be replaced. The exterior walls are now newly painted in the original red with green trim. A plaque at the bottom of the stairs signals the temple as a California Historic Landmark.

Through the efforts of the Hee family, the temple trustees, Mendocino youth groups involved in the North Coast Rural Challenge Network, the National Trust for Historic Preservation, and the California Coastal Resources Agency, the Temple of Kwan Tai was officially rededicated on October 13, 2001. The rededication ceremony included a parade from Little Lake Street to the temple, a Lion Dance, as well as *gong fu* (kung fu) and *taiji* (t'ai-chi) performances by the Chinese Redwood Empire Association of Santa Rosa. Lorraine Hee Chorley, the Temple of Kwan Tai director; Anthony VeerKamp, from the National Trust for Historic Preservation; Patty Campbell, the 4th District supervisor; and David Colfax, the 5th District supervisor, all addressed the people in attendance. In addition, Buddhist nuns from the City of Ten Thousand Buddhas at Ukiah performed a Buddhist blessing ritual.

Members of the Hee family packaged their own Kwan Tai Temple Tea, made of a special black Oolong tea from Shui Xian. Each box of tea carries a decorative label commemorating the temple's rededication. Proceeds from the sale of the Kwan Tai Temple Tea are used to support the temple museum. The restoration efforts did not go unnoticed. On October 10, 2002, at the National Preservation Conference in Cleveland, Ohio, the Temple of Kwan Tai was awarded the prestigious National Preservation Honor Award.

Description of the Temple

Leading up to the entrance is a building-wide staircase painted red with green trim. The exterior wallboards are also painted red with green trim. Before the restoration the exterior walls were weathered to an almost natural red-brown color. From the base of the staircase one can see a red board with gold Chinese characters flanking the top of the green entrance door; it reads (from right to left) "Wu di miao," meaning "Temple of the Military God."

Upon entering the temple, one sees that it is a small but cozy room. The main altar dedicated to Guandi is located against the north wall, directly in front of the main entrance. The altar is crafted of locally milled tongue-and-grove and plain boards with simple cornice features, similar to the two narrow secondary altar pedestals in the front. The altar is painted green, while the secondary pedestals have been painted red with faded green-blue and gold highlights. The altar is elaborately decorated with aged yellow drapery, peacock feathers, and a red painted signboard over the top and vertical memorial boards with large gold characters.

The original image of Guandi accompanied by his comrades Liu Bei and Zhang Fei was made of fabric. It was an old, unframed, incense-sooted canvas about two-and-a-half by five feet in size, the focal feature of the altar. The image, fragile with age, was unfortunately damaged during the restoration process, when both the front and rear doors were accidentally left open and a sudden gust of wind took its toll on the antique painting. However, on a trip to San Francisco's Chinatown, Lorraine Hee Chorley and Loretta Hee McCoard happened on an exact replica of the original Guandi painting. The image currently hanging on the main shrine has a black background, and the images of Guandi, Liu Bei, and Zhang Fei are made of mother-of-pearl, seashells, and colored glass.

On the left side of the main altar there is a display of ceremonial flags, along with antique Chinese drums and baskets. There are several green boards inscribed with gold Chinese characters that are mounted on the walls of the temple. Local Chinese residents, either as a way to initiate a prayer or as a way to return thanks, donated these boards to the temple. There is a little room in the rear of the temple. Historically, it may have been the sleeping quarters for the temple-keeper, but today it has been transformed into an office. There are awards from the city and state recognizing the Temple of Kwan Tai's cultural and historical significance. There are also a miniature lion costume, swords decorating the walls, an air conditioner, a bookshelf, and a desk. When I visited the Temple of Kwan Tai on May 24, 2003, I noticed two abalone shells with offerings of flowers, coins, and seashells, in addition to a Chinese rice bowl with cloves of garlic. Loretta Hee McCoard said that some members of the local community had placed them there because they understand the religious nature of the temple.

The life and history of the Temple of Kwan Tai, in addition to the Chinese community of Mendocino, reflect larger cultural patterns. Lorraine and Loretta Hee McCoard's diligent work in restoring the Temple of Kwan Tai in the memory of their father reflects a deep appreciation for history, community, and tradition. The Hee sisters recall memories of their childhood in which the little bright-red cabin was a reminder of how different they were from the rest of their community. Today, it is the opposite; it is this difference that is celebrated, embraced, and remembered. The historic landmark status of the temple makes it a permanent part of Chinese American religious history. On receiving the National Trust for Historic Preservation's National Preservation Honor Award on October 10, 2002, Lorraine Hee Chorley said:

We have kept a promise for four generations, and it is our ancestors who deserve the praise for their pioneer spirits. The Temple has withstood years of turmoil, change and peace. The restoration, rehabilitation ensures that its story will be told for years to come. The Temple of Kwan Tai stands as a reminder to us all that this country was built on diversity and cooperation.

Contemporary Period Case Study: Ma-tsu Temple U.S.A.

On March 14, 1986, the Ma-tsu Temple U.S.A. was established in San Francisco's Chinatown on 562 Grant Avenue and officially registered as a non-profit religious institution. This temple was established as a branch of the Chaotian Temple located in Beigang, Taiwan. In the mid-1990s the temple relocated to 30 Beckett Street. The temple's stated mission is to advocate the virtues of Mazu (Ma-tsu), uphold the Buddhist dharma, teach the principles of human kindness and relations, and promote social morality.

The establishment of the Ma-tsu Temple U.S.A. bears witness to the changing patterns of Chinese immigration that were brought about by the end of the 1882 Chinese Exclusion Act. The 1965 Immigration Act abolished the provision, first established in 1924 and retained in the Immigration and Nationality Act of 1952, that favored immigrants of Western European origin. Furthermore, amendments in 1981 were directed toward increasing Chinese immigration—including a separate quota of 20,000 for Taiwan, which Taiwan had previously shared with China and Hong Kong. The subsequent series of amendments in 1990, collectively referred to as the Immigration Act of 1990, provided for an overall increase in worldwide immigration and increased the allocation for both family-related and employment-related immigration. It also created a separate basis by which "diversity immigrants"—that is, nationals of countries previously under-represented since 1965, could enter the United States. It was that series of laws and amendments that enabled Chinese immigrants from Taiwan to enter the United States in the second half of the twentieth century. Like their earlier compatriots, they began to establish communities while negotiating life as new immigrant Americans. Their religion played a central role in their resettlement and the formation of their new ethnic-cultural identity.

Ritual Tradition and Veneration

Mazu's official imperial title is the Empress of Heaven (Tianhou). The Empress of Heaven is popularly venerated in Taiwan as Mazu, an affectionate kinship term denoting "Granny." However, in mainland China and Hong Kong she is venerated by her formal title, Tianhou (or in Cantonese as Tin Hau). Historically, the Empress of Heaven has also been worshiped as a sea goddess. It was this role that made her ideal for early Chinese immigrants: their journey to Gold Mountain included an arduous three-week journey across the Pacific Ocean and adjustment to a strange land. Upon arriving safely and alive they returned thanks by constructing a temple to her. The first Tianhou temple was, not surprisingly, founded in San Francisco's Chinatown in 1852. In the age of airplanes, Tianhou's role as sea goddess has given way to other roles: protector of women and children, hearer of prayers, healer of illnesses, giver of prosperity, and protector of family and community.

The biggest festival at Mazu temples takes place on her birthday. In traditional Chinese settings, Mazu's birthday celebrations feature huge bonfires, firecrackers, big banquets, and continuous religious rituals performed in the temple by Daoist masters, as well as performances of Chinese operas to entertain the goddess. This type of traditional celebration lasts for several days and is still practiced in Hong Kong, Taiwan, and Fujian at major Tianhou or Mazu temples. On Sunday, May 5, 2002, I attended Mazu's birthday celebration at the Ma-tsu Temple U.S.A. When I arrived at the temple at ten o'clock, it was already packed with worshipers. Temple volunteers were busily preparing a delicious vegetarian meal for all visitors. By noon there was an invocation and offering ritual for "American Mazu" (*Meiguo Mazu*). The temple also gave "good luck" noodles to everyone who visited the temple on that day.

The smaller-scale celebration of Mazu's birthday at the Ma-tsu Temple U.S.A. did not include the traditional "celestial inspection tour," in which the goddess views the state of her immediate realm and extends her protection to the community. Instead, the Ma-tsu Temple U.S.A. takes advantage of the Chinese New Year Parade, two to three months before her actual birthday, by participating in it to provide the goddess with an opportunity to make her celestial inspection tour. During the U.S. version of Mazu's inspection tour, she views the state of the world and extends her protection to the community, thus mediating between Chinese and non-Chinese culture while expanding the parameters of her religious sovereignty. One of the main functions of

Mazu's tour is to "unify" the community. Mazu is able to accomplish this because as a symbol of Chinese religious culture, she reminds both the Chinese and non-Chinese viewers of something that is distinctively Chinese.

Chinese New Year is also celebrated in the Sacramento Valley town of Marysville with a festival honoring Bok Kai, a Chinese water god. The Mazu from the Ma-tsu Temple U.S.A. is taken out of the temple and driven over to Marysville to participate in the annual Bok Kai Temple festival, held the first weekend of every March. Chinese immigrants built the Bok Kai Temple in 1879 because Bok Kai protects his devotees from floods and provides them with bountiful water for farming. The highlight of the annual festival is the Bok Kai Parade. This parade, produced annually for more than a hundred years, is the oldest continuing parade in California. Paul G. Chace, an anthropologist with an interest in Chinese American temples, suggests that despite its beginnings as a yearly celebration in southern Chinese villages, over time the parade's 121 years in Marysville have de-emphasized the religious nature of the parade. Instead, two U.S. threads have risen to the fore: commercialism, and coping with ethnic and cultural diversity (Chace 1992, 3–6, 588–605).

Chace explains the current nonreligiousness of the parade with the concept of "interpretive restraint," which means the purposeful withholding of symbolic meaning for traditional ritual performance. With interpretive restraints, the rites of Chinese popular religions could serve to celebrate the larger civic community and to promote interethnic and intercultural community relations. The theory of interpretive restraint thus suggests that Chinese Americans have politely concealed or downplayed the original reasons for the parade, thus allowing it to take on a new emphasis in the United States (ibid., 3–6).

Mazu's participation in the San Francisco Chinese New Year and Bok Kai parades can be interpreted in different ways. To many non-Chinese viewers of the parades, Mazu and Bok Kai are symbols of Chinese cultural heritage. The carriage carrying Mazu, her two attendants walking in front of her, and the loud firecrackers exploding in the San Francisco Chinese New Year Parade are distinctive aspects of the contemporary reality of U.S. cultural pluralism, comparable perhaps to dragon dances or young Chinese American children dressed in traditional Chinese clothes. To the Marysville community, who are mostly second-, third-, and fourth-generation Chinese Americans, the traditional religious meaning of these parades may also be downplayed in favor of civil, cultural symbolism.

The Ma-tsu Temple U.S.A. also plays a role in emphasizing the cultural value of these activities, and it actively invites visitors to participate in their celebrations as a form of cultural exchange. For example, during the Chinese New Year Parade, they warmly welcomed non-Chinese volunteers as flag carriers, horn blowers, and incense carriers. They even let volunteers wear the costumes of the two generals at Mazu's side. After the parade, they invited all the volunteers to participate in the ritual return of Mazu to her celestial throne, followed by a meal at which a special vegetarian soup was served. Lastly, they invited everyone to revisit the temple on any occasion. Some of the volunteers freely mentioned that they were not devotees, but that they were excited about volunteering to show their support for the Chinese American community, as well as to have some fun by participating in the parade.

To the immigrant Chinese Americans who join with Mazu on the parades, however, these activities are full of religious meaning. The firecrackers, for instance, are not simply aspects of Chinese heritage but fulfill an important religious function by symbolically scaring away demons as she inspects her precinct. Mazu's participation in the parade also foreshadows the celestial inspection tour that she will later undertake on her birthday. Interviews confirm the continuing religious meaning for some participants. During the 2003 Chinese New Year Parade, a seventy-four-year-old Taiwanese American woman shared her reason for participating in the parade: ten years ago, when she was diagnosed with a terminal heart condition, her son went to the Ma-tsu Temple U.S.A., petitioning Mazu to heal his mother. Immediately after his prayer, her mistaken diagnosis was corrected. It turned out that she had a thyroid problem, not a heart condition. Hence, she received proper medical care and medication. As a way to return thanks to Mazu, the mother and son have been attending every parade for the last ten years.

The contemporary U.S. version of Mazu's inspection tour serves both religious and secular functions. Each year during the parade, Mazu becomes an honored symbol of traditional Chinese culture both for Chinese Americans and for non-Chinese viewers. It would seem that a certain level of "interpretive restraint," to use Chace's term, concerning this activity has already begun. But even though for many people the role of Chinese deities in the parade is viewed purely in terms of cultural heritage, the continuing religious meaning of Mazu's participation in the Chinese New Year Parade has not disappeared—at least for recent Chinese American immigrants.

Creating Common Culture?

Mazu has been venerated for a thousand years by a considerable number of Chinese communities. Many Chinese Americans in the United States have venerated her for nearly 150 years. The development of new Mazu temples has related to the new and more complex composition of Chinese immigrants entering the United States, with an increasing percentage coming from Taiwan. New temples have been established in the 1990s in Los Angeles as well as in Houston. In Taiwan, Mazu is still considered to be the island's patron goddess, especially for Taiwanese whose ancestors arrived before World War II.

Vivian-Lee Nyitray posed several questions concerning Mazu's area of sovereignty. She states that

> the multiple and powerful forces of modernization and shifting world populations have redrawn the boundaries of Tianhou/Mazu's concern. What remains to be seen is the final map of the goddess' sovereignty: Will it be so localized that Chinese people worship Chinese Mazu, Taiwanese people worship Taiwanese Mazu, and North American devotees worship a Canadian or American or Mexican Mazu? Or will Tianhou/Mazu's sovereignty shift from the identity politics of nation-states and ethnic origins to a conceptual realm of common culture? (Nyitray 2000, 176)

Mazu's history provides insights into the question of her connection to issues of nationality and ethnicity. In Taiwan, Mazu had historically functioned as a symbol uniting the various Taiwanese ethnic groups—Hakka, Zhangzhou, Quanzhou, and other Fujianese "Taiwanese"—and distinguishing them from those "mainlanders" who fled to Taiwan in the wake of the communist victory in 1949 (ibid., 172). Earlier in Chinese history, the Empress of Heaven had also served to unite the people, and was promoted by state authorities as a symbol of imperial pacification and "approved Chinese culture" during periods of chaotic dynastic transition. Recently, similar co-optation programs have been initiated by mainland China in its efforts to reunify officially with Taiwan. Centuries later and a world away in San Francisco, will she once again redraw the boundaries of her religious sovereignty to include the various Chinese American communities?

This question also arises when we consider the various localized versions of Mazu. As Nyitray asks, will North American devotees worship a Canadian or American or Mexican Mazu? It seems likely that the answer to this question will be yes. First of all, Mazu is a territorial goddess: the territorial nature of her religious functions is evident in her celestial inspection tour, in which she views the state of the specific area over which she has religious authority. Secondly, there already is an American Mazu: she is enshrined at the Ma-tsu Temple U.S.A. and is referred to as American Mazu (*Meiguo Mazu*) in all religious rituals. Moreover, during the Chinese New Year Parade and during her birthday celebration, her American appellation is emphasized, clearly differentiating her from the Mazu in Beigang, Taiwan. What then is the relationship between the Beigang Mazu and the American Mazu? In the Ma-tsu Temple U.S.A. the relationship between the two is symbolized spatially: Beigang Mazu's honorary shrine is placed in front of American Mazu's main shrine. Moreover, the statue of Mazu housed in the Ma-tsu Temple U.S.A. comes directly from the Beigang temple, but nevertheless she is addressed by her own American name. Clearly, American Mazu is a relative—perhaps a sister or a daughter—of the original Beigang Mazu. The two are closely connected, but each has her own identity. This subtle religious difference parallels the difference in needs and concerns between the Chinese American and Chinese Taiwanese communities.

There is, therefore, the potential for American Mazu to function as a unifying symbol of Chinese identity for the various ethnic Chinese American groups in the United States. More questions about the connection between religious, cultural, and ethnic identity will form as the composition of the Chinese American communities continues to change in light of the newer Chinese immigration from the Republic of China on Taiwan, in addition to the plethora of ethnic Chinese coming from Southeast Asia.

From my participant-observations at the Ma-tsu Temple U.S.A., I have noticed that the majority of worshipers are immigrant Chinese Americans. I have rarely seen second- or third-generation Chinese Americans visiting or worshiping at the temple, other than children accompanying their parents. Fenggang Yang has noted this same generational pattern in the Chinese American religious communities in Houston. Yang says, "[T]he continuity of these temples in their current form will depend on continual influx of immigrants more than on the maturing second and later generations" of Chinese Americans (Yang 2002, 80–81). Currently, all the workers at the Ma-tsu Temple U.S.A. are recent Chinese immigrants who do not speak English. The question that arises, therefore, is what role, if any, Mazu will play in unifying the multiple generations of Chinese Americans.

The fact that most of Mazu's devotees are immigrants does not necessarily mean that her symbolic role in Chinese American culture will disappear in future generations. Possibly she will become identified with the Chinese aspect of Chinese American life and will continue to remind Chinese Americans of their Chinese heritage. Since 1992, the Ma-tsu Temple U.S.A. has received several first- and second-place community service awards for its participation in the San Francisco Chinese New Year Parade. These awards would suggest that Mazu is already active in her role as Chinese cultural ambassador. Mazu is therefore a carrier of traditional Chinese culture, a cultural broker bridging Chinese and non-Chinese cultures, and a cultural entrepreneur in her role in redefining and reinventing a new Chinese identity in the United States. From my observations of the large groups of tourists guided by a Chinese American tour guide at the Ma-Tsu Temple U.S.A., the identification of Mazu with that which is Chinese is key.

The Globalization of Chinese Religious Life in America

The local and global dimensions of Chinese-America continue to experience rapid transformation sociologically, politically, economically, linguistically, culturally, and religiously. This has resulted in unprecedented demographic changes and fragmentation along class, language, and religious lines among the various ethnic Chinese communities in the United States. The accelerated process of globalization, fueled in no small measure by rapid advances in telecommunications, transportation, and Internet technology—as well as by growing transnational financial, commercial, and cultural-religious ties—has helped cement connections and forge new relationships that have transformed the various ethnic Chinese communities across national boundaries and in ways previously not imagined.

Today's Chinese American religious organizations, institutions, and communities operate across traditional borders and boundaries. Consequently, border and boundary crossings not only imply change and mobility but also the potential for the transformation of prevailing social, cultural, economic, political, and religious practices. This section will provide an introductory examination of two emerging global and transnational Chinese religious communities that are redefining Chinese-America: the Buddhist Tzu Chi Compassion Relief Society and the Indo-Chinese Teo Chew Association.

Tzu Chi Compassion Relief Society

Tzu Chi is a worldwide Buddhist social outreach network founded in Taiwan in 1966 by Dharma Master Zhengyan (see Chapter 9 for more information on its founder). Today it has centers throughout Europe, Latin America, Southeast Asia, and North America. The headquarters of Tzu Chi in America is located in Monrovia, California, within Los Angeles proper in a predominantly Chinese immigrant community sometimes referred to as "Little Taipei." In the nearby city of Hacienda sits Hsi Lai Temple, the largest Buddhist temple in the United States, nestled on the side of a hill. Tzu Chi has established itself within the U.S. religious landscape through the promotion of social services. Typical of these social services is the Tzu Chi Free Clinic, established in 1993 under the leadership of Dharma Master Zhengyan. The clinic is a general health care facility providing medical assistance to financially disadvantaged residents of Los Angeles. It incorporates traditional Chinese healing and Buddhist philosophies of compassion to serve clients without regard to age, sex, race, class, or religious affiliation.

Tzu Chi clearly uses social service as a way of establishing community: recent Chinese immigrants donate to Tzu Chi and seek its assistance. But it is also a means for creating legitimacy for Chinese Buddhism. New immigrants recognize that they are up against false public perceptions and misunderstandings, so part of Tzu Chi's work lies in correcting their own image and establishing themselves in the public eye as capable of performing social services. Social services are valued as a U.S. ideal, and by engaging in altruistic activities the religious community will foster an image of being "good Americans," doing the things that good Americans do. The work of Tzu Chi is also redefining the form of religious activities for Chinese immigrant communities as they adapt their religious views to incorporate service into their religious activities.

The work of Tzu Chi also raises the question of the role of religion in the public sphere. Tzu Chi has refused to accept government funding, fearing that their services to those most in need might be compromised as a result of limitations or restrictions that could accompany such funds. For example, accepting government funding for social services might restrict them from

Tzu Chi volunteer Kane Chang bows at a Buddhist altar at the Tzu Chi Free Clinic in Alhambra, California. Tzu Chi is an international, nonprofit charitable organization with four major service areas: charitable services, medical services, education, and cultural services. Tzu Chi means giving with compassion. At left is a photo of Dharma Master Zhengyan, who founded Tzu Chi in Taiwan in 1966. (Damian Dovarganes/AP Photo)

serving residents who do not have proper legal documentation, which they compassionately refuse to do since a large percentage of their relief effort in urban areas like Los Angeles revolves around immigrant Americans.

Besides the free clinic and medical outreach, Tzu Chi participates in educational programs such as the Everyone Reads program. This literacy program organizes volunteers who meet monthly to read with an elementary school student. In addition, Tzu Chi celebrates U.S. holidays by donating Thanksgiving baskets and meals, Christmas gifts, and so on to needy local residents. Tzu Chi is also actively involved in new interfaith meeting and community events as ways of establishing U.S. roots. Chinese religious institutions have always served the community, but unlike earlier Chinese religious centers, Tzu Chi recognizes that it is located more broadly in a multiethnic, multireligious setting. Tzu Chi takes care to serve this larger community, as well as the Chinese immigrant community, through its social services.

Teo Chew Association

The Teo Chew Association is one of several Indo-Chinese associations whose members are Chinese from Vietnam, Cambodia, Thailand, and Laos that immigrated to the United States as refugees following the Vietnam War. In 1975 more than 130,000 refugees entered the United States from those countries as communist governments were established in them. In 1977, the U.S. Congress passed a law allowing Southeast Asians to become permanent residents upon request. Among the Southeast Asian refugees were thousands of Indo-Chinese immigrants.

In the 1990s the Teo Chew Association appeared in urban Chinatowns across the country, in such places as New York City, San Francisco, Seattle, Houston, Austin, Chicago, Honolulu, Boston, Atlanta, and Los Angeles. Teo Chew is the word in the southern Min dialect for the city of Chaozhou in Guangdong province, China. In Cantonese it is known as Chiu Chow. Teo Chow culture is known for its unique food and music, and distinctive Teo Chow subcultures can be found in Hong Kong and throughout Southeast Asia. Most members of the U.S. Teo Chow Association are Indo-Chinese immigrants who can trace their roots to Chaozhou. The Los Angeles Teo Chew Association was founded in 1982 by Chinese Cambodian immigrants as a social network and community center to foster solidarity among its members. It provides financial services and assists new immigrants in finding homes and referrals for social and medical services. It is also a place for worshiping the red-faced Guandi, the Chinese god of war, literature, wealth, and social harmony. The temple hall is located in a one-story building that was once a commercial bank. The front room is the main worship hall, while the back portion is a large community hall for banquets and meetings. Like the Elderly Indo-Chinese Association, the Teo Chew Association provides an annual scholarship to children of members who maintain an overall GPA of 3.5 or better. The Teo Chew Association is now a global association with centers throughout Southeast Asia, Europe, and North and South America. In 2002 during its twentieth anniversary, Governor Gray Davis extended a warm congratulations to the Los Angeles Teo Chew Association for "its commitment to the Asian American community" and "investment in the future of our state."

The Teo Chew Association and temple in Los Angeles are open every day and welcome visitors and participants of various backgrounds. Their printed material is usually in Chinese and Vietnamese, but sometimes English. Like traditional Chinese temples, the Teo Chew Association does not have a formal membership system, because all are welcome to worship there. However, the social, educational, and financial services are provided to those who are considered "official" members only. On any given day, one may find a dozen or so old-timers whiling their time away in the company of their friends, reading a Chinese newspaper, or sipping a cup of coffee. Teo Chew, like Tzu Chi, has integrated social service and civil responsibility into its operations in the United States. However, unlike Tzu Chi, they do not extend their social services beyond the immediate immigrant Indo-Chinese boundary.

Conclusion

The life of Chinese religions and religious communities in the United States has waxed and waned with shifting mainstream attitudes, from exclusion to assimilation to cultural pluralism. It has also correlated with immigration policies and the increasing connections forged by transnational networks of religious communities. In the past the pressure to assimilate influenced Chinese American religious life and experience, but the current situation is dramatically different. The Kwan Tai Temple exemplifies a period of Chinese American religious life and community that reflects exclusion and assimilation. Its historical landmark status demarcates it as a piece of Americana: a Chinese American museum and temple. Although the Chinese American community of Mendocino has greatly declined in size, the little historic temple has gained increased religious and cultural significance. The Kwan Tai Temple resembles Confucian temples in East Asia, a "Temple of Culture" (*wen miao*) that preserves Chinese American religious culture and history.

Contemporary Chinese communities in the United States have creatively negotiated the extremes of both assimilation and pluralism in terms of their religious life. They find themselves operating in an area that crosses community boundaries, religio-cultural boundaries, and national boundaries. Adapting to the principle of social and community service, Tzu Chi has been able to situate itself as an important religious-cultural nonprofit institution in the United States and throughout the world. Similarly, Indo-Chinese associations like Teo Chew, though directed toward the needs of member immigrants, have adopted the same principles of social and community service. Both Tzu Chi and the Teo Chew Association cross ethnic, cultural, and national boundaries. The Ma-tsu Temple U.S.A. has also creatively negotiated traditional religious duties while creating new rituals and traditions.

Chinese American religious life and community come in various shapes, sizes, and imaginations. Traditional assimilation is no longer seen as viable, necessary, possible, or ideal. The changes in religious communities have influenced Chinese American identity, boundaries, and boarders and will continue to do so. Geographical boundaries no longer inform solely citizenship, nationality, and identity, and Chinese identities in contemporary transnational and increasingly global communities are less bounded by distinct territorial boundaries, becoming defined more in terms of cultural heritage. The life of Chinese religions in contemporary U.S. society is being maintained and constructed in the Chinese American diaspora both apart from and within the so-called American mainstream. Contemporary Chinese religious life in the American diaspora crosses cultural, religious, social, economic, and national boundaries. It requires creative and imaginative investigation.

References

Chace, Paul. 1992. "Returning Thanks: Chinese Rites in an American Community." Ph.D. diss., University of California, Riverside.

Nyitray, Vivian-Lee. 2000. "Becoming the Empress of Heaven: The Life and Bureaucratic Career of Tianhou/Mazu." Pp. 165–180 in *Goddesses Who Rule*. Edited by Elisabeth Bernard and Beverly Moon. New York: Oxford University Press.

Takaki, Ronald. 1989. *Strangers from a Different Shore*. New York: Penguin.

Temple of Kwan Tai. N.d. http://www.kwantaitemple.org.

Yang, Fenggang. 2002. "Religious Diversity among the Chinese in America." Pp. 71–98 in *Religions in Asian America: Building Faith Communities*. Edited by Pyong Gap Min and Jung Ha Kim. Walnut Creek, CA: AltaMira.

11

Chinese Traditions in Euro-American Society

ELIJAH SIEGLER

Introduction

This chapter attempts to explain the contemporary Western fascination with ideas and practices based on Chinese religion. In general, this fascination derives not from China directly, so much as from Orientalist fantasies about China's past. Thus the chapter begins with a brief overview of Western scholarship on Chinese religion. Then the chapter shows how mid-twentieth, century Chinese immigrants to North America, who were the first generation to teach Chinese religious practices to non–Chinese Americans, combined these scholarly ideas with their own cultural and political background to create a new religious movement that may be termed American Daoism. In this chapter, therefore, the term "American Daoism" signifies a set of related practices and values that may have some connection to the Daoist tradition in China but have less connection, and a different kind of connection, than that which the movement claims for itself. It should be noted that the consumption of Chinese traditions in the West has been subsumed largely under the category of Daoism, whether or not that is historically justified. Westerners interested in Buddhism rarely practice a specifically Chinese form of it. Confucianism in the West appeals to an elite minority of tenured scholars. Thus this chapter uses the term "American Daoism" despite the fact that many of the concepts (for example, yin/yang and *qi*) and practices (such as *taiji* [t'ai-chi] and acupuncture) may have only a tenuous link to the historical practice of Daoist religion in China.

By the 1970s, American Daoism had coalesced into several organizations headed by charismatic masters, of whom four of the most important are described. Next, the chapter describes the most common practices of American Daoism, dividing them into three headings: reading, moving, and healing. Finally the chapter surveys the general worldview of the typical American Daoist.

Western Scholarship on Chinese Religions

The earliest firsthand accounts of Chinese religions came from Christian missionaries who looked upon them as devilish and wholly incompatible with the modern, Christian West. In the late nineteenth century the new field of sinology, which developed concurrently with the so-called science of religion, valued the classical traditions of China found in ancient texts while despising its modern manifestations. Twentieth-century scholars, while bringing to light new information on Chinese religions, in particular Daoism, helped to construct a romantic picture of Daoism that might cure the illnesses of the modern West. Popular writers took this idea further, seeing Daoism as a degenerated perennial philosophy that could be conserved in the West and restored to its original purity.

China has fascinated Europe at least since the time of Marco Polo (1254–1324). But it was in the eighteenth century that important European thinkers such as Gottfried Leibniz (1646–1716) and Denis Diderot (1713–1784) became intellectually stirred by Chinese philosophy though reading the often fragmentary and lopsided reports from Jesuits and other travelers to the country. In this way, China became important to the consciousness of the European Enlightenment.

The first important European scholar of Chinese religions was the Jesuit missionary Matteo Ricci (1552–1610), who arrived in China in 1582 and stayed until his death. To allow for the intellectual accommodation for which the Jesuits were known, Ricci claimed that the imperial ritual, and state Confucianism in general, were not religious. His interest in Confucianism and his downplaying of Buddhism and Daoism had lasting effects: Enlightenment philosophers, the first secularists in modern Europe, used reports from Jesuit missionaries for their own purposes, seeing China as model of deism and rational kingship. Voltaire, for example, valorized a Confucianism that he viewed as an enlightened philosophy that governed by reason and not superstition. Daoism, in its infrequent appearances in Voltaire's work, was seen as superstitious and corrupt and thus mirrored Voltaire's conception of the Catholic Church.

The nineteenth century saw the first appearance of professional sinologists, French scholars who translated the Chinese classics, as well as the first sustained English and U.S. interest in China as Protestant missionary societies sent hardy men and women into the field. Indeed, the only source of information on contemporary Chinese religion available to the United States came from missionaries. British Presbyterian Robert Morrison (1782–1834), the first Protestant missionary in China, wrote letters that appeared in U.S. publications. The first U.S. missionaries in China arrived in Guangzhou (Canton) in February 1830 and wrote letters back to the United States decrying Chinese idolatry.

James Legge (1815–1897), a Scottish Congregationalist missionary, became the leading scholar of Chinese religion from the late 1870s until the end of the century. Unlike previous missionary-scholars, Legge admired the Daoism of Laozi and Zhuangzi as serious and worthy. He allowed himself to understand, even to be moved by, the texts of classical Daoism, while at the same time denigrating present-day Daoism—thus instituting a conceptual dualism in thinking about Daoism that persists to this day. From the 1890s until quite recently, Americans who wrote on religions of the world relied mainly on Legge for their information about Chinese religion in general and Daoism in particular.

Returning from his many years in China to occupy the first professorship in Chinese at Oxford University, Legge introduced a substantial knowledge of Chinese religions to the West. He was the first scholar to translate into English the great Chinese classics, the ones that are still found in every bookstore and taught in any survey course on Asian religions, including the *Yijing* (*I Ching*), the *Zhuangzi* (*Chuang Tzu*), and the *Daode jing* (*Tao Te Ching*). These works were published as part of F. Max Muller's monumental series "The Sacred Books of the East," thereby placing Chinese religions into the emerging category of Religions of the World.

The modern concept of "world religions" and the place of Chinese religions within it took shape at the World's Parliament of Religion held in 1893 in Chicago, Illinois. This groundbreaking congress, held in conjunction with the Columbian Exposition, invited, for the first time, representatives of many religious traditions to speak on a more or less equal footing with their

Anglo-American hosts (despite the absence of any indigenous or African traditions, and the generally Protestant triumphalist tone). Pu Kwan Yu, a literatus who served as the Chinese legate in Washington, D.C., represented Confucianism. Buddhist delegates included a Japanese Zen abbot and a Ceylonese Theravada monk, but nobody from China. Significantly, Daoism was represented by an anonymous essay that excoriated modern-day Daoism as having "deteriorated" and expressed a hope that someone would "restore our religion, save it from errors" (quoted in Seager 1993, 247).

At the parliament, an audience member named Paul Carus made contact with the interpreter for the Zen abbot, a young Japanese man named D. T. Suzuki, who later popularized Zen for Americans. In 1898, the pair produced the first U.S. translation of the *Daode jing*. Carus saw the book as an example of the perennial philosophy, which paralleled Christianity in many ways. For example, Carus compared the word "Dao" with the "Logos" of the Gospel of John. Carus followed Legge's rhetoric in showing that Daoism was a "world religion" like Christianity and Buddhism but that it had degenerated from its historical glory days.

Carus's work was the first translation of the *Daode jing* published in the United States, but it would not be the last: by 1950 there were ten in print. The most widely read edition of its day was the 1944 "literary" rendition by Boston poet and saloniste Witter Bynner (1881–1961), which was the first of many English renderings of this short text by Americans who knew no Chinese. It was likewise noticeable for containing in the introduction the definitive Western dualistic statement about Daoism: "Taoist religion is an abuse of Taoist philosophy," wrote Bynner. The *Daode jing*'s fascination for Western scholars, as well as its status as the most translated text in the world after the Bible, can be attributed to its brevity, its lack of proper names, and especially its multiplicity of possible meanings. These traits continue to make the *Daode jing* central to the contemporary practice of U.S. Daoism.

Another subject of scholarly interest was Daoist physical practices, including alchemy. Although less research was done on those topics than on the "Daoist philosophy" of the *Daode jing* and the *Zhuangzi,* this research provided fodder for further Orientalist fantasies and had a huge impact on the formation of U.S. Daoism. In this case China was fantasized not, as it had been during the Enlightenment, as a rational, ethical kingdom, but as a romantic land of alchemists, hermits, and immortals.

Henri Maspéro's (1883–1945) article "Les procèdes de 'nourrir le principe vital' dans la religion taoïste ancienne" [Methods of nourishing the vital principle in ancient Chinese religion], published in 1937, was the first to explore the Daoist dimensions of the breathing, standing, and moving exercises that today would be called *qigong*.

Joseph Needham's (1901–1995) romanticized view of early China also influenced the subsequent study of Daoism. Needham was editor and chief author of the monumental multivolume work *Science and Civilization in China* (1956), which includes book-length studies on many areas of science and technology in China including textiles, agriculture, and mining. Writing at the end of World War II, he saw Chinese alchemy as an antidote to the disease of the West. Some of Needham's most thorough and important work was on Chinese alchemy. Needham saw in Daoism the potential for an archaic revival in the modern world. Daoism might restore what modernity had broken: the connection between morality and science, between humans and nature, and between branches of knowledge.

Another important source for U.S. Daoism was Dutch diplomat Robert van Gulik's *Sexual Life in Ancient China,* written in 1961. Van Gulik demonstrated that China had a "healthier" attitude toward sex, while titillating readers with hints of an "exotic" sexuality. Needham's volumes on alchemy (published in the 1970s and 1980s) contained much new material on sexual techniques as well.

The Swiss psychologist and philosopher Carl Gustav Jung (1875–1961) was the person most responsible for popularizing Chinese alchemy in the West. Although never terribly interested in Confucianism, Jung had demonstrated excitement for, and sympathy toward, Daoism—which he tended, erroneously, to look upon as typical of Chinese thinking as whole. Jung was first attracted to Daoism via *The Secret of the Golden Flower,* a Qing dynasty internal alchemical text for which he wrote an introduction in 1922.

The ideas advanced by scholars such as Maspéro, Needham, Jung, and Van Gulik about Daoist conceptions of health, longevity, and immortality appealed to the West's growing need for body-centered spirituality. Through them, the language of transformation and cultivation found its way into the popular discourse about Daoism and then into communities of practice.

Besides European scholarly and popular writing, Daoist terminology also entered North America through the macrobiotic movement of Japan. Like European scholarship, macrobiotics did not provide a direct link with traditional

Chinese Daoism, but rather ideas based on textual sources. The philosopher Ekken Kaibara (1630–1716), often called the "grandfather of macrobiotics" because of his work on healthful diet and lifestyle, used the Japanese words for *qi* and Dao, but his understanding of those terms came not from Daoist sources but from the philosophy of Neo-Confucianism. The founder of modern macrobiotics, George Ohsawa, used the word "tao" to refer to spiritual development, and he divided all food into yin and yang. Ohsawa's chief student, Michio Kushi, settled in the United States in 1950 and began promoting macrobiotic ideas, deepening Ohsawa's conception of *qi,* yin/yang, and Dao, as well as introducing the Chinese five element (*wu xing*) theory into the macrobiotic worldview (Kotzsch 1985, 132; Kushi 1977, 4). As macrobiotics was disseminated through magazines (notably the *East-West Journal*) and health food stores, a Daoist vocabulary was introduced to a larger population.

1940s–1970s: The Birth of "American Daoism"

It should be quite obvious by now that Daoism in the West was formed through a series of contacts. The encounters that make up "The Dao of the West" that took place in the realms of philosophy and intellectual history have been well expounded upon (see Clarke 2000). Less well known are the moments of contact that took place among real people in the real world. This section thus highlights a few of those moments of contact between a select group of Chinese immigrants and Euro-Americans interested in the counterculture. These immigrants were not Daoists in any sense of the word. Their most important common characteristic was a background of displacement and a sense of loss. As Fenggang Yang describes it:

> In the 1950s to 1970s, many Chinese immigrants were uprooted and rootless people. They were born in the mainland under the rule of Guomindang's Republic of China, escaped from wars or fled the Communist mainland, then wandered around in several places—Taiwan, Hong Kong, or Southeast Asia—before coming to the United States. Meanwhile, many also have a strong attachment to their birthplace in Mainland China and hold a vision of a united and strong Chinese nation (Yang 1999, 40).

This profile fits the Daoist teachers described below to an uncanny degree. American Daoist teachers have been particularly "uprooted and rootless" and have shown "a strong attachment to their birthplace." Their own sense of displacement, of belonging to a nation and a culture that no longer exists as they remember it—not just the physical China but also the social, educational, and cultural nexus of the Qing dynasty literati—was an important factor in creating American Daoism. Daoist masters' strong attachment to (and their nostalgic vision of) the China of their memories manifests itself in the utopian and restorationist character of American Daoism that persists to this day.

Another important characteristic of the teachers described below is their skill in performance. They are often self-conscious actors and sometimes even trained as such professionally. Indeed, especially in the case of ethnically Chinese teachers ministering to non-Chinese followers, certain costumes, music, and discourses would not be present if all the participants were Chinese.

Chao-li Chi and the Taoist Sanctuary

Chao-li Chi (1929–) neither trained as a Daoist in China nor did he claim to be a Daoist upon arrival in the United States, but he is the de facto prototype of the American Daoist. His wealthy and educated northern Chinese family left China on the heels of the Japanese invasion. In high school in New York City and later at the Great Books Program of St. John's College in Maryland, young Chi immersed himself in the Western classics. Later, he "went back to his roots" to study the *Daode jing* and the *Yijing,* a study that to him was a form of rebellion against his Western environment and upbringing. Chi also tried to find work as a stage actor in New York and studied yoga and comparative religion. These elements in Chao-li Chi's life put him at a far remove from the normative Daoism as practiced in China: his Western education, his lack of interaction with any form of organized Daoism (outside of seeing Daoist priests at family funerals), as well as his admittedly artistic and nonspiritual temperament. Yet it was just those qualities that made Chi the American Daoist pioneer he became. In 1948 he collaborated with the foremost U.S. avant-garde filmmaker of the day, a Ukrainian Jewish immigrant named Maya Deren, on a twelve-minute experimental film. In a bare room, Chi, the sole actor, performs a loose and speeded-up interpretation of taiji (t'ai-chi). Then, as the tempo of the Japanese-style drumming increases, he begins to do *gongfu* (kung fu). After that he leaps outdoors and performs a sword practice as the music becomes more martial. The whole effect is stylized and theatrical.

This film, *Meditation on Violence,* is historically important for a number of reasons. It is probably the first visual depiction of gongfu and taiji in the United States. References in the title card to "Shao-lin" and "Wu-tang" (two places in China associated with the martial arts) would have been more puzzling than evocative for most Americans in 1948. For most Chinese, however, Mt. Wudang and the Shaolin Temple complex were the stuff of ancient legend, as well as the subject of songs and popular novels. For Chi, those locations evoked nostalgia for his own childhood in a China forever lost. This film also prefigures American Daoism in Deren's explanatory notes, which link the movements of taiji as depicted in the film to the hexagrams of the *Yijing,* a connection that would become a keystone of American Daoism.

Chao-li Chi's role in the formation of American Daoism did not end with his appearance in this film. In the late 1960s, Chi met Khigh Dhiegh (1910–1991; the name is pronounced KAI DEE), the founder, rector, and spiritual mentor of the Taoist Sanctuary, the first Daoist religious organization in the United States to receive tax-exempt status as a church.

Although Dhiegh claimed to have held a doctorate in psychology and to have written a well-researched book on the *Yijing,* he made his living as a character actor, since his bald head, sallow complexion, and pointy black moustache allowed him to portray a series of stock Oriental villains. Indeed, his most famous role was that of Wo Fat, the nefarious "red Chinese agent" and Jack Lord's nemesis in the long-running detective series *Hawaii Five-O* on CBS from 1968 to 1980. Significantly, despite his success at playing Chinese characters on television, Dhiegh was not Chinese. He was born Kenneth Dickerson in New Jersey in 1910 and was of British and Egyptian descent.

Dhiegh founded the Taoist Sanctuary in 1970 in a church basement in North Hollywood, California. The name was not mere fancy: there actually was a sanctuary. Occasional rituals were held there during astrologically prescribed times following the Chinese almanac, presided over by Dhiegh, dressed in vestments of his own design. Dhiegh taught Daoist meditation and *Yijing* divination techniques at the sanctuary, but his lack of ability to read Chinese prevented him from being an effective teacher of the *Daode jing.* So in 1974, Dhiegh invited his friend Chao-li Chi (who had been directing the dance program for the Dayton, Ohio, public school system) to move to Los Angeles and teach at the Taoist Sanctuary. Chi became the "academic dean" of the Taoist Sanctuary, teaching taiji as well as a weekly seminar on the *Daode jing.*

The Taoist Sanctuary also provided a venue for Share K. Lew (1918–) to teach Euro-Americans for the first time. Lew was raised by Daoist monks at the Yellow Dragon Monastery on Mt. Luofu in Guangdong province, and thus he stands as one of the few American Daoist masters with documented Daoist training. Interestingly, he does not generally teach the *Daode jing*, the *Yijing*, or taiji (the most common American Daoist practices), but rather *qi* development techniques and hard martial arts.

Al Huang and Alan Watts

American Daoism, perhaps more than any other Asian-inspired tradition, is conceptually linked to the human potential movement, a generic name for a gamut of therapeutic techniques based on self-transfor-

Alan Watts and his daughter Ann Watts experiment with bamboo poles. (Time Life Pictures/Getty Images)

mation and often thought to have been born at the famed California retreat center, Esalen. This link was forged though the efforts of two men, Alan Watts and Al Huang. Al Chungliang Huang (1937–), like Chao-li Chi, was born into a privileged family in China. Huang's family left for Taiwan in 1949, where he had an Americanized upbringing, and in 1955 Huang moved to Los Angeles to pursue degrees in architecture. There he met Alan Watts (1915–1973), a British self-made Buddhist and amateur scholar, in 1961 and they began teaching classes together at Esalen in 1965. Their final collaboration was the book *Tao: The Watercourse Way*, which Watts wrote and Huang edited and illustrated with free-flowing Chinese calligraphy. It was published in 1975. Later Huang founded the Living Tao Institute, a loosely organized nonprofit based in Huang's hometown of Urbana, Illinois. Huang continues to teach free-form taiji, Chinese philosophy, and calligraphy.

Although Huang publicly acknowledges his debt to other great perennial and popular philosophers such as John Blofeld, Joseph Campbell, and Huston Smith, it is Watts whose influence on American Daoism should not be underestimated. In many ways, Watts was the pivotal figure in the shift from the American interest in Daoism as a philosophical and literary curio to the involvement in Daoism as a practical way of life.

The 1970s: The Organization of American Daoism

As we have seen, Daoism did not arrive in the United States as a coherent religious system, but rather as a piecemeal series of texts and ideas—and, later, teachers and practices. Until fairly recently, Daoism was best known in the West, if at all, as a quaint and exotic philosophy of quietism and mysticism. That was how Daoism was depicted in most readily available sources of information, including anthologies of Chinese philosophy and world religion textbooks. According to Confucian-influenced scholars, Daoism may have inspired a lot of Chinese art and poetry, but it was not a contemporary spiritual option for Chinese—and certainly not for North Americans. However, in the 1970s, Daoism's image changed in North America because of a confluence of factors. Foremost perhaps were the 1965 changes in the immigration laws of the United States and Canada, which brought more Chinese to North America. Since the 1960s the Chinese population has been doubling every decade, and by 1990 the Chinese population in the United States was put at 1,645,472 (ibid., 35). That growth had several effects on the consumption of Chinese religion in the West. First, with so many Chinese living in North America, Chinese culture—from martial arts to eating with chopsticks—no longer seemed as exotic as it had from the 1940s through the early 1970s. Second, a handful of these immigrants were experienced in various Chinese religiophysical techniques and were eager to teach their skills to willing Americans. At approximately the same time, young North Americans' search for spirituality outside of traditional institutions (often called the "new religious consciousness") led them to embrace teachers and practices from Asia.

Thus, the situation was ripe for the creation of American Daoist masters and organizations. Four of the most important are presented below. All are quite different in their presentations and methods, though all make similar claims to authenticity. Indeed, one aspect of the charismatic presence of these American Daoist masters is their claim to possess a unique personal transmission of authentic Daoism. All of the masters tell a similar story: how they found their own Daoist master (often a mountain hermit) and were given license to teach by that master, after which that master then died or disappeared. Thus the spiritual pedigree of American Daoist masters is untraceable and irreproducible.

Hua-ching Ni

Hua-ching Ni is a prolific author and doctor of Chinese medicine. He was born in Wenzhou, a coastal city in Zhejiang province, and came to Taiwan in 1949, where he had two sons. In 1976, two students at the Taoist Sanctuary who had been studying in Taiwan brought Ni to California. Ni was installed in a house at Malibu, where he opened a shrine called the Eternal Breath of Tao and began teaching classes privately in a venue he named the College of Tao. Over the years, Ni-sponsored organizations have multiplied. His private acupuncture clinic was known as the Union of Tao and Man. He also founded Yo San University of Traditional Chinese Medicine in 1989, an accredited, degree-granting college. Both the clinic and the university are now headed by his sons, Maoshing and Daoshing, while Master Ni lives in semi-seclusion when not traveling.

Some aspects of his biography are controversial: reports are contradictory, his own story changes, and opinions vary wildly. One of several official biographical statements about Ni has it that

> as a young boy he was educated in spiritual learning by his family, and was then chosen to study with Taoist masters in the high mountains of mainland China. . . . After more than 31 years of intensive training, he was fully acknowledged and empowered as a true master of the traditional Tao, including all aspects of Taoist science and metaphysics. In Taiwan for 28 years, Master Ni taught and practiced Daoist arts such as Tai Chi Chuan, Kung Fu, Daoist meditation and internal alchemy (Seven Star Communications n.d.).

This statement suggests that Ni was born in the early twentieth century, something Ni neither confirms nor denies. Ni began publishing books in English in 1979 and today, with the help of his students (who have worked as volunteer editors, designers, and publishers) Ni has some sixty or seventy self-published books in print.

The subjects of his earliest classes in the United States were the *Daode jing* and the *Yijing;* his renditions of those texts were two of his earliest publications. The movement arts he first taught were forms of taiji, albeit exotically named ("gentle path," "sky journey," and "infinite expansion").

Mantak Chia and Healing Tao

Mantak Chia, an ethnic Chinese born in Thailand in 1941, was trained in Hong Kong and has a background in both Oriental and Western medicine, as well as in traditional Daoist practices. Chia is said to have begun self-cultivation at the very young age of six with Buddhist meditation, martial arts, taiji quan, and kundalini yoga. Of his many teachers the most influential, and the one from whom he claims lineage transmission, was a hermit of the Dragon's Gate (Longmen) branch of Complete Perfection (Quanzhen) Daoism named One Cloud, who gave Chia a mandate to teach and heal.

Chia systematized his knowledge of various alchemical techniques, and in 1974 he established the first of his schools in Thailand. In 1979 he moved to New York and opened the Taoist Esoteric Yoga Center. (Note that he changed the name of his center to include the word "Taoist" upon arrival in the United States.) That center, which was renamed the Healing Tao Center, attracted Euro-American students who helped him to organize a national seminar circuit. In 1994, Mantak and his wife, Maneween (whom he has since divorced), moved back to Thailand to establish an international healing Tao center in Chiang Mai, Tao Garden, where wealthy Europeans and Americans take cultivation classes in a luxurious resort spa atmosphere.

Chia presents a cosmology (1993) based on *qi* formation similar to Ni's, but Chia's written material, unlike Ni's, contains little in the way of philosophy, ethics, or everyday advice. Chia's material is best described as a popularized, streamlined system of qigong based on Chinese internal alchemy (*neidan*). These exercises have all been described in Chia's books, but the program emphasizes personal instruction. The full Mantak Chia program consists of fifteen courses, the first nine being introductory, the next three intermediate, and the final three advanced.

Healing Tao's practices are taught by franchised instructors all over the world and in a more concentrated manner year-round at Chia's Tao Garden retreat in Thailand. In North America, the Healing Tao program has been adapted by Michael Winn, Chia's coauthor on many books. Winn's revised

Healing Tao curriculum, which is available on audiotape and videotape, is slightly different in form and philosophy. His annual summer program (to which Mantak Chia is an invited guest instructor) is notable for the highly commercialized language it uses to describe the benefits of such cultivation practices. According to its brochure, students who practice Healing Tao will be able to "reach new levels of health," "lose pounds permanently without dieting," "profoundly improve sexual health," and "help their career" (Healing Tao 2001, 2).

Moy Lin-shin and Taoist Tai Chi

Moy Lin-shin founded the Taoist Tai Chi Society (TTCS) in 1970. This is perhaps the largest Daoist group in the Western Hemisphere, although it is largely unknown within the American Daoist community, in part because it is based in Canada. Moy, like other Daoist masters, has a somewhat vague biography. He was born in Taishan county, Guangdong province, in 1931. He moved to Hong Kong in 1948 or 1949. There he trained at various Daoist institutes. Moy came to New York City for a short stay and then immigrated to Canada in 1970, where he quickly began teaching in a small studio in downtown Toronto, which he also made his home. He called his group the Toronto Tai Chi Society. He taught gongfu as well as a martial arts–oriented style of taiji. Later, he softened the style and called it Taoist Tai Chi. Moy and his students bought a permanent center and registered the society as a charitable organization. As his original students left Toronto, Taoist Tai Chi clubs sprang up around Canada and the United States. Eva Wong, a Hong Kong immigrant doing graduate work in neuroscience in Buffalo, New York, became one of Moy's chief students and later helped establish the Denver branch of the society. She is no longer a member of the organization but works independently as a popular author and translator (see Wong 1990; 1997; 2001). The TTCS claims to teach thousands of classes in more than four hundred locations on four continents and to have some 10,000 dues-paying members worldwide. Representatives of twenty-five nations (including Aruba, Poland, and Malaysia) attended the 2000 annual meeting, which was also the thirtieth anniversary of the society.

Fung Loy Kok Institute (FLK), dedicated in 1981, is the religious arm of the Moy organization. The original temple was located upstairs from the taiji studio. The Fung Loy Kok Taoist temple derives from popular Hong

Kong lay Daoism and claims to follow the teachings of Confucianism, Buddhism, and Daoism. These are represented by the central triad of the temple altar: the Jade Emperor, the Buddhist bodhisattva Guanyin, and the Daoist immortal Lü Dongbin, respectively. Committed members were formally initiated into the temple beginning in the early 1980s, but that practice ended in the late 1980s. Today lay members perform religious activities, and chanting is practiced in Cantonese, which is transliterated phonetically for the non-Chinese members, who are unaware of the meaning of the words. Most Taoist Tai Chi studios around the world dedicate at least a corner of their space to a small shrine.

Liu Ming and Orthodox Daoism in America

The final American Daoist master to be discussed is in many ways the most unusual. Liu Ming was born Charles Belyea in 1946 to a Boston Methodist family of French Canadian background. Belyea moved to Taiwan in 1977, where he took Mahayana Buddhist vows in the Tibetan tradition. According to Liu Ming's own reports, which he has since modified, while in Taiwan he trained with a Daoist hermit who initiated him into the Liu family tradition, which claims an unbroken lineage of 115 generations. For Belyea to continue on the tradition, he was adopted into the family and given the name Liu Ming.

Belyea returned to the United States in 1980 and began offering classes based on his Daoist experiences, called "dragon training," which culminated in the publication of a book, *Dragon's Play,* in 1991. In 1992, Belyea gave up this more "universalist" instruction and began "teaching Daoism to Daoists." He thus established a nonprofit religious organization called Orthodox Daoism in America (ODA) and taught a "curriculum for lay priests" geared toward textual study and culminating in ritual investiture. A rented house in Santa Cruz served as the ODA headquarters, including Belyea's residence, a Daoist altar (*daotan*), and space for a mail-order business specializing in incense and books about Daoism.

Liu Ming's writings, principally in the official ODA journal *Frost Bell,* demonstrate a penetrating critique of the practice of popularized Western Daoism, as exemplified by the techniques of Mantak Chia and Hua-ching Ni (though Liu Ming does not mention them by name in writing). In Liu Ming's view, these cultivation techniques emphasize personal spiritual development and self-help in ways similar to the modern Western "spiritual quest culture."

Thus, to Liu Ming, most American Daoist techniques are products of cultural appropriation in the service of a liberal Protestant ethic in its latest guise as New Age spirituality. Liu Ming's writings in *Frost Bell* develop this point, often in the form of questions and answers:

> *Q:* Many Americans now view spiritual practice as a healing device. So many people in the modern west feel abused, injured, diseased and betrayed. Can Daoism address these issues?
> *A:* No (Liu 1998, 1.42).

Liu Ming's single word response is perhaps somewhat disingenuous. Some of his students surely train with him to rid themselves of the effects of abuse, injury, or disease. Liu Ming's deliberately contrarian attitude is used to define his own Daoist identity.

This section, of course, has presented only a sampling of Daoist teachers in North America, but it should provide an idea of some of the major figures, and of the broad spectrum of American Daoism that they represent. Other notable Daoist teachers include Alex Anatole, a Russian who was initiated as a Daoist priest in Moscow and who currently leads a private temple outside Boston; Harrison Moretz, a Euro-American who runs the Taoist Studies Institute in Seattle; and Hsien Yuen, an ordained Daoist priest from Taiwan who founded the American Taoist & Buddhist Association in New York City.

The Practice of American Daoism

American Daoism promotes self-improvement and physical, mental, and spiritual health by offering a series of modular, voluntary practices that both produce and are produced by an overall "Daoist" worldview. These practices provide both immediate benefits (for example, increased physical stamina and emotional well-being) and more long-term rewards (for example, feeling reconnected to nature and to the cosmos). The practices come from China, but the way they are marketed, conceptualized, and inserted into daily life are North American. Indeed part of the appeal of these Daoist practices is their instrumentality. They can be taught and learned in discrete units and can be performed individually or in groups, when and where needed. Indeed, these practices may well outlive American Daoism itself, which lacks both strong institutions and solid connections with its Chinese counterpart.

In North America, Daoism is no longer defined as an ancient, quietist philosophy but as an individual's regime of practice. American Daoist groups teach practices through a combination of weekly classes and yearly, or seasonal, retreats or seminars. What all these practices have in common is that they can be performed individually, not collectively, as a modular part of a daily regimen; this may well be inevitable in the American context.

Each practice has been radically recontextualized in North America: the *Daode jing* and the *Yijing* entered the American scene through the academic field of sinology, which never imagined that these texts would be construed as modern practice. Once taiji was in common circulation in the early 1970s and linked to the philosophy of the *Daode jing* and the *Yijing*, spiritual practice groups could offer courses in the study of those two texts, as well as in taiji, linking them by a common vocabulary of *qi*, yin/yang, and Dao. That is exactly what the Taoist Sanctuary did in 1970, setting the stage for the current group of contemporary North American Daoist institutions. (This is also the approach taken in several seminal books on the history of American Daoism, notably by Al Huang [1973] and Gia-fu Feng [1970].)

Although American Daoists engage in many practices, the overall variety is limited and consistent. The most commonly mentioned practices are qigong, meditation (including guided visualizations), taiji, and *Yijing* study. The next most common grouping consists of text study, diet (including fasting), and Chinese medicine (both as patient and healer). Less commonly mentioned practices include invocations, lucid dreaming, *fengshui*, and calligraphy.

Reading Chinese Classics as an American Daoist Practice

A visit to a typical North American bookstore will retrieve some ten or twelve versions of the *Daode jing*, along with two or three translations of the *Zhuangzi*, and few if any other Daoist texts. The rate of appearance of new translations of the *Daode jing* has not abated since scholars of Chinese religion first remarked upon it as a cause for the lack of attention paid to the thousands of other important Daoist texts.

The proliferation of *Daode jing* translations has had another, largely unnoticed effect: it allows American Daoists to become their own interpreters. The *Daode jing* occupies an important place in the home of American Daoists; its study, alone or in groups, has become a regular part of their routine. In these ways, the *Daode jing* works like the Bible. *Daode jing* lovers will often own five or ten different translations of Laozi's "five-thousand-word" classic. By choosing one of the eighty-one chapters, looking up that chapter in several translations at once, and noting the similarities and divergences among the texts, readers can elicit their own preferred reading; reflecting on that meaning can become a meditative experience. In short, reading the *Daode jing* functions as a spiritual practice.

The second so-called Daoist classic, the *Zhuangzi,* although a favorite among professional postmodernists, has seen a fewer number of new translations. And it does not seem to have been incorporated at all into the religious practice of American Daoists. The next most important text in the practice of American Daoism is the *Yijing* (*The Book of Changes*), regardless of the fact that it is not technically a Daoist text at all—or if it is, it is equally Confucian and Chinese Buddhist.

A difficult text to unpack, the *Yijing* has not been subject to as many English translations as the *Daode jing.* The Wilhelm/Baynes translation, with the famous foreword by C. G. Jung, became an unexpected bestseller for Princeton University Press from 1950 onward. By the early 1960s, the *Yijing* was as much a part of the countercultural elite's library as were D. T. Suzuki's treatises on Zen. There were two significant English-language editions that appeared in the 1960s, those by John Blofeld in 1965 and R. G. H. Siu in 1968. Blofeld's *Yijing* was particularly user-friendly, addressed to a countercultural elite, while Siu's version incorporated psychology and world literature. Together, these three renditions helped the *Yijing* become part of the "new spiritual consciousness," and an essential element in American Daoist practice. Using the *Yijing* as a spiritual practice, unlike using the *Daode jing,* does not depend on possessing a large number of translations so much as one reliable edition—preferably one well worn from constant use. Silently asking the question to the book, casting the hexagram, and looking up and reading the commentary all require and produce a meditative frame of mind.

Body Practice in American Daoism

Daoism in China has always placed more value on knowledge acquired through the body than through philosophical inquiry. The deepest truths of Daoism are often expressed through ritual movements and learned sets of physical practices, rather than doctrines of faith or statements of belief. American Daoism, while generally ignoring the physicality of learned ritual

A group of people perform taiji quan *(t'ai-chi) on a loading dock near San Francisco, California. (Morton Beebe/Corbis)*

forms, has embraced gymnastic and meditative physical practice, in particular taiji quan and qigong.

Taiji quan (often referred to simply as taiji or t'ai-chi) translates literally as "supreme ultimate fist." Taiji, surely the single most popular of the practices that make up American Daoism, is a series of slow movements done while standing. Despite its oft-cited connection to Daoism via the mythical Daoist immortal Zhang Sanfeng, taiji is historically traced to the eighteenth-century military. A retired soldier named Chen returned to his ancestral village and developed the exercise there, based on his previous training. The practice stayed within the Chen family until the end of the nineteenth century, when the Yang family began teaching it publicly in Beijing, and from there throughout China.

There is no record of the first taiji quan class taught in America, but we can assume that both the teacher and the students were from China; we can also assume that it was not taught under the rubric of Daoism. Indeed, it is doubtful that the first wave of Chinese immigrants practiced what we know today as taiji at all. They were mostly from South China, and taiji was centered in North China. Moreover, the first generation of immigrants arrived from the 1850s to the 1880s; yet taiji gained public popularity only in the late nineteenth and early-twentieth centuries thanks to Yang Cheng Fu (1886–1935), to whom most of the original Yang-style taiji instructors in North America trace their lineage. (Yang style remains the most common style of taiji in North America.) Significantly, the first North American taiji books published in English were by white authors Edward Maisel (1963) and Sophia Delza (1961). These books focused on health benefits and made no mention of taiji as either "spiritual" or "Daoist."

One of the first Chinese to teach taiji to non-Chinese in North America was Cheng Man-ch'ing (1901–1975). Fitting the pattern established by Huang and Chi, Cheng (1967) was from an educated Nationalist family. By the late 1960s and early 1970s, taiji was remarked on as a "fad." Taiji spread to second-generation non-Chinese teachers, even as a new generation of post-1965 immigrants from China and Taiwan, younger and not so tied to a nostalgic version of lost China, began teaching taiji. Many came to North America to attend graduate school, and they taught taiji at their university.

Qigong literally translates as "breath work," and while the term itself was coined in China in the 1930s and used to define longevity and meditative practices that spread throughout China beginning in the mid-1950s, some of those practices are many thousands of years old (see Chapter 7). In North America qigong was not widely known until the late 1980s, and it seems that "Taoist Yoga" was the more common English term for it before that time. As in the case with taiji (and Daoist practice in general), there is little data on whether the first generation of Chinese immigrants practiced what we would call qigong. More established American Daoist masters, those who left China before 1949, do not use the term at all. Probably the first English-language book to mention qigong by name is called simply *Chi Kung;* it was written by Hawaii-based teacher Lily Siou and privately published in Hong Kong in 1973. Siou went on to claim the title of the 64th Celestial Master. In the mid-1980s, martial arts teacher Yang Jwing-ming (1989), best known for teaching Shaolin-style gongfu and Yang-style taiji, began publishing a series of books about qigong, beginning with *Chi Kung—Health and Martial Arts* (1985). (It should be made clear that Yang does not identify himself as a Daoist, and his references to Daoism are often cursory.)

Health and Medicine in American Daoism

Although a lack of written sources makes exact data rare, Chinese pharmacology and acupuncture were undoubtedly the main form of health care for Chinese laborers in nineteenth-century America. Meanwhile, as early as the eighteenth-century, a few Anglo-American physicians were learning acupuncture techniques in France. Chinese medicine was always more acceptable in Europe, and, indeed, the very first issue of the influential British medical journal *Lancet* in 1823 carried a report on acupuncture (Melton 1990, 5). Acupuncture was even mentioned as a successful treatment for sciatica and lumbago in two mainstream U.S. medical texts. But the real integration of Chinese medicine into American Daoism began in the late 1960s, when Americans were first taught acupuncture by Chinese. It was then that Chinese medicine became conceived of as a cohesive, alternative, and "more natural" system than official Western biomedicine. Americans first began to study at Chinese medical colleges in Hong Kong or Macao in the early 1970s.

Awareness of acupuncture by the mainstream American media can be dated to 1972, when James Reston, a reporter with the *New York Times,* was on assignment in Beijing covering President Richard Nixon's historic visit to China. Reston came down with appendicitis, and his surgery was performed with acupuncture as the only anesthetic. He wrote about this remarkable "new" form of anesthesia for the *Times,* and since then Chinese medicine has been gaining acceptance by the culture at large. One sign of that acceptance has been its professionalization, and licensing organizations and accreditation processes for schools have been in place since the mid-1980s. By 1994, half a million Americans had paid for acupuncture from one of nearly ten thousand active licensed acupuncturists who may have graduated from one of more than fifty licensed Traditional Chinese Medicine colleges in the United States alone (Yang, Gan, and Hong 1997, 245).

On a conceptual level, the importance of healing and health in American Daoism far transcends any instruction in acupuncture or pharmacology. Almost all self-identified American Daoist groups place the metaphor of healing at the center of their worldview and therefore incorporate some kind of healing technique into their practice, be it Traditional Chinese Medicine (TCM), movement exercises, direct transmission of healing energy, or some combination of the three.

The Future of Chinese Traditions in Euro-American Society

Chinese movement and healing practices are no longer dependent on Daoist organizations for support or the Daoist worldview for validation. For example, some TCM practitioners are pushing for TCM to become fully integrated into mainstream American medicine. To become acceptable to state licensing boards, insurance companies, and the medical profession in general, the TCM curriculum in the United States must be standardized. Insurance companies now pay for it; hospitals offer it as part of therapy. Thus, more and more accredited, standardized degrees are offered. Ginseng and other Chinese herbs have become part of the larger market for herbal supplements, and Chinese medicine is unquestionably a growth industry.

Taiji and qigong too are easily commodified: they are now taught in nursing homes and community centers by teachers many generations removed from the charismatic "Daoist masters" discussed previously. Mass-marketed products minimize the Daoist influence on taiji and qigong, thus ironically, if unknowingly, mimicking the way in which the Chinese communists despiritualized qigong in the 1950s (see Chapter 7).

Today, Daoist cultivation practice in the United States is primarily an individual activity. A permanent American Daoist community is simply not yet here, and may never be, and so most American Daoists are by definition do-it-yourselfers. A hereditary priesthood supported by the community, or by secluded monastic communities supported by the state, have been two options in China for the intensive practice of Daoist cultivation. In North America, Daoist cultivation techniques must be optional and part-time, merged with family or career. The historical legacy of American Daoism may be that it provides a mode of transmission and a legitimizing structure for a variety of practices that twenty or fifty years hence may be seen as commonplace and American.

The Fluidity of American Daoism

There are anywhere from 10,000 to 30,000 American Daoists in the United States and Canada. Typically, they are well educated, middle class, and white. The majority of them first heard about Daoism in a college or high school class, or were lent a book (usually the *Daode jing*) by a friend or family member. The *Daode jing* remains the single greatest influence on North Americans who self-identify as Daoists. Many read it at a young age: "I read the *Tao Te Ching* when I was thirteen and began meditating on its meaning" is a typical quotation from an American Daoist.

Perhaps the current best-selling book about Daoism (and thus at least partially responsible for increasing interest in the subject) is *The Tao of Pooh* by Benjamin Hoff. This 1982 book is made up of whimsical dialogue between characters of A. A. Milne's classic volumes of children's literature, *Winnie-the-Pooh* and *The House at Pooh Corner*. Each chapter explains a term taken from the *Daode jing*, such as nonaction (*wuwei*) or naturalness (*ziran*). As Hoff tells it, he got the idea to "write a book that explained the principles of Taoism through Winnie-the-Pooh, and explained Winnie-the-Pooh through the principles of Taoism" (Hoff 1982, 3). It is used as a teaching tool in everything from management training seminars to seventh-grade English classes, even as scholars decry it for obscuring historical Chinese Daoism (see Kirkland 1999).

While American Daoist masters often use the trappings of Chinese exoticism to present their teachings (for example, by playing the bamboo flute or dressing in Chinese tunics), they generally ignore the specific ways that Daoism is rooted in Chinese culture and instead emphasize Daoism's universality. This emphasis accounts for the fact that very few American Daoists express interest in deepening their knowledge of Chinese language, culture, or history as a way of approaching Daoism.

The concept of Daoism is fluid enough that anyone can claim it without fear of contradiction, and it signifies a generally mystical attitude as opposed to any specific knowledge. People for whom Daoism provides a basic orientation to life but who find the word "Daoist" too limiting might use the expression "to follow the Dao."

Perhaps the easiest location to demonstrate the fluidity of American Daoism is in cyberspace. There are hundreds if not thousands of Daoist sites on the web, including more than a hundred linked to the web ring known as the "Wandering Taoist," marked by the easily identifiable logo of a Chinese sage with a walking staff. Most popular American Daoist sites reject any kind of historical or cultural definition of Daoism in favor of a gospel of contentment and acceptance. These sites are typically linked to websites about health practices (including sometimes *reiki*, a Japanese form of energy healing), *fengshui*, the *Yijing*, and the *Daode jing*. The occasional website represents a "virtual Daoist organization" that allows membership and encourages a more active identification as a Daoist—but still in the most fluid and personal terms. Most notable among these is "Western Reform Taoism," founded in 1998 and currently with more than fifty members, who are charged a modest yearly fee (see www.wrt.org). Most Daoist websites, though, are purely personal. The fluidity and privacy inherent in cyberspace lend themselves to maintaining a similarly fluid and private Daoist identity, which knows no national boundaries.

Those spiritual questers curious enough to buy a book or magazine on American Daoism might soon learn the name Solala Towler, who through his *Empty Vessel* magazine and two books has done more to expose North Americans to popular American Daoism than anyone. Americans who gain this introduction soon learn that Daoism is nothing if not fluid. For example, in his *Embarking on the Way: A Guide to Western Taoism*, Towler writes:

> [Daoism] works well for highly individuated Westerners and can be approached on any level, from the rank beginner to the evolved aspirant. There is nothing to join, no vows to take, no special naming, clothing style or diet to follow. It is strictly up to the individual to apply whatever aspect of the tradition he or she wishes (Towler 1997, xi–xii).

The historical inaccuracy of this passage (in fact, throughout Chinese history, becoming a Daoist generally meant joining something, taking vows, and taking up a new name, clothing style, and diet) is less significant than its succinct expression of the basic tenets of American Daoism, which happen to correspond to popular Euro-American spirituality in general: fluidity, universalism, and individualism.

References
Blofeld, John. (1968/1965). *I Ching*. New York: E. P. Dutton.
Bynner, Witter. 1944. *The Way of Life according to Laotzu: An American Version*. New York: John Day.
Carus, Paul. 1898. *Lao-tze's Tao-Te-King*. Chicago: Open Court.
Cheng Man-ch'ing and Robert K. Smith. 1967. *T'ai Chi: The Supreme Ultimate Exercise for Health, Sport, and Self-Defense*. Rutland, VT: Tuttle.
Chia, Mantak, and Maneewan Chia. 1993. *Awaken Healing Light of the Tao*. Huntington, NY: Healing Tao.
Clarke, J. J. 2000. *The Tao of the West*. London: Routledge.
Delza, Sophia. 1961. *Body and Mind in Harmony: T'ai Chi Ch'uan (Wu Style): An Ancient Chinese Way of Exercise*. New York: David McKay.
Dhiegh, Khigh Alx. 1973. *The Eleventh Wing: An Exposition of the Dynamics of the I Ching for Now*. New York: Dell.

Feng, Gia-fu. 1970. *Tai Chi, a Way of Centering and I Ching*. London: Collier.

Healing Tao. 2001. *Chi Newsletter*. Huntington, NY: Healing Tao.

Hoff, Benjamin. 1982. *The Tao of Pooh*. New York: Dutton.

Huang, Al Chung-liang. (1984/1973). *Embrace Tiger, Return to Mountain: The Essence of T'ai Chi*. Moab, UT: Real People.

Jung, Carl G. (1962/1922). "Commentary." Pp. 81–137 in *The Secret of the Golden Flower*. Translated by Richard Wilhelm. New York: Harcourt, Brace.

Kirkland, Russell. 1999. "Teaching Taoism in the 1990s." *Teaching Theology and Religion* 1: 111–119.

Kotzsch, Ronald E. 1985. *Macrobiotics: Yesterday and Today*. New York: Japan Publications.

Kushi, Michio. 1977. *The Book of Macrobiotics: The Universal Way of Health and Happiness*. Tokyo: Japan Publications.

Liu Ming. 1998. *The Collected Frost Bell*. 2 vols. Santa Cruz, CA: Orthodox Daoism in America.

Maisel, Edward. 1963. *Tai Chi for Health*. New York: Holt, Rinehart.

Melton, J. Gordon, ed. 1990. *New Age Encyclopedia*. Detroit: Gale.

Needham, Joseph. 1956. *Science and Civilization in China*. Vol. 2. Cambridge: Cambridge University Press.

Seager, Richard Hughes, ed. 1993. *The Dawn of Religious Pluralism: Voices from the World's Parliament of Religion, 1893*. LaSalle, IL: Open Court.

Seven Star Communications. N.d. *Ageless Wisdom for Modern Life*. Santa Monica, CA: Seven Star Communications.

Siou, Lily. 1973. *Chi Kung*. Hong Kong: Lily Siou's School of the Six Chinese Arts.

Siu, R. G. H. 1968. *The Man of Many Qualities: A Legacy of the I Ching*. Cambridge: MIT Press.

Towler, Solala. 1997. *Embarking on the Way: A Guide to Western Taoism*. Eugene, OR: Abode of the Eternal Tao.

Van Gulik, Robert. 1961. *Sexual Life in Ancient China*. Leiden: E. J. Brill.

Watts, Alan. 1975. *Tao: The Watercourse Way*. New York: Pantheon.

Wilhelm, Richard. 1951. *The I Ching or The Book of Changes*. Translated by Cary F. Baynes. London: Routledge.

Wong, Eva. 1990. *Seven Taoist Masters*. Boston: Shambhala.

———. 1997. *The Shambhala Guide to Taoism*. Boston: Shambhala.

———. 2001. *A Master Course in Feng Shui*. Boston: Shambhala.

Yang, Fenggang. 1999. *Chinese Christians in America: Conversion, Assimilation, and Adhesive Identities*. University Park: Pennsylvania State University Press.

Yang, Jeff, Dina Gan, and Terry Hong, eds. 1997. *Eastern Standard Time: A Guide to Asian Influence on American Culture*. Boston: Houghton Mifflin.

Yang, Jwing-ming. 1989. *The Root of Chinese Chi Kung: The Secrets of Chi Kung Training*. Jamaica Plain, MA: Yang's Martial Arts Association.

12

Confucian Spirituality
in an Ecological Age

HE XIANG AND JAMES MILLER

The Contemporary Invention of Confucian Spirituality

According to the vast majority of intellectuals, China's modernization and secularization at the beginning of the twentieth century dealt a death blow to Confucianism. Confucianism was inextricably associated with China's feudal past and was thought to be incompatible with the values of modernity (see Levenson 1958). Yet, as Lin Tongqi notes, just as most scholars were consigning Confucianism to the history books, a small but influential new generation of intellectuals including Qian Mu (1895–1990), Tang Junyi (1909–1978), and Mou Zongsan (1909–1995) set about the task of reinventing the tradition (Lin 2004, 323). Based originally in East Asia, this "New Confucianism" (*xinrujia*) has spread to North America through the work of key interpreters such as Cheng Chung-ying at the University of Hawai'i, Julia Ching at the University of Toronto, and Tu Weiming at Harvard University. Their work has been complemented by that of Euro-American scholars such as Roger Ames (University of Hawai'i), Robert Neville, and John Berthrong (both at Boston University). Together, this group of intercultural intellectuals has succeeded in positioning Confucianism as a viable philosophical and religious option on the world stage. This chapter examines the way in which these North American scholars have constructed a view of Confucianism in a way that directly appeals to the twenty-first century issues of spirituality and ecology.

The novel emphasis on Confucian spirituality, however, is not shared by all scholars of Confucianism. In fact, the bulk of studies concerning the revival of Confucianism in the late twentieth century have not focused on religion in any way, but rather on the political and economic connections between Confucianism and East Asian modernization. In contrast to the radical modernizers of the early twentieth century, conservative East Asian intellectuals in the late twentieth century began to trumpet Confucianism as the cultural underpinning of the rapid economic development of the so-called minidragons: Hong Kong, Korea, Taiwan, and Singapore. Scholars rushed to investigate the correlation between Confucian values and economic prosperity in the light of Max Weber's famous theory about the affinity between Protestantism and the development of the capitalist economy in Europe. The economic excitement and interest in Confucianism fizzled out, however, somewhat as a result of the Asian financial crisis of 1997–1999. On the other hand, interest remains keen in the political appropriation of Confucianism as a repertoire of sociocultural techniques to ensure cultural stability and to ward off social ills associated with Western forms of modernization (see Elman 2002, 5). The South Korean military leader Park Chung Hee, for instance, promoted conservative Confucian values at the same time as he suspended the constitution and imposed martial law in 1971 (Duncan 2002, 453).

Although most scholars have associated Confucianism with a kind of social conservatism enshrined in a hierarchical worldview, not all advocates of New Confucianism are happy to see their work used to resist efforts toward the democratization of East Asia. Tu Weiming warns that the precepts of Confucian humanism "can easily be co-opted by social engineering as a mechanism of control" (Tu 2004, 489). To ignore the deep spiritual purposes of Confucianism would be, in Tu's view, to lose Confucianism's penetrating critique of the Enlightenment mentality and its accompanying social ills. In short, Confucianism must be revived not as the handmaid of an East Asian bureaucratic scientism but as a critique of, and solution to, the social alienation and ecological devastation that are the by-products of industrial modernity.

Of the contemporary North American scholars interested in Confucianism as a philosophical orientation that is more than just a means for political control and economic development, not all are keen to define Confucianism in terms of religion. The work of the Hawai'ian scholars, for instance, can be categorized chiefly in terms of the academic study of comparative philosophy—and indeed operates out of that university's philosophy department.

Tu Weiming, the most prominent exponent of New Confucianism in the West, participates in a debate on "identity and conflict" during the World Economic Forum in Davos, Switzerland, January 2000. (Jerome Delay/AP Photo)

On the other hand, the work of the East Coast scholars evinces a sincere desire to revive Confucianism as a spiritual tradition for the twenty-first century. That group of scholars, known collectively as the Boston Confucians, views Confucianism as a profound religious tradition capable of orienting human beings toward the transcendent truths of ultimate reality (see Neville 2000). They do not see Confucianism as synonymous with a nationalistic, authoritarian Chinese culture, but as a tradition of human civilization that carries profound and unique insights about the human condition. For the Boston Confucians, what is of significance in the Confucian tradition are those key motifs and core values that are applicable universally and not simply within the East Asian cultural context.

The religious character of Confucianism, however, remains an elusive issue, not least because many scholars are reluctant to use the term "religion" to describe Confucianism. Mary Evelyn Tucker, for instance, notes that religion

> tends to be associated with formal institutional structures and most often
> with characteristics of Western religions. . . . The term "religion" may thus

obscure rather than clarify the distinctive religious and spiritual dimensions of Confucianism (Tucker 2003, 2).

A similar sentiment can be discerned in the following statement made by Tu Weiming. Although here he is talking about the Neo-Confucian renaissance that took place in the Song dynasty, his comment applies equally to the tradition as a whole:

> The problem of whether Neo-Confucianism is a religion should not be confused with the more significant question: what does it mean to be religious in the Neo-Confucian community? The solution to the former often depends on the particular interpretive position we choose to take on what constitutes the paradigmatic example of a religion, which may have little to do with our knowledge about Neo-Confucianism as a spiritual tradition (Tu 1985, 132).

In other words, if modern Westerners are at all prepared to call Confucianism a religion, they may also have to be prepared to change or redefine their concept of religion. Here Tu sets the ground for defining Confucianism not as a religion in the conventional Western sense—that is, a social organization with religious leaders, temples, rituals, and so forth—but as a "way of being religious." This type of approach is evident in the increasingly common adoption of the term "spirituality" and the adjective "religious," rather than the noun "religion," to describe Confucianism. Instead of forthrightly claiming Confucianism as a religion, for instance, Mary Evelyn Tucker suggests that a "religious worldview" is manifested in the "spiritual practices" and "cosmological orientation" of Confucianism:

> This cosmological orientation is realized in the connection of the microcosm of the self to the macrocosm of the universe through spiritual practices of communitarian ethics, self-transformation, and ritual relatedness (Tucker 2003, 3).

In Tucker's view, therefore, Confucianism has a religious character because it fulfills one of the most important functions of religion—namely, providing a worldview or orientation for the believer (see Berger 1990). Whereas in most religions this worldview provides for social institutions and mechanisms of social control, Confucianism is in the unusual position of having had its social apparatus effectively dismantled. What remains, therefore, are the more vague elements that Tucker cites—namely, communitarian ethics, self-transformation, and ritual relatedness. Ironically, it is the near-total dev-astation and disestablishment of Confucianism in East Asian society that renders it attractive as a contemporary spiritual vehicle, focused not on maintaining patriarchal privilege through rigid social controls but on a highly spiritualized relationship between the individual and the universe. Since Confucianism has had no social power in the twentieth century, it has enjoyed the freedom to become reinvented and reappropriated by contemporary liberal intellectuals.

As a matter of fact, the history of Confucianism has been marked by many such attempts to rethink, reinterpret, and re-evaluate the tradition as a whole. When contemporary scholars argue over whether to understand Confucianism as a religion, a spirituality, a politics, or a philosophy—although the terms of the debate are newly derived from Western thinking—that type of intellectual reframing is not. The task of this chapter is not to solve the problem of whether New Confucianism is a religion, but rather to explore the way in which the tradition is being reconceptualized in a light that is highly compatible with contemporary social values.

Overall, there are two major positions regarding the question of how to interpret the religious character of Confucianism. The first position, held by such scholars as Herbert Fingarette, David L. Hall, Roger T. Ames, and Henry Rosemont, Jr., tends to focus on classical Confucianism, emphasizing the atheistic, secular, or humanistic nature of Confucian religiousness. It might seem surprising that some of these scholars, though emphasizing Confucianism's secular, atheistic, and nontranscendent nature, are still inclined to view Confucianism in religious terms. Hall and Ames (1987; 1998) argue that the notion of transcendence, loaded with Western theological implications, does not apply to the Confucian experience. Yet at the same time, Ames unequivocally states that classical Confucianism is

> at once a-theistic and profoundly religious. It is a religion without a God, a religion that affirms the cumulative human experience itself (Ames 2003, 165).

How can Confucianism be religious without being a religion? In an attempt to generate an alternative vocabulary with which to understand Confucian religiousness, Ames introduces a distinction between notions of "creativity" and "power." Creativity is to be understood in terms of self-actualization, while power is to be understood in terms of relationships with others. Ames interprets all the key elements of Confucian tradition (benevolence, sincerity, spirit, harmony, and the like) in terms of the dynamic between subjective creativity and objective power relations: together these form a "co-creative" process. Ames thus understands Confucian religiousness to be a co-creative process of self-actualization in which "ontological distinctions are abandoned in favor of cosmological parity among all things" (ibid., 167). In other words, Confucianism, in its religious aspect, is not concerned with the nature of the existence of humans, gods, or ultimate reality, but rather with the qualities of relationships between the various dimensions of the universe.

In making this interpretive claim, Ames is not simply attempting to define Confucianism; he is also pointing the way toward a new way of understanding religion. Because of the influence of Christianity and Judaism, the concept of religion as it has developed in the West has revolved chiefly around gods, their priestly representatives, and their theologies. The process of secularization that has taken place in the West since the Enlightenment has removed this concept of religion from the public sphere and associated it with private belief. At the same time, the rise of rationality and science has made belief in gods as superhuman figures highly implausible for many people. Despite these changes in the social and intellectual arenas, it seems that people still have a desire for many of the elements of religion that are collected under the human-centered and highly personalized term "spirituality." Ames's atheistic, nontranscendent religion may well be more compatible with the scientific, secularized worldview of the twenty-first century.

The more explicitly religious view of Confucian religion is held by Julia Ching, Tu Weiming, Robert Neville, and others. That view tends to focus on Neo-Confucianism and emphasize the "transcendent dimensions" of Confucianism. Julia Ching, for instance, states that Confucianism "does not deny God's existence" but talks about discovering "transcendence in immanence" (Ching 2003, 94). In a similar move, Ying-shih Yü proposes the idea of "inward transcendence" to interpret the Chinese mentality (Yü 2003). In both these cases, what is seen as essential in Confucian religiousness is not its positing of a transcendent realm populated by the gods and spirits of traditional Chinese mythology, but rather the way in which the tradition affords its adherents the ability to apprehend "transcendence" in the interior depths of the self.

The contemporary Western attraction to spirituality in fact is transforming the character of religion for many people. The transcendent realm is no longer held to be totally transcendent, a kind of alien world beyond all imagining, but rather intimately connected with the deepest purposes of human life. This theology is not new, but its increasingly broad acceptance in religious culture is. This shift is responding in part to the way in which science has successfully appropriated the domains of physics, cosmology, and astronomy, disciplines formerly associated with religion. Whereas in premodern times the transcendent literally implied the heavens—that is, the realm above and beyond the earth—now the term "transcendence" must denote something altogether more subtle and figurative.

For this reason the contemporary fascination with Confucianism as a religion without transcendence, or as a type of inward or immanent transcendence, is altogether understandable. It fits perfectly with contemporary Western cultural understandings about where the realm of religion ought to be located—namely, deep within the soul. As Ewert Cousins explains:

> The spiritual core is the deepest center of the person. It is here that the person is open to the transcendent dimension; it is here that the person experiences ultimate reality (Cousins 2003, xii).

Tu Weiming has provided one of the most interesting cases of this attempt to reinterpret Confucianism for the present day. He readily acknowledges the problems with all of the existing Western definitions of religion:

> It should be obvious that some of the conceptual apparatuses widely employed in religious studies are inadequate in dealing with the Confucian tradition. Virtually all familiar exclusive dichotomies have lost their explanatory power: spirit/matter, body/mind, sacred/profane, creator/creature, and transcendence/immanence (Tu 1993, 198).

Despite this large caveat, Tu does not manage to escape these Western terms entirely. He defines the Confucian way of being religious as "ultimate self-transformation as a communal act and as a faithful dialogical response to the transcendent" (Tu 1989, 94). To be religious in the Confucian sense thus means to be engaged in the process of self-transformation, located within a community, and in relationship with the transcendent realm. This definition invokes familiar Western categories of ultimacy, fidelity, and transcendence. His view of Confucianism is one that makes sense to contemporary Westerners schooled in thousands of years of Western religious history.

Sorting through all of these various approaches to Confucian religiousness we can discern two basic approaches. The first is focused on ordinary human experience, or in Ames's words, "ritualized living through the roles and rela-tionships of family and community," as the source of religious experience (Ames 2003, 166). The second is often Heaven-centered, with Heaven (*tian*) understood as the symbol of transcendence, be it "inward transcendence" or "immanent transcendence." Both, however, emphasize self-transformation and cultivation. Both regard the ultimate religious goal as to achieve a "harmonious union of the Heavenly and the human (*tian ren he yi*)." It is clear, therefore, that the scholars who wish to emphasize the transcendent, overtly religious side of Confucianism do so by emphasizing creativity and self-transformation. All would agree in emphasizing Confucianism as a form of human "spirituality." This modern spirituality focused on the inner core of human experience, or on an "immanent transcendence," resonates well with the way contemporary Con-fucian scholars have come to interpret their tradition.

To demonstrate this spiritualized reading of the Confucian tradition, it is worth examining the way in which contemporary Confucians have inter-preted two famous Confucian texts, the *Great Learning* (*Daxue*) and the *Doc-trine of the Mean* (*Zhongyong*). These two books were canonized by the Neo-Confucian philosopher Zhu Xi (1130–1200) as two of the four key texts of the Confucian tradition. Before Zhu Xi's efforts in promoting the texts, they were formerly two small chapters from an ancient Chinese classic known as the *Book of Ritual* (*Liji*). In Thomas Berry's words, these two books

> express the quintessence of the entire Chinese tradition. . . . They have a sim-plicity, a power, and a comprehensiveness in establishing the contours of the Confucian tradition that is not likely to be surpassed (Berry 2003, 45–46).

In other words, these two texts lie at the heart of the contemporary revival of Confucian spirituality.

The key passage of the *Great Learning* is as follows:

> The ancients who wished to manifest their clear character to the world would first bring order to their states. Those who wished to bring order to their states would first regulate their families. Those who wished to regu-late their families would first cultivate their personal lives. Those who wished to cultivate their personal lives would first rectify their minds. Those who wished to rectify their minds would first make their wills sin-cere. Those who wished to make their wills sincere would first extend their knowledge. The extension of knowledge consists in the investigation of things (Chan 1963, 86–87).

This passage places the "investigation of things" at the starting point or first action of which everything else, from family harmony to world peace, are consequences. The passage suggests both an internal and external chain of causation. On the one hand, the solution to the social problems of the state lies in the "personal life" of the Confucian sage-ruler. On the other hand, the rectification of his personal life lies in extending knowledge outward and in investigating things. The sage thus brings the world into himself and then radiates his transformed self back out through the world. In so doing he establishes harmony, which is understood as the dynamic flourishing together of all the various elements that go to make up the world. The passage then goes on to summarize the whole message as "From the Son of Heaven down to the common people, all must regard cultivation of the personal life as the root or foundation" (ibid., 87). The crucial question is what exactly the investigation of things means. As it turned out, the mainstream wing of the Confucian tradition has come to interpret this phrase not, as one might think, as a kind of scientific investigation of the world, but rather as the investigation of oneself and one's relations—that is, as moral self-cultivation. Because of this, the starting point for Confucian development has not been something akin to the instrumental empiricism that developed in the West (know the world in order to transform it), but rather a focus on personal morality and social ethics. In fact the Ming dynasty Confucian Wang Yangming (1472–1529) went so far as to interpret the investigation of things (*gewu*) as the investigation of the mind (*gexin*). In so doing he set the stage for the present-day emphasis on Confucianism as moral and spiritual self-cultivation.

As a result of the emphasis given to this passage in the *Great Learning* by a certain stream of Confucian intellectuals including Zhu Xi and Wang Yangming, modern commentators today hold up this passage as the defining example of Confucian spirituality. Henry Rosemont points out that this passage "conveys a religious message that is unique in its overall thrust" (Rosemont 2003, 184). According to Tu Weiming, the implication of this particular passage is that "the more we broaden ourselves to involve others, the more we are capable of deepening our self-awareness; our persistence in deepening our self-awareness is the basis for our fruitful interaction with an ever-expanding network of human-relatedness" (Tu 1993, 144). Tu depicts a diagram of concentric circles starting with the self in the center and expanding to the family, community, country, world, and beyond. Tu's interpretation, following Wang Yangming, rests on interpreting "the investigation of things" in terms of the moral center of the self, rather than something akin to science: the investigation of trees, rivers, animals, winds, heavenly bodies such as the sun and the moon—in short, everything within nature.

To give yet another example of how the ongoing transmission of the Confucian tradition is subject to this particularly "spiritual" line of interpretation, we may turn to another Confucian classic, the *Doctrine of the Mean* (*Zhongyong*). According to Wing-tsit Chan, the *Doctrine of the Mean* is "perhaps the most philosophical in the whole body of ancient Confucian literature"; its extensive discussion of the idea of the Confucian concept of sincerity (*cheng*) makes it "at once psychological, metaphysical, and religious" (Chan 1963, 96). A key passage is found in chapter 26:

> Therefore absolute sincerity is ceaseless. Being ceaseless, it is lasting. Being lasting, it is evident. Being evident, it is infinite. Being infinite, it is extensive and deep. Being extensive and deep, it is high and brilliant. It is because it is extensive and deep that it contains all things. It is because it is high and brilliant that it overshadows all things. It is because it is infinite and lasting that it can complete all things. In being extensive and deep, it is a counterpart of Earth. In being high and brilliant, it is a counterpart of Heaven. In being infinite and lasting, it is unlimited. Such being its nature, it becomes prominent without any display, produces changes without motion, and accomplishes its ends without action (ibid., 109).

The religious significance of this paragraph lies in the way it manages to create a complete worldview out of the single concept of "absolute sincerity"—a concept that comes close in meaning to the Western concept of "ultimate reality" (Tu 1989, 84). Apart from this ultimate reality, there is nothing else. As the previous chapter of the text puts it, "[Without] sincerity there would be nothing." This ultimate reality is "sincere" because it is single, whole, and without any counterpart. As Tu Weiming puts it, "[Sincerity] as the ultimate reality is not the unity of opposites but a continuous, lasting, and homogeneous whole" (ibid.). Within this wholesome and holistic universe, all are parts of the totality: the sky with all its stars, the earth with all its mountains, waters, and inhabitants. In spite of the numerous forms of existence, everything is essentially the same. This is the meaning of sincerity, which we might also translate as "homogeneity"—that is, belonging to the same kind, or sharing the same genetic roots. The crucial distinction, however, between the Confucian ideal of "sincerity" and the modern Western notion of "ultimate reality" is that Confucianism treats this concept not just as an ontological fact, a description of the fundamental nature of the universe, but also as a value to be embodied by human beings. Since the universe is whole, humans too ought to encompass all things within their moral capacity. In other words, nature itself conveys a certain intrinsic value to human beings.

This way of thinking is unfamiliar to Western modernity, which has by and large been predicated on the split between facts and values (Neville 2004, 451). Facts are objective and belong to the realm of science. Values are subjective and belong to the realm of personal or cultural ethics. The by-product of this split between nature and ethics has been the general reluctance on the part of Western ethics to regard the natural world as having intrinsic worth. Rather, nature is valuable only insofar as human beings place a subjective value on it or are capable of using it for their own purposes. This viewpoint makes possible the ongoing exploitation of nature that fuels modern economic development. The Confucian tradition, however, suggests the alternative point of view, that ethics cannot ultimately be divorced from our knowledge of the world. For this reason, many advocates of New Confucianism are focusing on the role that the tradition might play in engaging the current problems of environmental ethics. The Confucian realization that "the ontological reality of man is none other than the ontological reality of Heaven," and that the relationship between Heaven and man is "an indivisibly single oneness" (Tu 1989, 84), points to the most recent development in Confucian spirituality—namely, its engagement with the current ecological crisis as a key area of religious concern.

The Ecological Turn in New Confucian Spirituality

Those unfamiliar with the broad reorientation of religion that is underway in the religion and ecology movement might be surprised by the convergence of religion and ecology. Ecology, it might be supposed, is concerned with the scientific laws governing the relations among species and between species and their habitats. Religion, on the other hand, is focused on the transcendent realm, on the end of time and the hope of eternity. This characterization of religion may well have been broadly accurate in the Enlightenment period. It also fits in perfectly with the split between facts and values that is so characteristic of European modernity and has led to the rejection of objective religion in favor of a multicultural postmodern world of subjective spiritualities.

A man walks near a stone sculpture guarding a tomb in the cemetery at the Garden of Confucius, Qufu, Shandong province. (Lowell Georgia/Corbis)

This modern psychological view of spirituality, however, does not completely exhaust what is meant by the term "immanent transcendence" used to describe the New Confucian view of spirituality. The fact is that for many New Confucians, as well as a broad swath of contemporary religious people, spirituality is not simply a matter of the subjective, personal experience of the transcendent, but about the immanence or indwelling of the transcendent realm within nature. Nature, in fact, becomes the field for spiritual experience, for encountering the transcendent realm, and for pursuing the goals of spiritual self-cultivation. This task is described by the Confucian tradition as the harmonious unity of heaven and earth (*tian ren he yi*). For the contemporary ecological Confucians, this concept is seen not as a metaphysical statement about the unity of the cosmos but as a call to environmental action and spiritual cultivation. For this reason, modern Confucian spiritualists have been at the forefront of the movement to connect nature and religion. Scholars such as Mary Evelyn Tucker, Tu Weiming, and Thomas Berry, for example, were instrumental in establishing the Harvard-based Forum on Religion and Ecology (FORE) and serve on its steering committee.

Central to the promotion of this ecological Confucianism has been the positive reassessment of the Song dynasty Confucian Zhang Zai (1020–1077) and his philosophy of *qi* (ch'i). Zhang Zai's most famous statement is known as the *Western Inscription*. It begins thus:

> Heaven is my father and Earth is my mother, and even such a small crea-
> ture as I find an intimate place in their midst. Therefore that which fills
> the universe I regard as my body and that which directs the universe I
> consider as my nature. All people are my brothers and sisters, and all
> things are my companions (Chan 1963, 497).

The contemporary significance of Zhang Zai's work is that he seems to be proposing what we would today call an ecological view of the self, or, as Tu Weiming terms it, an "anthropocosmic" self. Tu uses this term to denote the Confucian sense that the true human self is best understood not in the modern Enlightenment terms of individuality, freedom, and autonomy, but rather in terms of the deep network of connections between the self and the contexts in which it is located. For Robert Neville, this is one of the most significant advances made by the Confucian tradition. He writes:

> The attempt to broaden the concerns of individuals and communities in
> order to be able to frame ecological issues fairly is sorely taxed by custom-
> ary Western and South Asian conceptions of the self. The former are
> shaped by a strong distinction between self and other, . . . and expressed in
> languages that use reflexive pronouns extensively to talk about the self. The
> result is that it is barely possible to relate to other selves except perhaps as
> mirrors of our own, let alone to natural processes and contexts that have
> their integrities in irrelevance to human selves (Neville 1998, 265).

In other words, if humans are to be successful in understanding, relating to, and empathizing with the processes of nature, they are best equipped to do so if they have a concept of the self that can anticipate and embrace these larger natural concerns. Zhang Zai's work is thus key to the way in which contemporary Confucians have begun to reorient their tradition toward a "spiritual ecology." In Zhang Zai's view, self-cultivation is not a personal, psychological, or ego-centered activity, because "there is nothing under heaven that is not me" (Zhang Zai 1978, 7.24.12). The true nature of the self, according to Zhang

Zai, is the cosmic self—namely, the self that incorporates the "ten thousand things" (*wanwu*) of nature. (Zhang Zai's work in fact contains a wealth of observations, knowledge, and tentative theories in such scientific fields as astronomy, physics, and biology.)

Zhang Zai came to these conclusions as a result of the prominent place he gave in his philosophy to *qi*, the universal cosmic power. He writes:

> [*Qi*] fills the universe. And as it completely provides for the flourish[ing] and transformation of all things, it is all the more spatially unrestricted. As it is not spatially restricted, it operates in time and proceeds with time. From morning to evening, from spring to summer, and from the present tracing back to the past, there is no time at which it does not operate, and there is no time at which it does not produce. Consequently, as one sprout bursts forth it becomes a tree with a thousand big branches, and as one egg evolves, it progressively becomes a fish capable of swallowing a ship (quoted in Tu 1998, 112).

The fact that all in the cosmos is *qi*, the whole *qi*, and nothing but *qi* leads Tu Weiming to coin the phrase "the continuity of being" to describe the Confucian view of the world. According to this monistic worldview, there is nothing in the universe that can be considered radically separate from, or other than, anything else. Everything is connected to everything else by virtue of being composed of the same *qi*. This worldview is important in two respects: firstly, it follows from this view that there can be nothing in Confucian thinking that is parallel to the biblical god—a being with power so utterly unique and awesome that it is capable of bringing the universe into existence or destroying it absolutely; secondly, the "continuity of being" demands that humans accept that they are not intrinsically, ontologically, or genetically different from other animals, or other processes of nature. In short, the universe is a single, natural power; human life, like everything else, is just one part of it.

Following Tu's lead, contemporary Confucians have therefore begun to incorporate this expanded, holistic, ecological view into their doctrine of moral self-cultivation. John Berthrong writes that it is now impossible to imagine a New Confucianism without imagining also that it would deal with the ecological crisis:

> The crux of the matter is that, whereas . . . the primary concern of the tradition was focused on human life and its salvation, the basis of the present intellectual and moral crisis is to discover how to preserve the

best of Confucian self-cultivation and social ethics and expand it into the new area of concern for nature as the arena for ecological reflection (Berthrong 1998, 239).

This notion of an expanded or inclusive humanism fits well into the mainstream view of Confucianism as a humanistic philosophy. Cheng Chung-ying, for instance, describes the Confucian contribution to environmental ethics as proposing an "inclusive humanism" in which self-transformation is always understood as being grounded in the underlying reality of nature (Cheng 1998, 214). Moreover, when the Confucian emphasis on creative harmony is understood as incorporating both human and natural harmony, Confucian inclusive humanism provides an alternative to the humanism that developed in the modern West, which is "nothing more than a secular will for power or a striving for domination, with rationalistic science at its disposal" (ibid., 213). The Japanese Confucian Okada Takehiko, for instance, understands this inclusive humanism as necessarily implying ethical responsibilities to all forms of life. When asked directly about this by Confucianism scholar Rodney Taylor, he responds:

> Yes I think we do [have this responsibility], and such an ideal should be extended to all forms of life, animals and plants alike. The Confucian concept of being in community (forming one body) with other human beings can be extended to the community of life itself. . . . All humankind has a mind that cannot bear to see the suffering of others and this is something that should be applied to all life (Taylor 1998, 47).

This focus on the inclusive, ecological self has, perhaps surprisingly, not led to the total rejection of the notion of spirituality or transcendence within the Confucian tradition. From a modern Western perspective, it is hard to understand how a universe of continuous being composed solely of *qi* could permit the notion of transcendence, a term normally associated with the concept of going beyond or transcending the realm of being. It is clear from the version of Confucianism advocated by Zhang Zai that this type of transcendence is out of the question. Moreover, according to the inclusive humanism advocated by Cheng Chungying, it is unnecessary. Rather, contemporary Confucian notions of transcendence come to mean something akin to the Chinese phrase of forming a harmonious unity with heaven and earth (*tian ren he yi*). Transcendence is not, as the term conventionally implies, about going beyond the ordinary realm, but about incorporating the entirety of the universe within one's body. In this redefined "immanent transcendence," ecology and spirituality become interrelated as defining elements of human life. Humans are biological creatures who depend for their very lives on plants, which remove carbon dioxide from the atmosphere and replace it with oxygen through the process of photosynthesis. Humans are also spiritual creatures capable of harmonizing and uniting the processes of the universe in their moral being. As such the Confucian view is clearly different from contemporary Christian or Islamic views about human stewardship over the earth and has the potential to make a unique contribution to this ongoing dialogue.

Ecology, Spirituality, and Modernity

This remarkable ecospiritual reinvention of Confucianism is not universally shared by contemporary Confucians. An uneasy relationship still exists between advocates of science and advocates of Confucianism in its more traditional humanistic form, and the binary logic of science versus religion has not been completely overcome. Okada writes:

> I have a concern about the way in which science has developed. Its development has reached the point where it threatens the very existence of human life (quoted in ibid., 46).

This suggests that, for him, the perils of modernization are to be undone by some sort of return to tradition, a move that is clearly conservative and traditionalist. Tu Weiming writes: "The New Confucian ecological turn has great significance for China's spiritual self-definition, for it urges China to return to its home base and rediscover its own soul" (Tu 2004, 505). Again this motif of return, though not couched in terms of a distrust of science, also implies a somewhat conservative, traditionalist mentality. The difference, however, is that Tu has a clear vision that China's reappropriation of its own Confucian heritage can be of benefit to the world community in its quest for a sustainable future (ibid.).

In all the debates about whether Confucianism can legitimately be construed as a religious tradition, about the nature of transcendence and the moral self, we can detect the forming of a new type of religiosity, one that is particularly responsive to the needs of the twenty-first century. This form of religion is secular, in that it has no institutional social power. It is atheistic, in that it does not focus on a personal divine being. It is ecological, in that it regards the self as the nexus of biological as well as sociological connections.

Yet these three elements, remarkably, are not forged into a modern scientific synthesis but into a spiritual one. It is hard to overestimate how odd this would sound to the radical modernizers of the early twentieth century, and even to the first wave of New Confucian humanists. They could not have believed that there would be reputable Confucians at Harvard and Boston universities—some not even Chinese—who would talk openly of taking two thousand years of Confucian humanism and extracting from this a spiritual framework capable of engaging with nature. This spiritual framework, open to science, ecologically friendly, and divested of authoritarian social institutions, seems remarkably suited to a contemporary and progressive global culture.

References

Ames, Roger T. 2003. "*Li* and the A-theistic Religiousness of Classical Confucianism." Pp. 165–182 in *Confucian Spirituality*. Vol. 1. Edited by Tu Weiming and Mary Evelyn Tucker. New York: Crossroad.

Berger, Peter L. 1990. *The Sacred Canopy: Elements of a Sociological Theory of Religions.* New York: Anchor.

Berry, Thomas. 2003. "Individualism and Holism in Chinese Tradition: The Religious Cultural Context." Pp. 39–55 in *Confucian Spirituality,* vol. 1. Edited by Tu Weiming and Mary Evelyn Tucker. New York: Crossroad.

Berthrong, John H. 1998. "Motifs for a New Confucian Ecological Vision." Pp. 237–263 in *Confucianism and Ecology.* Edited by Mary Evelyn Tucker and John Berthrong. Cambridge: Harvard University Press.

Chan, Wing-tsit. 1963. *A Source Book in Chinese Philosophy.* Princeton: Princeton University Press.

Cheng Chung-ying. 1998. "The Trinity of Cosmology, Ecology, and Ethics in the Confucian Personhood." Pp. 211–235 in *Confucianism and Ecology.* Edited by Mary Evelyn Tucker and John Berthrong. Cambridge: Harvard University Press.

Ching, Julia. 2003. "What Is Confucian Spirituality?" Pp. 81–95 in *Confucian Spirituality,* vol. 1. Edited by Tu Weiming and Mary Evelyn Tucker. New York: Crossroad.

Cousins, Ewert. 2003. "Preface to the Series." Pp. xi–xii in *Confucian Spirituality,* vol. 1. Edited by Tu Weiming and Mary Evelyn Tucker. New York: Crossroad.

Duncan, John B. 2002. "The Uses of Confucianism in Modern Korea." Pp. 431–462 in *Rethinking Confucianism: Past and Present in China, Japan, Korea, and Vietnam.* Edited by Benjamin A. Elman, John B. Duncan, and Herman Ooms. Los Angeles: UCLA Asian Pacific Monograph Series.

Elman, Benjamin A., with John B. Duncan and Herman Ooms. 2002. "Introduction." Pp. 1–29 in *Rethinking Confucianism: Past and Present in China, Japan, Korea, and Vietnam.* Edited by Benjamin A. Elman,

John B. Duncan, and Herman Ooms. Los Angeles: UCLA Asian Pacific Monograph Series.

Forum on Religion and Ecology (FORE). http://environment.harvard.edu/religion.

Hall, David L., and Roger T. Ames. 1987. *Thinking through Confucius.* Albany: State University of New York Press.

———. 1998. *Thinking from the Han: Self, Truth and Transcendence in Chinese and Western Culture.* Albany: State University of New York Press.

Levenson, Joseph. 1958. *Confucian China and its Modern Fate.* Vol. 1: *The Problem of Intellectual Continuity.* Berkeley: University of California Press.

Lin Tongqi. 2004. "Mou Zongsan's Spiritual Vision: How Is *Summum Bonum* Possible?" Pp. 323–352 in *Confucian Sprituality,* vol. 2. Edited by Tu Weiming and Mary Evelyn Tucker. New York: Crossroad.

Neville, Robert Cummings. 1998. "Orientation, Self, and Ecological Posture." Pp. 265–271 in *Confucianism and Ecology.* Edited by Mary Evelyn Tucker and John Berthrong. Cambridge: Harvard University Press.

———. 2000. *Boston Confucianism: Portable Tradition in the Late-Modern World.* Albany: State University of New York Press.

———. 2004. "Contemporary Confucian Spirituality and Multiple Religious Identity." Pp. 440–462 in *Confucian Spirituality,* vol. 2. Edited by Tu Weiming and Mary Evelyn Tucker. New York: Crossroad.

Rosemont, Jr., Henry. 2003. "Is There a Universal Path of Spiritual Progress in the Texts of Early Confucianism?" Pp. 183–196 in *Confucian Spirituality,* vol. 1. Edited by Tu Weiming and Mary Evelyn Tucker. New York: Crossroad.

Taylor, Rodney L. 1998. "Companionship with the World: Roots and Branches of a Confucian Ecology." Pp. 37–58 in *Confucianism and Ecology.* Edited by Mary Evelyn Tucker and John Berthrong. Cambridge: Harvard University Press.

Tu Weiming. 1985. *Confucian Thought: Selfhood as Creative Transformation.* Albany: State University of New York Press.

———. 1989. *Centrality and Commonality: An Essay on Confucian Religiousness (A Revised and Enlarged Edition of Centrality and Commonality: An Essay on Chung-yung).* Albany: State University of New York Press.

———. 1993. "Confucianism." Pp. 139–228 in *Our Religions.* Edited by Arvind Sharma. New York: HarperSanFrancisco.

———. 1998. "The Continuity of Being: Chinese Visions of Nature." Pp. 105–121 in *Confucianism and Ecology.* Edited by Mary Evelyn Tucker and John Berthrong. Cambridge: Harvard University Press.

———. 2004. "Epilogue: The Ecological Turn in New Confucian Humanism: Implications for China and the World." Pp. 480–508 in *Confucian Spirituality,* vol. 2. Edited by Tu Weiming and Mary Evelyn Tucker. New York: Crossroad.

Tucker, Mary Evelyn. 2003. "Introduction." Pp. 1–35 in *Confucian Spirituality*, vol. 1. Edited by Tu Weiming and Mary Evelyn Tucker. New York: Crossroad.

Yü Ying-shih. 2003. "Between the Heavenly and the Human." Pp. 62–80 in *Confucian Spirituality*, vol. 1. Edited by Tu Weiming and Mary Evelyn Tucker. New York: Crossroad.

Zhang Zai. 1978. *Zhang Zai ji* [The collected works of Zhang Zai]. Beijing: Zhonghua shuju.

Index

About the Authors

He Xiang is a doctoral candidate in philosophy of religion at Boston University. He is pursuing a public service career in the field of international development in Canada.

Ven. Jing Yin received his Ph.D. from the School of Oriental and African Studies at University of London and is director of the Buddhist studies program at Hong Kong University.

Kim Sung-Hae is professor of religion at Sogang University, Seoul. Her research is in the comparative study of Christianity and East Asian religions.

Jonathan H. X. Lee is a doctoral candidate in religious studies at the University of California, Santa Barbara. His research interests are in contemporary Chinese popular religion and Daoism, material culture, and postcolonial studies.

Alison Marshall received her Ph.D. from the University of Toronto and is associate professor and chair of the department of religious studies at Brandon University, Manitoba.

James Miller is assistant professor of East Asian Traditions at Queen's University, Canada, and coordinator of its graduate program in religion and modernity. He has published *Daoism: A Short Introduction* (OneWorld 2003) and coedited *Daoism and Ecology* (Harvard 2001).

David A. Palmer completed his doctoral work at the École pratique des hautes études in Paris and is director of the Hong Kong office of the École française d'Extrême-Orient.

Elijah Siegler is assistant professor of religion at the College of Charleston, South Carolina, and author of *New Religious Movements* (Prentice Hall 2006).

Tam Wai Lun is associate professor of cultural and religious studies at Chinese University of Hong Kong. He is undertaking a research project with John Lagerwey of the École pratique des hautes études on local religion in southeast China.

Tak-ling Terry Woo graduated from the University of Toronto in 2000. She is a research assistant in the department of cultural and religious studies at Chinese University of Hong Kong and is affiliated with its new Centre for the Study of Humanistic Buddhism.

Francis Ching-wah Yip received his doctorate from Harvard Divinity School and now teaches at Chinese University of Hong Kong.